Foundations of the Theory of Learning Systems

This is Volume 101 in
MATHEMATICS IN SCIENCE AND ENGINEERING
A series of monographs and textbooks
Edited by RICHARD BELLMAN, *University of Southern California*

The complete listing of books in this series is available from the Publisher upon request.

Foundations of the Theory of Learning Systems

YA. Z. TSYPKIN

The Institute of Automation and Telemechanics
Moscow, U.S.S.R.

Translated by

Z. J. NIKOLIC

Esso Production Research Company
Houston, Texas

ACADEMIC PRESS New York and London 1973

A Subsidiary of Harcourt Brace Jovanovich, Publishers

ACADEMIC PRESS, INC.
111 Fifth Avenue, New York, New York 10003

United Kingdom Edition published by
ACADEMIC PRESS, INC. (LONDON) LTD;
24/28 Oval Road, London NW1

LIBRARY OF CONGRESS CATALOG CARD NUMBER: 72-82655

PRINTED IN THE UNITED STATES OF AMERICA

First published in the Russian language
under the title
OSNOVY TEORII OBUCHAYUSHCHIKHSYA SISTEM
Nauka, Moscow, 1970

In fond memory of

ALEKSANDR ARONOVICH FEL'DBAUM

Contents

Chapter III Algorithms of Optimal Learning

Chapter IV Elements of Statistical Decision Theory

Chapter V Learning Pattern Recognition Systems

Chapter VIII Learning Filters

Chapter IX Examples of Learning Systems

Preface to the Russian Edition

The construction of learning systems is currently receiving much attention. Such systems can improve their performance in the course of their own operation. The necessity for applying learning systems arises in cases when a system must operate in conditions of uncertainty, and when the available information is so small that it is impossible to design in advance a system that has fixed properties and also operates sufficiently well.

The principle of constructing learning systems is based on the learning accomplished through probabilistic iterative algorithms. These algorithms are here called algorithms of learning. The algorithms of learning, described by stochastic difference or differential equations, can compensate for the lack of *a priori* information by processing the current information and then reaching a performance that is best in a certain specific sense.

Basic attention is given to learning systems. Many known and new approaches to the design of learning systems are considered.

Unlike the preceding book by this author, "Adaptation and Learning in Automatic Systems," which was devoted to the development of general concepts and to the presentation of a unified approach to the solution of the problems of adaptation and learning, this book does not consider a very wide circle of questions related to adaptation and learning. This permits the development in depth of specific approaches to the problems of learning and adaptation. Of all the possible approaches to the theory of adaptation and learning, only a few which are related to the construction of learning pattern recognition systems and learning filters are presented. Learning models are also considered, and a special chapter is devoted to the examples of various learning systems.

This book has an extensive bibliography. References to the literature are given in the commentaries at the end of each chapter.

Obviously, there are three stages of knowledge: the first stage is a pleasant feeling that the arguments presented in a book are understood; the second stage is one when the arguments can be repeated and used; and, finally, the third stage is when the arguments can be disproved.

This book will have reached its goal if the reader, after reading it, proves himself on any one of these stages.

Acknowledgments

The development of the views presented here was greatly influenced by Aleksandr Aronovich Fel'dbaum, the author of many works on adaptive and learning systems, ending with the creation of dual control theory. In spite of serious illness, he took an active part in evaluating many aspects of the developing theory.

This book was being written at the time when many of us, friends of Alexandr Aronovich, were losing and then again regaining the hope that he would overcome his serious ailment. But it was not destined that this hope be fulfilled. On January 15, 1969, the life of this extraordinary scientist and man, who has done so much for the development of science and who could have done even more, came to an end.

The author is grateful to his co-workers and colleagues for their help in the preparation of the manuscript. E. Avedyan, G. Kel'mans, and Yu. Popkov carefully read various chapters of the book, and provided numerous corrections and additions. N. Loginov and L. Epstein carried out extensive theoretical and experimental investigations of specific learning systems and algorithms. G. Arhipova typed many versions of the manuscript. Without such active help, the completion of this book could have taken an indefinite period of time.

Chapter I

Goal of Learning

Nothing happens in the universe that does not have a sense of either certain maximum or minimum.

L. EULER

1.1 Introduction

When we talk about learning, we always have in mind the existence of a certain goal that has to be reached through the learning process. Very often this goal of learning cannot be specified explicitly due to insufficient *a priori* information. In other words, the goal of learning is not completely defined. In the opposite case, that is, when the goal of learning is given in an explicit form, there is no need for learning since such a goal can be reached without any learning, for instance, by designing the system in advance. The characteristic feature of learning is that the lack of *a priori* information, that is, incomplete definition of the goal of learning, is compensated by necessary processing of current information.

In this introductory chapter, we present the concept of the goal of learning. In addition to the simple goal of learning, this chapter also considers the complex goals of learning; the constraints under which learning must proceed are also mentioned; finally, various forms of learning are evaluated.

1.2 Concept of the Goal of Learning

In its general form, the goal of learning represents the state that has to be reached by the learning system in the process of learning. It is thus appropriate to differentiate such a state from all other possible states. The selection of such a desired state is actually achieved by a proper choice of a certain functional that has an extremum which corresponds to the state. The modification of the state of the system is performed either by modification of the control action or by a change in the system parameters. Let us introduce vector

$$\mathbf{c} = (c_1, \ldots, c_N), \tag{1.1}$$

the components of which are either the values characterizing the control actions or the values of the parameters. Then a functional of the vector **c**, for instance

$$J(\mathbf{c}) = \int_X Q(\mathbf{x}, \mathbf{c}) p(\mathbf{x}) \, d\mathbf{x} \tag{1.2}$$

can be selected to define the goal of learning. Here,

$$\mathbf{x} = (x_1, \ldots, x_M) \tag{1.3}$$

is the random vector of a stationary discrete or continuous process with probability density function $p(\mathbf{x})$, and $Q(\mathbf{x}, \mathbf{c})$ is a certain function specified in advance. Actually, $Q(\mathbf{x}, \mathbf{c})$ is a random functional for each realization of **x**, and its expectation, as can be seen from (1.2), is equal to $J(\mathbf{c})$. Therefore, (1.2) can briefly be written in another form:

$$J(\mathbf{c}) = \mathsf{M}_{\mathbf{x}}\{Q(\mathbf{x}, \mathbf{c})\}. \tag{1.4}$$

If we assume that functional $Q(\mathbf{x}, \mathbf{c})$ is continuous with respect to **c**, then the necessary conditions of the extremum (1.4) can be presented in the form of the equation

$$\nabla J(\mathbf{c}) = \mathsf{M}_{\mathbf{x}}\{\nabla_{\mathbf{c}} Q(\mathbf{x}, \mathbf{c})\} = 0, \tag{1.5}$$

where

$$\nabla J(\mathbf{c}) = \operatorname{grad} J(\mathbf{c}) = (\partial J(\mathbf{c})/\partial c_1, \ldots, \partial J(\mathbf{c})/\partial c_N) \tag{1.6}$$

is the gradient of the functional $J(\mathbf{c})$ with respect to the "argument"

$$\nabla_{\mathbf{c}} Q(\mathbf{x}, \mathbf{c}) = \operatorname{grad}_{\mathbf{c}} Q(\mathbf{x}, \mathbf{c}) = (\partial Q(\mathbf{x}, \mathbf{c})/\partial c_1, \ldots, \partial Q(\mathbf{x}, \mathbf{c})/\partial c_N) \tag{1.7}$$

and is the gradient of the random functional $Q(\mathbf{x}, \mathbf{c})$ with respect to **c**.

If the functional $J(\mathbf{c})$ does not have a gradient in the ordinary sense at a certain point $\mathbf{c}^0$, then $\nabla J(\mathbf{c})$ (1.6) is not defined uniquely. However, if the collection of values $\nabla J(\mathbf{c})$ consists of points that belong to the convex hull of values $\mathbf{c}$ in any neighborhood of the point $\mathbf{c}^0$, then, as before, the necessary condition of the extremum is obtained by equating the gradient with zero, that is, condition (1.5). We shall not consider this case.

If the functional $J(\mathbf{c})$ is convex and has a single extremum, the condition (1.5) is both necessary and sufficient. In this case, the root of the equation (1.5) defines the optimal value $\mathbf{c} = \mathbf{c}^0$ for which the functional (1.4) reaches an extremum.

Learning becomes necessary only when *a priori* information is incomplete, and thus insufficient to define completely the functional (1.4). This case, which will basically be considered from now on, takes place when the probability density function $p(\mathbf{x})$ is unknown. Learning must be organized in such a fashion that the optimal vector $\mathbf{c} = \mathbf{c}^0$ is determined with the passage of time on the basis of the observed process $\mathbf{x}$ and the measured gradient of the random functional $\nabla_{\mathbf{c}} Q(\mathbf{x}, \mathbf{c})$. When the probability density function $p(\mathbf{x})$ is known in advance, and this corresponds to the case of sufficiently complete *a priori* information, the functional $J(\mathbf{c})$ (1.4) and its gradient $\nabla J(\mathbf{c})$ (1.5) can be written in explicit form, and the optimal vector $\mathbf{c} = \mathbf{c}^0$ can be defined, at least in principle, on the basis of presently well-developed methods of optimal control theory.

It should be clear now that learning systems are, generally speaking, asymptotically optimal systems, since optimal vector $\mathbf{c} = \mathbf{c}^0$ is not obtained immediately but with the passage of time through learning.

1.3 Complex Goals of Learning

More complex goals of learning, which correspond to the extremum of the functional that is a function of already known functionals (1.4), may become important in many cases.

This functional can be written, for instance, in the form

$$J_q(\mathbf{c}) = \Phi(\mathsf{M}_{\mathbf{x}_1}\{Q_1(\mathbf{x}_1, \mathbf{c})\}, \ldots, \mathsf{M}_{\mathbf{x}_q}\{Q_q(\mathbf{x}_q, \mathbf{c})\}). \tag{1.8}$$

In order to present $J_q(\mathbf{c})$ in a more compact form, we introduce the following notation for the component vector:

$$\vec{\mathbf{x}} = (\mathbf{x}_1, \ldots, \mathbf{x}_q), \tag{1.9}$$

where

$$\mathbf{x}_m = (x_{1m}, \ldots, x_{Mm}), \qquad m = 1, 2, \ldots, q,$$

and the vector function

$$\mathbf{Q}(\vec{\mathbf{x}}, \mathbf{c}) = (Q_1(\mathbf{x}_1, \mathbf{c}), \ldots, Q_q(\mathbf{x}_q, \mathbf{c})). \tag{1.10}$$

Then instead of (1.8), we obtain

$$J_q(\mathbf{c}) = \Phi(\mathsf{M}_{\vec{\mathbf{x}}}\{\mathbf{Q}(\vec{\mathbf{x}}, \mathbf{c})\}). \tag{1.11}$$

A more complex goal of learning is defined by the extremum of the functional

$$J_{q+s}(\mathbf{c}) = \mathsf{M}_{\vec{\mathbf{y}}}\{\Phi(\mathsf{M}_{\vec{\mathbf{x}}}\{\mathbf{Q}(\vec{\mathbf{x}}, \mathbf{c})\}, \mathbf{S}(\vec{\mathbf{y}}, \mathbf{c}))\}, \tag{1.12}$$

where in addition to (1.9) and (1.10) are introduced the symbols of the component vector

$$\vec{\mathbf{y}} = (\mathbf{y}_1, \ldots, \mathbf{y}_s) \tag{1.13}$$

and of the vector function

$$\mathbf{S}(\vec{\mathbf{y}}, \mathbf{c}) = (S_1(\mathbf{y}_1, \mathbf{c}), \ldots, S_s(\mathbf{y}_s, \mathbf{c})). \tag{1.14}$$

When $\mathbf{S}(\vec{\mathbf{y}}, \mathbf{c}) \equiv 0$, the functional (1.12) is transformed into the functional (1.11).

In order to obtain necessary conditions for the extremum of the functional (1.12) and, in particular, that of the functional (1.11), we set the gradient of the functional (1.12) at zero. We then obtain

$$\nabla J_{q+s}(\mathbf{c}) = \mathsf{M}_{\vec{\mathbf{y}}}\{\nabla_{\mathbf{c}}\Phi(\mathsf{M}_{\vec{\mathbf{x}}}\{\mathbf{Q}(\vec{\mathbf{x}}, \mathbf{c})\}, \mathbf{S}_{\vec{\mathbf{y}}}(\vec{\mathbf{y}}, \mathbf{c}))\} = 0. \tag{1.15}$$

In the cases when the functional $J_{q+s}(\mathbf{c})$ is convex and has unique extremum, the conditions (1.15) are at the same time sufficient, and the root of the equation (1.15) defines the optimal value $\mathbf{c} = \mathbf{c}^0$ for which the functional (1.12) has several extrema. This means that there are several local goals of learning. One of these local goals, which corresponds to the smallest (in the case of minimum) or largest (in the case of maximum) value of the functional, is the global goal of learning. Speaking of goals of learning, we shall consider only local goals of learning in the following unless the opposite is stated.

1.4 Constraints

Very frequently in the course of learning, the vectors $\mathbf{x}$, $\mathbf{c}$ must satisfy certain constraints. These constraints are expressed either in the form of equalities or inequalities. We shall distinguish constraints of two kinds.

The constraints of the first kind are given by equations that express certain natural laws, for instance, equations of motion.

The constraints of the second kind usually describe the limits of variations in given physical equalities. These limits cannot be exceeded. For instance, it is undesirable to exceed the limits of resources, energy, power, speed, etc.

The constraints of the second kind are usually described in the form of equalities and inequalities involving mathematical expectations of certain functions

$$g_\nu(\mathbf{c}) = \mathsf{M}_\mathbf{z}\{h_\nu(\mathbf{z}, \mathbf{c})\} = 0, \qquad \nu = 1, 2, \ldots, r < N, \tag{1.16}$$

or

$$g_\nu(\mathbf{c}) = \mathsf{M}_\mathbf{z}\{h_\nu(\mathbf{z}, \mathbf{c})\} < 0, \qquad \nu = 1, 2, 3, \ldots. \tag{1.17}$$

Therefore, these constraints include the process equations and the limits in process variables.

The existence of constraints, although narrowing the region of search for the optimal vector, complicates the process of finding the optimal vector. We shall mention that the constraints (1.16), (1.17) are also frequently incompletely defined as is the functional defining the goal of learning by its extremum.

1.5 Types of Learning

The need for learning arises whenever available *a priori* information is incomplete. The type of learning depends on the degree of completeness of this *a priori* information.

We shall distinguish two types of learning: learning with supervision (or with reinforcement) and learning without supervision (or without reinforcement).

In learning with supervision, it is assumed that at each instant of time we know in advance the desired response of the learning system, and we use the difference between the desired and actual response, that is, the error of the learning system, to correct its behavior. For instance, in learning to classify situations or to recognize patterns using reinforcement, there is a sequence of situations and patterns of known classification (so-called learning sequence), and this fact is used to form the classification errors in the process of learning while observing situations and patterns.

In learning without supervision, we do not know the desired response of the learning system, and thus we cannot explicitly formulate and use the errors of the learning system in order to improve its behavior.

For instance, in the case of learning to classify the situations or to recognize patterns, learning must be accomplished on the basis of observed situations or patterns of unknown classifications when a learning sequence is not available.

Learning without supervision is appropriately called self-learning. It may seem at first that self-learning is, in principle, impossible. The classified situations are characterized by many different features, and it seems improbable that a learning system by itself can find which features should be considered in classification and which should be neglected. The system cannot guess which classification was in the mind of a man evaluating the system. And if classification performed by such a system are arbitrary, only a few people may be satisfied.

However, regardless of the apparent justification of such pessimistic conclusions, they become unfounded under more careful considerations. The designer–teacher provides essential solutions to the system. For instance, the selection of input transducers predefines the features of the classified situations. If the input transducers are photoelements, then the features can be shape (dimensions), and not weight or density. The teacher also defines the goal of learning that has to be reached in the course of self-learning, and this eliminates the arbitrariness of classification.

1.6 Discussion

Let us briefly consider the questions of terminology, and the comparison between learning with supervision and learning without supervision. Frequently these two types of learning are called *learning with a teacher* and *learning without a teacher*. We think that this terminology is inappropriate. Learning without a teacher is actually impossible. The role of a teacher is not only to provide correct classification of the observed situations (in the case of learning with supervision), but also to formulate the goal of learning (in learning both with and without supervision). It is appropriate to use the following analogy. Learning with supervision corresponds to classroom learning where, in the course of the class, the teacher can answer any questions asked by the student (learning system). Learning without supervision, or self-learning, corresponds to learning by correspondence, using the methods and directions formed by a teacher, and the student cannot get explanations of certain unclear questions. It follows from this analogy that the term "learning without a teacher" does not reflect the true physical nature of self-learning, and thus we shall avoid it.

1.7 Conclusion

In this chapter we have become familiar with the concept of the goal of learning. A goal of learning is specified by the extremum of an incompletely defined functional, or, which is equivalent, by the roots of an incompletely defined functional equation. We have stated that complex goals of learning are also possible.

Learning must frequently be conducted in such a fashion that certain constraints are satisfied. We have also explained that learning may take two forms: learning with reinforcement and learning without reinforcement or self-learning. It is now time to show how learning can be accomplished and how to use it in the construction of various learning systems.

Comments

1.2 The concept of the goal of learning is closely related to the criteria of optimality which have been extensively discussed in the author's book [1]. Of course, the goal of learning specified by an extremum of the optimality criterion, has a meaning only in those cases when the criterion of optimality cannot be explicitely defined due to the lack of *a priori* information. The methods of the theory of optimal systems have been presented in numerous books and articles. Here, we shall only mention books related to the optimization of stochastic system.

First of all is the book by Fel'dbaum [1]. With his characteristic brilliance, the author has covered all aspects of the theory of optimal control theory, including his own theory of dual control.

The books by Aoki [1] and Sworder [1] present extensions of Fel'dbaum's ideas with respect to discrete systems. Although we cannot agree with all the statements in the latter book, we recommend the book to the readers that have an interest in the game-theoretic approach.

M. A. Krasnoselskii and P. P. Zabreyko suggested the possibility for generalization of the concept of gradient when the gradient in the simple sense does not exist.

1.3 The functional of the form (1.8), (1.11) was introduced in the correlation theory of statistical optimal systems by Andreev [1]. This and a more complex functional (1.12) had not been considered thus far in the theory of learning systems.

1.4 We casually mention the constraints not that they are unimportant, but because it would lead us away from the basic theme. Certain details related to the consideration of constraints can be found in the author's book [1].

1.5 The details related to various forms of learning are presented in the extremely interesting book by Fu [1]. Various approaches to the problem of learning can also be found in the works by the author [1, 2].

1.6 The term "learning without a teacher" was used by Aizerman *et al.* [1] of Chapter 5, and Braverman [1], Dorofeyuk [1], and Spragins [1] of Chapter 6.

REFERENCES

Andreev, N. I.

[1] "Correlation Theory of Statistical Optimal Systems." Nauka, Moscow, 1966 (in Russian).

Aoki, M.

[1] "Optimization of Stochastic Systems." Academic Press, New York, 1967.

Fel'dbaum, A. A.

[1] "Optimal Control Systems." Academic Press, New York, 1965.

Fu, K. S.

[1] "Sequential Methods in Pattern Recognition and Machine Learning." Academic Press, New York, 1968.

Sworder, D.

[1] "Optimal Adaptive Control Systems." Academic Press, New York, 1966.

Tsypkin, Ya. Z.

[1] "Adaptation and Learning in Automatic Systems." Academic Press, New York, 1971.

[2] Probleme der Adaptation in Automatische Systemen," Vol. 10, No. 10. Messen, Steuern, Regelung, 1967.

Chapter II

Algorithms of Learning

A cat that once sat on a hot stove will never again sit on a hot stove. Or on a cold one either.

M. TWAIN

2.1 Introduction

Learning in various learning systems is accomplished with the help of algorithms. These algorithms of learning actually represent stochastic difference or differential equations. Of course, the goal of learning can actually be achieved if the algorithms of learning converge, or in other words, if the solutions of the stochastic equations converge in a certain sense to the optimal values $\mathbf{c} = \mathbf{c}^*$, or more generally, if the values of the functionals defined over these solutions converge toward the optimal values.

This chapter introduces a method for obtaining the algorithms of learning, not only for simple, but also for complex goals of learning. The conditions for convergence of the algorithms are evaluated and the methods of treating the constraints are also considered. The presentation of the learning algorithms is preceded by a brief review of the algorithmic approach.

2.2 Algorithmic Approach

Let us assume for a moment that the probability density function $p(\mathbf{x})$ is known, and that the functional $J(\mathbf{c})$ can be written in the explicit form.

The necessary condition for the extremum of the functional is then given in the form of the equation

$$\nabla J(\mathbf{c}) = 0. \tag{2.1}$$

In order to be more specific, we shall assume that the extremum is the minimum.

In its general form, Eq. (2.1) cannot be solved unless certain gross simplifications are made (for instance, approximating a nonlinear equation (2.1) with a linear one). Since such approximation often leads us far from the solution of the posed problem, we shall use the algorithmic approach that is closely related to the iterative methods instead of the analytic one.

The "physical" meaning of the algorithmic approach consists of the substitution of the "statistical" equation (2.1) by a "dynamic" equation that converges in time to the optimal vector $\mathbf{c} = \mathbf{c}^*$. This dynamic equation —difference or differential—is indeed the algorithm for obtaining an optimal vector $\mathbf{c} = \mathbf{c}^*$. A discrete algorithm can be given in the form of a difference equation

$$\mathbf{c}[n] = \mathbf{c}[n-1] - \Gamma[n]\,\nabla J(\mathbf{c}[n-1]) \tag{2.2}$$

or equivalently by

$$\Delta\mathbf{c}[n-1] = -\Gamma[n]\,\nabla J(\mathbf{c}[n-1]). \tag{2.3}$$

The difference equation (2.2) actually represents a recursive relationship that permits us to determine the current value $\mathbf{c}[n]$ from the preceding value $\mathbf{c}[n-1]$.

A continuous algorithm can be written as a differential equation

$$d\mathbf{c}(t)/dt = -\Gamma(t)\,\nabla J(\mathbf{c}(t)). \tag{2.4}$$

In Eqs. (2.3) and (2.4), Γ is an $N \times N$ matrix. The elements of Γ are either constant or, generally speaking, depend on the current values of the vector $\mathbf{c}[n-1]$ or $\mathbf{c}[n]$.

The selected matrix Γ must guarantee the convergence of $\mathbf{c}[n]$ or $\mathbf{c}(t)$ to the optimal value $\mathbf{c}^*$. For various choices of $\Gamma[n]$, Algorithm (2.3) also covers many iterative formulas of numerical analysis. However, we shall not cover this here.

Discrete and continuous algorithms are easily realized respectively on digital and analog computers. A discrete system with feedback corresponds to the discrete algorithm (2.3), and a continuous feedback system corresponds to the continuous algorithm (2.4). The block diagram of these systems is shown in Fig. 2.1. It consists of a nonlinear functional converter $\nabla J(\mathbf{c})$, a matrix amplifier with variable gain coefficients Γ and discrete or continuous integrators. Double arrows indicate the vector connections, and the black arrow designates the sign reversal.

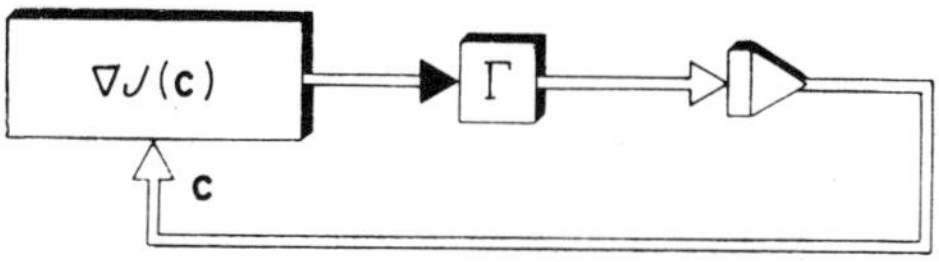

FIG. 2.1

It is important to emphasize that the block diagram shown in Fig. 2.1 is autonomous. All available and sufficiently complete *a priori* information is also included in the functional transformer. Therefore, learning is not needed here.

2.3 Algorithms of Learning

In the case of insufficient *a priori* information, that is, when the probability density function $p(\mathbf{x})$ is unknown and there is no possibility for estimating it in advance, the condition (2.1)

$$\nabla J(\mathbf{c}) = \mathsf{M}_{\mathbf{x}}\{\nabla_{\mathbf{c}} Q(\mathbf{x}, \mathbf{c})\} = 0 \tag{2.5}$$

cannot be specified explicitly. In these cases, the optimal vector $\mathbf{c} = \mathbf{c}^*$ is determined on the basis of learning algorithms. Learning algorithms have to provide an estimate of the vector $\mathbf{c}[n]$ or $\mathbf{c}(t)$ that converges in time to the optimal vector $\mathbf{c}^*$ using the observations $\mathbf{x}$, $\mathbf{c}$, and $\nabla_{\mathbf{c}} Q(\mathbf{x}, \mathbf{c})$.

The algorithms of learning are similar to the iterative formulas discussed in Section 2.2. The only difference is that the gradient of a stochastic functional $\nabla_{\mathbf{c}} Q(\mathbf{x}, \mathbf{c})$ now plays the role of the gradient $\nabla J(\mathbf{c})$. Therefore, we arrive at the following algorithms:

Discrete algorithm of learning:

$$\mathbf{c}[n] = \mathbf{c}[n-1] - \Gamma[n]\, \nabla_{\mathbf{c}} Q(\mathbf{x}[n], \mathbf{c}[n-1]); \tag{2.6}$$

Continuous algorithm of learning:

$$d\mathbf{c}(t)/dt = -\Gamma(t)\, \nabla_{\mathbf{c}} Q(\mathbf{x}(t), \mathbf{c}(t)). \tag{2.7}$$

Besides these algorithms, we shall introduce discrete-continuous or hybrid algorithms of learning

$$d\mathbf{c}(t)/dt = -\Gamma(t)\, \nabla_{\mathbf{c}} Q(\mathbf{x}[t], \mathbf{c}(t)), \tag{2.8}$$

where

$$\mathbf{x}[t] = \mathbf{x}(nT) \qquad \text{when} \quad nT \leq t < (n+1)T \tag{2.9}$$

is a stepwise function formed by discrete samples $\mathbf{x}[n] = \mathbf{x}(nT)$. In the algorithms of learning (2.6)–(2.8), Γ is in general a symmetric matrix, complete or diagonal. Its elements depend on the current instant (n or t), and perhaps, on the values of the vectors $\mathbf{x}$ and $\mathbf{c}$.

Discrete, continuous, and hybrid algorithms are realized, respectively, on the digital, analog, and hybrid computers. The block diagram of the system representing these algorithms is shown in Fig. 2.2.

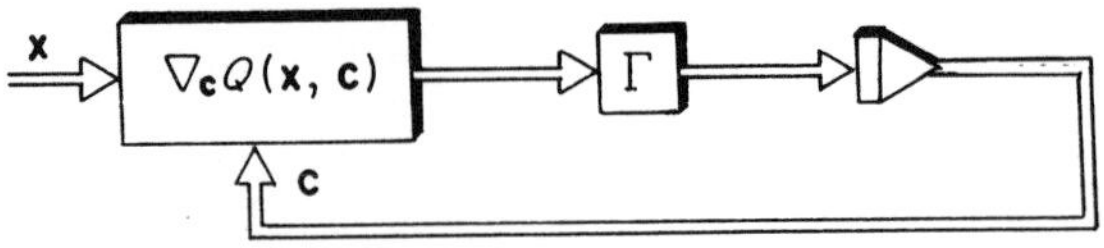

FIG. 2.2

Unlike the block diagram in Fig. 2.1, the block diagram in Fig. 2.2 represents a nonautonomous system. The functional transformer $\nabla_{\mathbf{c}} Q(\mathbf{x}, \mathbf{c})$ has two inputs, one of which carries the current information. The randomness of the gradient $\nabla_{\mathbf{c}} Q(\mathbf{x}, \mathbf{c})$ and the presence of additional disturbances impose definite constraints on the character of time variation in the coefficients of the matrix Γ. For instance, the matrix elements must converge to zero in time, because only under these conditions can the vectors $\mathbf{c}$ converge to the optimal values with probability one. It could be stated without any limitations that Γ is a diagonal matrix, that is,

$$\Gamma = \begin{pmatrix} \gamma_1 & 0 & \cdots & 0 \\ 0 & \gamma_2 & \cdots & 0 \\ \vdots & \vdots & & \vdots \\ 0 & 0 & \cdots & \gamma_N \end{pmatrix}, \tag{2.10}$$

since a complete matrix corresponds to a linear transformation of a diagonal matrix. In particular, when all elements in the diagonal matrix (2.10) are equal,

$$\Gamma = I\gamma, \tag{2.11}$$

where I is a unity matrix. The algorithms of learning (2.6) and (2.7) with (2.11) correspond to the discrete and continuous algorithms of the stochastic approximation method.

From the block diagram in Fig. 2.2, which corresponds to the algorithms of learning, it is easy to see the meaning and the essence of learning. Learning permits us to reduce the insufficient *a priori* information by processing the current information contained in the samples received from the external environment as time goes on.

2.4 Convergence of the Algorithms

The learning process will be successful if the attainment of the goal of learning can be guaranteed, or in other words, if the algorithms of learning converge. Convergence can be defined in various ways. For instance, we shall say that discrete algorithms converge in the mean-square sense and (or) almost surely if the sequence $\mathbf{c}[n]$ generated by these algorithms satisfy the conditions

$$\lim_{n\to\infty} \mathsf{M}\{\| \mathbf{c}[n] - \mathbf{c}^* \|^2\} = 0, \tag{2.12}$$

and (or)

$$\mathsf{P}\left\{\lim_{n\to\infty} \| \mathbf{c}[n] - \mathbf{c}^* \| = 0\right\} = 1. \tag{2.13}$$

Similarly, the convergence of continuous and hybrid algorithms in the mean-square sense and (or) with probability one take place when the function $\mathbf{c}(t)$ generated by the algorithms satisfies the conditions

$$\lim_{t\to\infty} \mathsf{M}\{\| \mathbf{c}(t) - \mathbf{c}^* \|^2\} = 0, \tag{2.14}$$

and (or)

$$\mathsf{P}\left\{\lim_{t\to\infty} \| \mathbf{c}(t) - \mathbf{c}^* \| = 0\right\} = 1, \tag{2.15}$$

where $\mathbf{c}^*$ is the optimal vector.

These definitions are convenient in cases when only one extremum of the functional exists. In order to cover more complicated cases, such as when the extremum of the functional lies on a closed set of points or segments, and when the functional has several extrema, it is useful to slightly modify such definitions of convergence. We shall say that a discrete algorithm converges almost surely if the functional $J(\mathbf{c}[n])$, defined over the sequence $\mathbf{c}[n]$ generated by the algorithm, satisfies the condition

$$\mathsf{P}\left\{\lim_{n\to\infty} [J(\mathbf{c}[n]) - \operatorname{extr} J(\mathbf{c})] = 0\right\} = 1, \tag{2.16}$$

and similarly for continuous and hybrid algorithms

$$\mathsf{P}\left\{\lim_{t\to\infty} [J(\mathbf{c}(t)) - \operatorname{extr} J(\mathbf{c})] = 0\right\} = 1. \tag{2.17}$$

From the convergence conditions (2.17) and (2.16), almost surely follow the conditions (2.13) and (2.15) that correspond to the case when the extremum is reached at the single optimal point $\mathbf{c} = \mathbf{c}^*$.

2.5 Criterion of Convergence of the Algorithms

The sufficient criterion of convergence of discrete algorithms of learning toward the goal of learning, which is the minimum or the lower branch of the functional, can be formulated in the following manner:

Discrete algorithms of learning converge almost surely if

(a) $\mathsf{M}_{\mathbf{x}}\{\nabla_{\mathbf{c}}{}^{\mathrm{T}} Q(\mathbf{x}, \mathbf{c})\, \nabla_{\mathbf{c}} Q(\mathbf{x}, \mathbf{c})\} \leq d(\alpha + \| \mathbf{c} \|^2), \quad \alpha = 0 \text{ or } 1;$ (2.18)

(b) the elements $\gamma_\nu[n]$ of the diagonal matrix $\Gamma[n]$ are such that

$$0 < \gamma_\nu[n] \leq \gamma_0(\alpha, \beta), \quad \sum_{n=1}^{\infty} \gamma_\nu[n] = \infty, \quad (\alpha + \beta) \sum_{n=1}^{\infty} \gamma_\nu{}^2[n] < \infty, \tag{2.19}$$

where $\beta = 1$ if the random gradient $\nabla_{\mathbf{c}} Q(\mathbf{x}, \mathbf{c})$ is measured with the errors of finite variance and mean zero, and $\beta = 0$ if such errors do not exist.

The meaning of these requirements for sufficient criterion of convergence is very simple. Requirement (a) imposes a constraint on the rate of increase in the functional, and thus on the gradient; the gradient $\nabla J(\mathbf{c})$ must not grow faster than a linear function of the norm of $\mathbf{c}$. Requirement (b) indicates that the discrete algorithm must guarantee the minimum or the lower branch in the functional. In this case $\gamma_\nu[n]$ $(\nu = 1, 2, \ldots, N)$ have to decrease in order to remove the influence of disturbances, but not so rapidly that a point different from the optimal one is reached. When noise is not present, $\beta = \alpha = 0$ and $\gamma_\nu[n]$ $(\nu = 1, 2, \ldots, N)$ can be either constant or decreasing sequences that converge to constant values.

For continuous (and hybrid) algorithms of learning, the sufficient criterion of convergence is formulated in an analogous fashion:

Continuous (and hybrid) algorithms converge almost surely if

(a) $$\mathsf{M}_{\mathbf{x}}\{\nabla_{\mathbf{c}}^{\mathrm{T}} Q(\mathbf{x}, \mathbf{c})\, \nabla_{\mathbf{c}} Q(\mathbf{x}, \mathbf{c})\} \leq d(\alpha + \| \mathbf{c} \|^2); \tag{2.20}$$

(b) the elements $\gamma_\nu(t)$ of the diagonal matrix $\Gamma(t)$ are such that

$$0 < \gamma_\nu(t), \qquad \int_0^\infty \gamma_\nu(t)\, dt = \infty, \qquad \int_0^\infty \gamma_\nu^2(t)\, dt < \infty. \tag{2.21}$$

This assumes that $\mathbf{x}$ is a random process with independent increments. The meaning of these requirements is the same as for discrete algorithms.

It should be remembered that if there is a finite number of local minima of the functional, these discrete and continuous algorithms lead to one of them.

Sufficient criteria of convergence in the case of convex functionals guarantee the convergence of the functional $J(\mathbf{c})$ to the values that correspond to the optimal $\mathbf{c}$ satisfying the equation

$$\mathsf{M}_{\mathbf{x}}\{\nabla_{\mathbf{c}} Q(\mathbf{x}, \mathbf{c})\} = 0. \tag{2.22}$$

2.6 Modified Algorithms

Let us introduce the operator $\mathfrak{B}$ that has the property

$$\mathsf{M}_{\mathbf{x}}\{\mathfrak{B}\, \nabla_{\mathbf{c}} Q(\mathbf{x}, \mathbf{c})\} = \mathsf{M}_{\mathbf{x}}\{\nabla_{\mathbf{c}} Q(\mathbf{x}, \mathbf{c})\}. \tag{2.23}$$

Various averaging or smoothing operators are related to the operators of this type. In the discrete case, for instance,

$$\mathfrak{B}_n\, \nabla_{\mathbf{c}} Q(\mathbf{x}[m], \mathbf{c}) = n^{-1} \sum_{m=1}^{n} \nabla_{\mathbf{c}} Q(\mathbf{x}[m], \mathbf{c}), \tag{2.24}$$

or

$$\mathfrak{B}_n\, \nabla_{\mathbf{c}} Q(\mathbf{x}[m], \mathbf{c}) = N_0^{-1} \sum_{m=n-N_0}^{n} \nabla_{\mathbf{c}} Q(\mathbf{x}[m], \mathbf{c}). \tag{2.25}$$

Similarly, in the continuous case

$$\mathfrak{B}_t\, \nabla_{\mathbf{c}} Q(\mathbf{x}(\tau), \mathbf{c}) = t^{-1} \int_0^t \nabla_{\mathbf{c}} Q(\mathbf{x}(\tau), \mathbf{c})\, d\tau, \tag{2.26}$$

or

$$\mathfrak{B}_{\mathrm{t}}\, \nabla_{\mathbf{c}} Q(\mathbf{x}(\tau), \mathbf{c}) = T^{-1} \int_{\mathrm{t}-T}^{t} \nabla_{\mathbf{c}} Q(\mathbf{x}(\tau), \mathbf{c})\, d\tau. \tag{2.27}$$

Using the identity (2.23), the condition (2.5) can be written as

$$\mathsf{M}\{\mathfrak{B}\, \nabla_{\mathbf{c}} Q(\mathbf{x}, \mathbf{c})\} = 0. \tag{2.28}$$

From this last relationship, we obtain the modified algorithms of learning:

Discrete algorithm:

$$\mathbf{c}[n] = \mathbf{c}[n-1] - \Gamma[n]\mathcal{B}_n \nabla_{\mathbf{c}} Q(\mathbf{x}[m], \mathbf{c}[n-1]); \tag{2.29}$$

Continuous algorithm:

$$d\mathbf{c}(t)/dt = -\Gamma(t)\mathcal{B}_{\mathrm{t}} \nabla_{\mathbf{c}} Q(\mathbf{x}(\tau), \mathbf{c}(t)); \tag{2.30}$$

Hybrid algorithm:

$$d\mathbf{c}(t)/dt = -\Gamma(t)\mathcal{B}_{\mathrm{t}} \nabla_{\mathbf{c}} Q(\mathbf{x}[\tau], \mathbf{c}(t)). \tag{2.31}$$

In Algorithms (2.23)–(2.31), the smoothing (complete and running) is carried simultaneously with the estimation of the sought optimal vector $\mathbf{c}^*$. Therefore, these modified algorithms can be called modified algorithms of simultaneous action. The block diagram representing these algorithms is shown in Fig. 2.3.

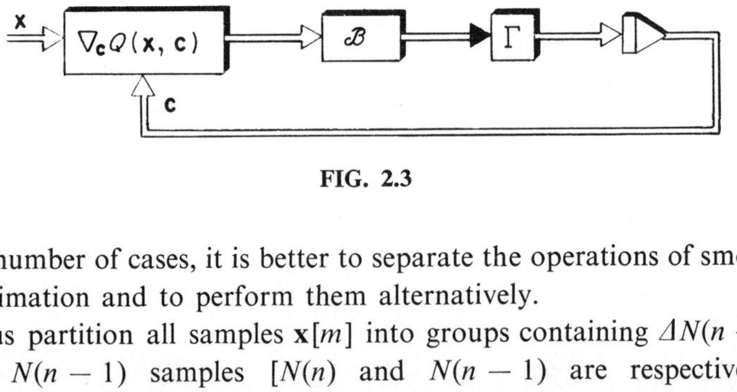

FIG. 2.3

In a number of cases, it is better to separate the operations of smoothing and estimation and to perform them alternatively.

Let us partition all samples $\mathbf{x}[m]$ into groups containing $\Delta N(n-1) = N(n) - N(n-1)$ samples [$N(n)$ and $N(n-1)$ are respectively the number of samples observed before the $(n-1)$st and the nth estimate of the vector $\mathbf{c}^*$ are computed]. Let us also introduce the averaging operator for each group of samples:

$$\mathcal{B}_N \nabla_{\mathbf{c}} Q(\mathbf{x}[m], \mathbf{c}) = [\Delta N(n-1)]^{-1} \sum_{m=N(n-1)+1}^{N(n)} \nabla_{\mathbf{c}} Q(\mathbf{x}[m], \mathbf{c}). \tag{2.32}$$

Then the discrete algorithm can be written in a complex, but still sufficiently clear form

$$\mathbf{c}[N(n)] = \mathbf{c}[N(n-1)] - \frac{\Gamma[n]}{\Delta N(n-1)} \sum_{m=N(n-1)+1}^{N(n)} \nabla_{\mathbf{c}} Q(\mathbf{x}[m], \mathbf{c}[N(n-1)]). \tag{2.33}$$

This algorithm will be called modified algorithm of alternating action. Using the property (2.23) of the averaging operator $\mathfrak{B}$, it is easy to conclude that if the simple algorithms converge, then their corresponding modified algorithms also converge.

2.7 General Algorithms of Learning

Let us now consider the functional (1.12) with the extremum, or, to be more specific, with the minimum that represents a complex goal of learning. It will be convenient to describe this functional in the form

$$J_{q+s}(\mathbf{c}) = \mathsf{M}_{\vec{\mathbf{y}}}\{\Phi(m, \mathbf{S}(\vec{\mathbf{y}}, \mathbf{c}))\}, \tag{2.34}$$

where

$$\mathbf{m} = \mathsf{M}_{\vec{\mathbf{x}}}\{\mathbf{Q}(\vec{\mathbf{x}}, \mathbf{c})\}. \tag{2.35}$$

The necessary conditions for the minimum (1.15) of the functional are explicitly given by

$$\nabla J_{q+s}(\mathbf{c}) = \mathsf{M}_{\vec{\mathbf{y}}}\left\{\left(\frac{d\mathbf{m}}{dc}\right)^{\mathrm{T}} \nabla_{\mathbf{m}}\Phi(\mathbf{m}, \mathbf{S}(\vec{\mathbf{y}}, \mathbf{c})) + \left(\frac{d\mathbf{S}(\mathbf{y}, \mathbf{c})}{d\mathbf{c}}\right)^{\mathrm{T}} \nabla_{\mathbf{s}}\Phi(\mathbf{m}, \mathbf{S}(\vec{\mathbf{y}}, \mathbf{c}))\right\} = 0. \tag{2.36}$$

However, from (2.35),

$$\frac{d\mathbf{m}}{d\mathbf{c}} = \mathsf{M}_{\vec{\mathbf{x}}}\left\{\frac{d\mathbf{Q}(\vec{\mathbf{x}}, \mathbf{c})}{d\mathbf{c}}\right\}. \tag{2.37}$$

By assuming that the stochastic processes $\vec{\mathbf{y}}$ and $\vec{\mathbf{x}}$ are statistically independent, we write the condition (2.36) in the form

$$\mathsf{M}_{\vec{\mathbf{x}}\vec{\mathbf{y}}}\left\{\left(\frac{d\mathbf{Q}(\vec{\mathbf{x}}, \mathbf{c})}{d\mathbf{c}}\right)^{\mathrm{T}} \nabla_{\mathbf{m}}\Phi(\mathbf{m}, \mathbf{S}(\vec{\mathbf{y}}, \mathbf{c})) + \left(\frac{d\mathbf{S}(\vec{\mathbf{y}}, \mathbf{c})}{d\mathbf{c}}\right)^{\mathrm{T}} \nabla_{\mathbf{s}}\Phi(\mathbf{m}, \mathbf{S}(\vec{\mathbf{y}}, \mathbf{c}))\right\} = 0. \tag{2.38}$$

Also, from (2.35) we obtain

$$\mathsf{M}_{\vec{\mathbf{x}}}\{\mathbf{m} - \mathbf{Q}(\vec{\mathbf{x}}, \mathbf{c})\} = 0. \tag{2.39}$$

Therefore, we have obtained two vector equations (2.38) and (2.39) relative to the unknown vectors $\mathbf{c}$ and $\mathbf{m}$. In Eq. (2.38),

$$\left(\frac{d\mathbf{Q}(\vec{\mathbf{x}}, \mathbf{c})}{d\mathbf{c}}\right)^{\mathrm{T}}, \qquad \left(\frac{d\mathbf{S}(\vec{\mathbf{y}}, \mathbf{c})}{d\mathbf{c}}\right)^{\mathrm{T}} \tag{2.40}$$

designate transposed matrices of dimensions $(N \times q)$ and $(N \times s)$, respectively. From Eqs. (2.38) and (2.39) directly follow general algorithms of learning:

Discrete algorithms:

$$\mathbf{c}[n] = \mathbf{c}[n-1] - \Gamma_1[n]\Bigg[\left(\frac{d\mathbf{Q}(\vec{\mathbf{x}}[n], \mathbf{c}[n-1])}{d\mathbf{c}}\right)^{\mathrm{T}} \times \nabla_{\mathbf{m}}\Phi(\mathbf{m}[n-1], \mathbf{S}(\vec{\mathbf{y}}[n], \mathbf{c}[n-1])) + \left(\frac{d\mathbf{S}(\vec{\mathbf{y}}[n], \mathbf{c}[n-1])}{d\mathbf{c}}\right)^{\mathrm{T}} \nabla_{\mathbf{s}}\Phi(\mathbf{m}[n-1], \mathbf{S}(\vec{\mathbf{y}}[n], \mathbf{c}[n-1]))\Bigg], \quad (2.41)$$

$$\mathbf{m}[n] = \mathbf{m}[n-1] - \Gamma_2[n][\mathbf{m}[n-1] - \mathbf{Q}(\vec{\mathbf{x}}[n], \mathbf{c}[n-1])]; \quad (2.42)$$

Continuous algorithms:

$$\frac{d\mathbf{c}(t)}{dt} = -\Gamma_1(t)\Bigg[\left(\frac{d\mathbf{Q}(\vec{\mathbf{x}}(t), \mathbf{c}(t))}{d\mathbf{c}}\right)^{\mathrm{T}} \nabla_{\mathbf{m}}\Phi(\mathbf{m}(t), \mathbf{S}(\vec{\mathbf{y}}(t), \mathbf{c}(t))) + \left(\frac{d\mathbf{S}(\vec{\mathbf{y}}(t), \mathbf{c}(t))}{d\mathbf{c}}\right)^{\mathrm{T}} \nabla_{\mathbf{s}}\Phi(\mathbf{m}(t), \mathbf{S}(\vec{\mathbf{y}}(t), \mathbf{c}(t)))\Bigg], \quad (2.43)$$

$$d\mathbf{m}(t)/dt = -\Gamma_2(t)[\mathbf{m}(t) - \mathbf{Q}(\vec{\mathbf{x}}(t), \mathbf{c}(t))]. \quad (2.44)$$

Hybrid algorithms differ from the continuous algorithms only by the

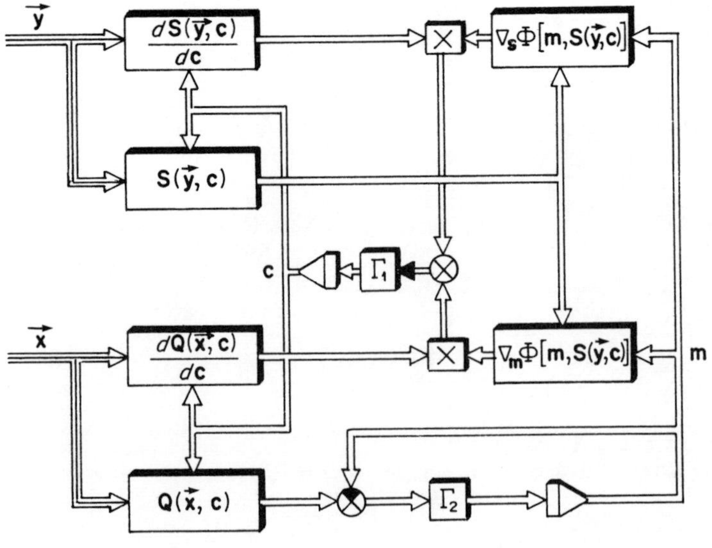

FIG. 2.4

presence of stepwise vector functions $\vec{x}[t]$, $\vec{y}[t]$, and thus we shall not write them down.

The block diagram representing these algorithms is given in Fig. 2.4.

2.8 Special Cases

Let us consider special cases of the algorithms given above.

1. When $\mathbf{S}(\vec{y}, \mathbf{c}) \equiv 0$, we obtain from (2.34) and (2.35)

$$\mathbf{J}_q(\mathbf{c}) = \Phi(\mathbf{m}), \tag{2.45}$$

$$\mathbf{m} = \mathsf{M}_{\vec{x}}\{\mathbf{Q}(\vec{x}, \mathbf{c})\}, \tag{2.46}$$

and from (2.41)–(2.44) follow

Discrete algorithms:

$$\mathbf{c}[n] = \mathbf{c}[n-1] - \Gamma_1[n]\left(\frac{d\mathbf{Q}(\vec{x}[n], \mathbf{c}[n-1])}{d\mathbf{c}}\right)^{\mathrm{T}} \nabla_{\mathbf{m}}\Phi(\mathbf{m}[n-1]), \tag{2.47}$$

$$\mathbf{m}[n] = \mathbf{m}[n-1] - \Gamma_2[n][\mathbf{m}[n-1] - \mathbf{Q}(\vec{x}[n], \mathbf{c}[n-1])]; \tag{2.48}$$

Continuous algorithms:

$$\frac{d\mathbf{c}(t)}{dt} = -\Gamma_1(t)\left(\frac{d\mathbf{Q}(\vec{x}(t), \mathbf{c}(t))}{d\mathbf{c}}\right)^{\mathrm{T}} \nabla_{\mathbf{m}}\Phi(\mathbf{m}(t)), \tag{2.49}$$

$$d\mathbf{m}(t)/dt = -\Gamma_2(t)[\mathbf{m}(t) - \mathbf{Q}(\vec{x}(t), \mathbf{c}(t))]. \tag{2.50}$$

The block diagram representing these algorithms is shown in Fig. 2.5.

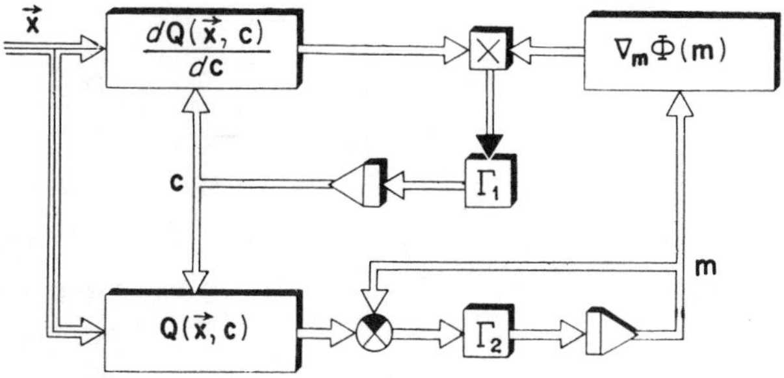

FIG. 2.5

2. If in addition to $\mathbf{S}(\vec{\mathbf{y}}, \mathbf{c}) \equiv 0$, we also assume that $q = 1$, instead of (2.34) and (2.35) we obtain

$$J_1(\mathbf{c}) = \Phi(\mathsf{M}_{\mathbf{x}_1}\{Q_1(\mathbf{x}_1, \mathbf{c})\}). \tag{2.51}$$

In this case

$$\nabla_{\mathbf{m}}\Phi(\mathbf{m}) = \Phi'(\mathbf{m}_1), \tag{2.52}$$

$$(d\mathbf{Q}(\vec{\mathbf{x}}, \mathbf{c})/d\mathbf{c})^{\mathrm{T}} = \nabla_{\mathbf{c}} Q_1(\mathbf{x}_1, \mathbf{c}), \tag{2.53}$$

and from Algorithms (2.41)–(2.44) follow

Discrete algorithms:

$$\mathbf{c}[n] = \mathbf{c}[n-1] - \Gamma_1[n]\Phi'(m_1[n-1])\,\nabla_{\mathbf{c}} Q_1(\mathbf{x}_1[n], \mathbf{c}[n-1]), \tag{2.54}$$

$$m_1[n] = m_1[n-1] - \gamma_2[n][m_1[n-1] - Q_1(\mathbf{x}_1[n], \mathbf{c}[n-1])]; \tag{2.55}$$

Continuous algorithms:

$$d\mathbf{c}(t)/dt = -\Gamma_1(t)\Phi'(m_1(t))\,\nabla_{\mathbf{c}} Q_1(\mathbf{x}_1(t), \mathbf{c}(t)), \tag{2.56}$$

$$dm_1(t)/dt = -\gamma_2(t)[m_1(t) - Q_1(\mathbf{x}_1(t), \mathbf{c}(t))]. \tag{2.57}$$

The block diagram representing these algorithms is shown in Fig. 2.6.

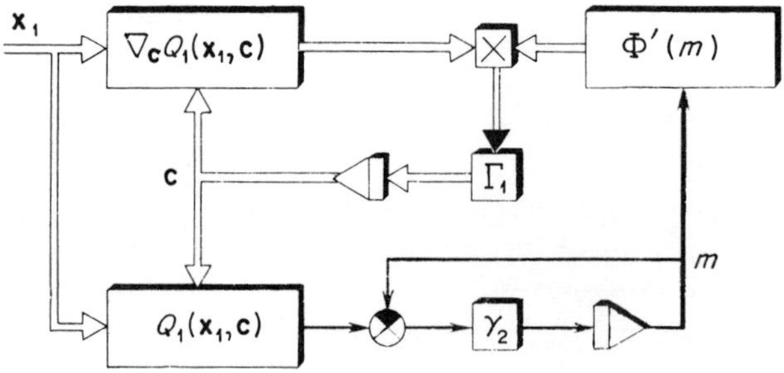

FIG. 2.6

If $\Phi(m_1)$ is linear, $\Phi'(m_1)$ is a constant, and Algorithms (2.54) and (2.56) become Algorithms (2.6) and (2.7) that correspond to the simple goals of learning. Regarding Algorithms (2.55) and (2.57), these can be used to estimate the value of the functional $m_1 = J_1(\mathbf{c})$ in the process of learning, and this may often be very useful.

3. When $\mathbf{Q}(\vec{\mathbf{x}}, \mathbf{c}) \equiv 0$, or, more specifically, when $\mathbf{m} \equiv 0$, we obtain from (2.34)

$$J_s(\mathbf{c}) = \mathsf{M}_{\vec{\mathbf{y}}}\{\Phi(\mathbf{S}(\vec{\mathbf{y}}, \mathbf{c}))\}, \tag{2.58}$$

and from Algorithms (2.41)–(2.44) follow

Discrete algorithms:

$$\mathbf{c}[n] = \mathbf{c}[n-1] - \Gamma_1[n]\left(\frac{d\mathbf{S}(\vec{\mathbf{y}}[n], \mathbf{c}[n-1])}{d\mathbf{c}}\right)^{\mathrm{T}} \times \nabla_s \Phi(\mathbf{S}(\vec{\mathbf{y}}[n], \mathbf{c}[n-1])); \tag{2.59}$$

Continuous algorithms:

$$\frac{d\mathbf{c}(t)}{dt} = -\Gamma_1(t)\left(\frac{d\mathbf{S}(\vec{\mathbf{y}}(t), \mathbf{c}(t))}{d\mathbf{c}}\right)^{\mathrm{T}} \nabla_s \Phi(\mathbf{S}(\vec{\mathbf{y}}(t), \mathbf{c}(t))). \tag{2.60}$$

The block diagram representing these algorithms is shown in Fig. 2.7.

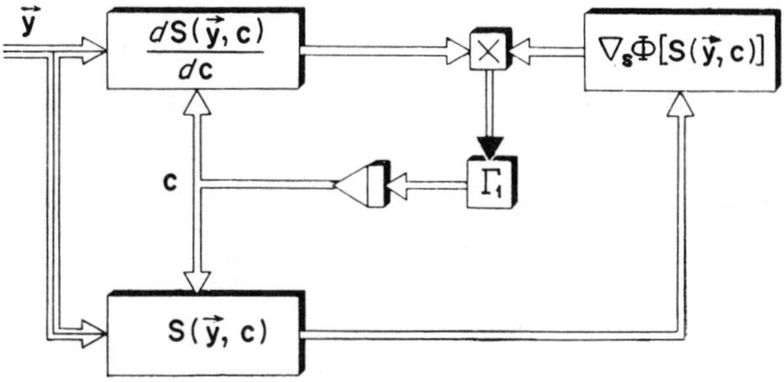

FIG. 2.7

It is not difficult to verify that in the special case for $\mathbf{S} = 1$ and a linear function $\Phi(\,\cdot\,)$, Algorithms (2.59) and (2.60) are transformed into the simple algorithms (2.6) and (2.7) that correspond to the simplest goals of learning.

2.9 Algorithms of Learning in the Presence of Constraints

Let us assume that the vector $\mathbf{c}$ must reach the complex goal of learning and simultaneously satisfy the constraints given in the form of Eq. (1.16),

$$\mathbf{g}(\mathbf{c}) = \mathsf{M}_{\vec{\mathbf{z}}}\{\mathbf{h}(\vec{\mathbf{z}}, \mathbf{c})\} = 0, \tag{2.61}$$

where the stationary random process $\vec{\mathbf{z}}$ does not depend upon random processes $\vec{\mathbf{x}}$ and $\vec{\mathbf{y}}$ that appear in the functional (2.34) and (2.35).

Using the method of Lagrange multipliers, we form a new functional

$$J_{q+s}(\mathbf{c}, \boldsymbol{\lambda}) = \mathsf{M}_{\vec{\mathbf{y}}}\{\Phi(\mathbf{m}, \mathbf{S}(\vec{\mathbf{y}}, \mathbf{c}))\} + \boldsymbol{\lambda}^{\mathrm{T}}\mathsf{M}_{\vec{\mathbf{z}}}\{\mathbf{h}(\vec{\mathbf{z}}, \mathbf{c})\}, \tag{2.62}$$

or

$$J_{q+s}(\mathbf{c}, \boldsymbol{\lambda}) = \mathsf{M}_{\vec{\mathbf{y}}\vec{\mathbf{z}}}\{\Phi(\mathbf{m}, \mathbf{S}(\vec{\mathbf{y}}, \mathbf{c})) + \boldsymbol{\lambda}^{\mathrm{T}}\mathbf{h}(\vec{\mathbf{z}}, \mathbf{c})\}, \tag{2.63}$$

and obtain necessary conditions for extremum

$$\begin{aligned} \nabla_{\mathbf{c}} J_{q+s}(\mathbf{c}, \boldsymbol{\lambda}) = \mathsf{M}_{\vec{\mathbf{y}}\vec{\mathbf{z}}}\Big\{&\left(\frac{d\mathbf{Q}(\vec{\mathbf{x}}, \mathbf{c})}{d\mathbf{c}}\right)^{\mathrm{T}} \nabla_{\mathbf{m}}\Phi(\mathbf{m}, \mathbf{S}(\vec{\mathbf{y}}, \mathbf{c})) \\ &+\left(\frac{d\mathbf{S}(\vec{\mathbf{y}}, \mathbf{c})}{d\mathbf{c}}\right)^{\mathrm{T}} \nabla_{\mathbf{s}}\Phi(\mathbf{m}, \mathbf{S}(\vec{\mathbf{y}}, \mathbf{c})) + \left(\frac{d\mathbf{h}(\vec{\mathbf{z}}, \mathbf{c})}{d\mathbf{c}}\right)^{\mathrm{T}}\boldsymbol{\lambda}\Big\} \\ = 0, \end{aligned} \tag{2.64}$$

$$\begin{aligned} \nabla_{\boldsymbol{\lambda}} J_{q+s}(\mathbf{c}, \boldsymbol{\lambda}) &= \mathsf{M}_{\vec{\mathbf{z}}}\{\mathbf{h}(\vec{\mathbf{z}}, \mathbf{c})\} \\ &= 0, \end{aligned} \tag{2.65}$$

and

$$\mathsf{M}_{\vec{\mathbf{x}}}\{\mathbf{m} - \mathbf{Q}(\vec{\mathbf{x}}, \mathbf{c})\} = 0. \tag{2.66}$$

In Eq. (2.64)

$$(d\mathbf{h}(\vec{\mathbf{z}}, \mathbf{c})/d\mathbf{c})^{\mathrm{T}} \tag{2.67}$$

designates a transposed matrix of dimension $N \times r$.

The algorithms of learning obtained from Conditions (2.64)–(2.66) can be presented in the following form:

Discrete algorithms:

$$\begin{aligned} \mathbf{c}[n] = \mathbf{c}[n-1] - \Gamma_1[n]\Big[&\left(\frac{d\mathbf{Q}(\vec{\mathbf{x}}[n], \mathbf{c}[n-1])}{d\mathbf{c}}\right)^{\mathrm{T}} \\ &\times \nabla_{\mathbf{m}}\Phi(\mathbf{m}[n-1], \mathbf{S}(\vec{\mathbf{y}}[n], \mathbf{c}[n-1])) \\ &+\left(\frac{d\mathbf{S}(\vec{\mathbf{y}}[n], \mathbf{c}[n-1])}{d\mathbf{c}}\right)^{\mathrm{T}} \nabla_{\mathbf{s}}\Phi(\mathbf{m}[n-1], \mathbf{S}(\vec{\mathbf{y}}[n], \mathbf{c}[n-1])) \\ &+\left(\frac{d\mathbf{h}(\vec{\mathbf{z}}[n], \mathbf{c}[n-1])}{d\mathbf{c}}\right)^{\mathrm{T}} \boldsymbol{\lambda}[n-1]\Big], \end{aligned} \tag{2.68}$$

$$\boldsymbol{\lambda}[n] = \boldsymbol{\lambda}[n-1] + \Gamma_2[n]\mathbf{h}(\vec{\mathbf{z}}[n], \mathbf{c}[n-1]), \tag{2.69}$$

$$\mathbf{m}[n] = \mathbf{m}[n-1] - \Gamma_3[n][\mathbf{m}[n-1] - \mathbf{Q}(\vec{\mathbf{x}}[n], \mathbf{c}[n-1])]; \tag{2.70}$$

Continuous algorithms:

$$\frac{d\mathbf{c}(t)}{dt} = -\Gamma_1(t)\left[\left(\frac{d\mathbf{Q}(\vec{\mathbf{x}}(t), \mathbf{c}(t))}{d\mathbf{c}}\right)^{\mathrm{T}} \nabla_{\mathrm{m}}\Phi(\mathbf{m}(t), \mathbf{S}(\vec{\mathbf{y}}(t), \mathbf{c}(t))) + \left(\frac{d\mathbf{S}(\vec{\mathbf{y}}(t), \mathbf{c}(t))}{d\mathbf{c}}\right)^{\mathrm{T}} \nabla_{\mathrm{s}}\Phi(\mathbf{m}(t), \mathbf{S}(\vec{\mathbf{y}}(t), \mathbf{c}(t))) + \left(\frac{d\mathbf{h}(\vec{\mathbf{z}}(t), \mathbf{c}(t))}{d\mathbf{c}}\right)^{\mathrm{T}} \boldsymbol{\lambda}(t)\right], \tag{2.71}$$

$$d\boldsymbol{\lambda}(t)/dt = \Gamma_2(t)\mathbf{h}(\vec{\mathbf{z}}(t), \mathbf{c}(t)), \tag{2.72}$$

$$d\mathbf{m}(t)/dt = -\Gamma_3(t)[\mathbf{m}(t) - \mathbf{Q}(\vec{\mathbf{x}}(t), \mathbf{c}(t))]. \tag{2.73}$$

Hybrid algorithms are not written down since they can be obtained from the continuous algorithms by substituting continuous samples $\vec{\mathbf{x}}(t), \vec{\mathbf{y}}(t), \vec{\mathbf{z}}(t)$ with the stepwise samples $\vec{\mathbf{x}}[t], \vec{\mathbf{y}}[t], \vec{\mathbf{z}}[t]$.

The block diagram representing these algorithms is shown in Fig. 2.8.

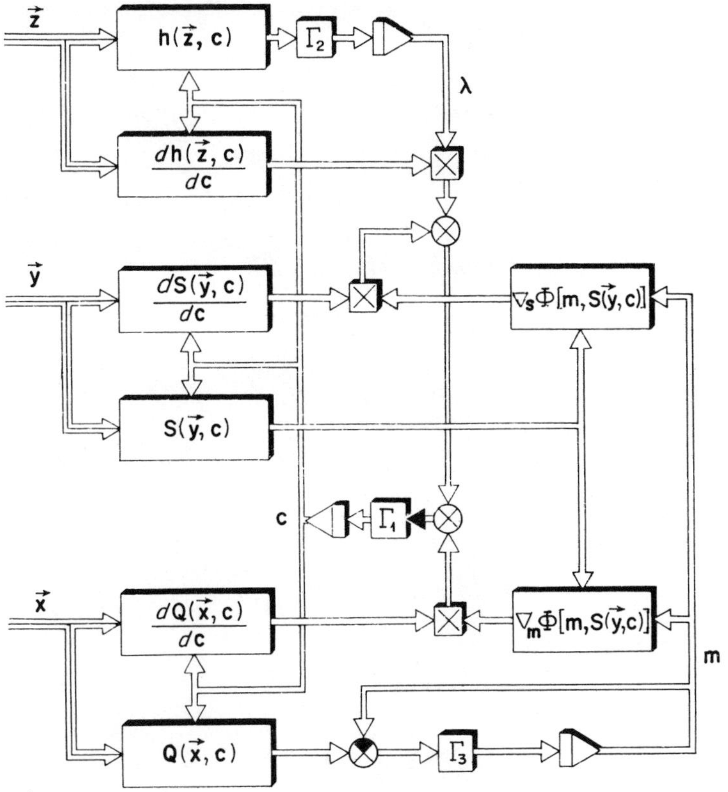

FIG. 2.8

2.10 Special Cases

Let us consider the special cases of the algorithms under constraints.

1. When $\mathbf{S}(\vec{\mathbf{y}}, \mathbf{c}) \equiv 0$, that is, for the functional (2.45), (2.46), and the constraints (2.61), we obtain from (2.68)–(2.73):

Discrete algorithms:

$$\mathbf{c}[n] = \mathbf{c}[n-1] - \Gamma_1[n]\Bigg[\left(\frac{d\mathbf{Q}(\vec{\mathbf{x}}[n], \mathbf{c}[n-1])}{d\mathbf{c}}\right)^{\mathrm{T}} \times \nabla_{\mathbf{m}}\Phi(\mathbf{m}[n-1]) + \left(\frac{d\mathbf{h}(\vec{\mathbf{z}}[n], \mathbf{c}[n-1])}{d\mathbf{c}}\right)^{\mathrm{T}}\boldsymbol{\lambda}[n-1]\Bigg], \tag{2.74}$$

$$\boldsymbol{\lambda}[n] = \boldsymbol{\lambda}[n-1] + \Gamma_2[n]\mathbf{h}(\vec{\mathbf{z}}[n], \mathbf{c}[n-1]), \tag{2.75}$$

$$\mathbf{m}[n] = \mathbf{m}[n-1] - \Gamma_3[n][\mathbf{m}[n-1] - \mathbf{Q}(\vec{\mathbf{x}}[n], \mathbf{c}[n-1])]; \tag{2.76}$$

Continuous algorithms:

$$\frac{d\mathbf{c}(t)}{dt} = -\Gamma_1(t)\Bigg[\left(\frac{d\mathbf{Q}(\vec{\mathbf{x}}(t), \mathbf{c}(t))}{d\mathbf{c}}\right)^{\mathrm{T}} \nabla_{\mathbf{m}}\Phi(\mathbf{m}(t)) + \left(\frac{d\mathbf{h}(\vec{\mathbf{z}}(t), \mathbf{c}(t))}{d\mathbf{c}}\right)^{\mathrm{T}}\boldsymbol{\lambda}(t)\Bigg], \tag{2.77}$$

$$d\boldsymbol{\lambda}(t)/dt = \Gamma_2(t)\mathbf{h}(\vec{\mathbf{z}}(t), \mathbf{c}(t)), \tag{2.78}$$

$$d\mathbf{m}(t)/dt = -\Gamma_3(t)[\mathbf{m}(t) - \mathbf{Q}(\vec{\mathbf{x}}(t), \mathbf{c}(t))]. \tag{2.79}$$

The block diagram representing these algorithms is shown in Fig. 2.9.

2. If in addition to $\mathbf{S}(\vec{\mathbf{y}}, \mathbf{c}) \equiv 0$, it is also assumed that $q = 1$, from (2.74) and (2.75) we obtain

Discrete algorithms:

$$\mathbf{c}[n] = \mathbf{c}[n-1] - \Gamma_1[n]\Bigg[\Phi'(m[n-1])\,\nabla_{\mathbf{c}}Q_1(\mathbf{x}_1[n], \mathbf{c}[n-1]) + \left(\frac{d\mathbf{h}(\vec{\mathbf{z}}[n], \mathbf{c}[n-1])}{d\mathbf{c}}\right)^{\mathrm{T}}\boldsymbol{\lambda}[n-1]\Bigg], \tag{2.80}$$

$$\boldsymbol{\lambda}[n] = \boldsymbol{\lambda}[n-1] + \Gamma_2[n]\mathbf{h}(\vec{\mathbf{z}}[n], \mathbf{c}[n-1]), \tag{2.81}$$

$$m[n] = m[n-1] - \gamma_3[n][m[n-1] - Q_1(\mathbf{x}_1[n], \mathbf{c}[n-1])]; \tag{2.82}$$

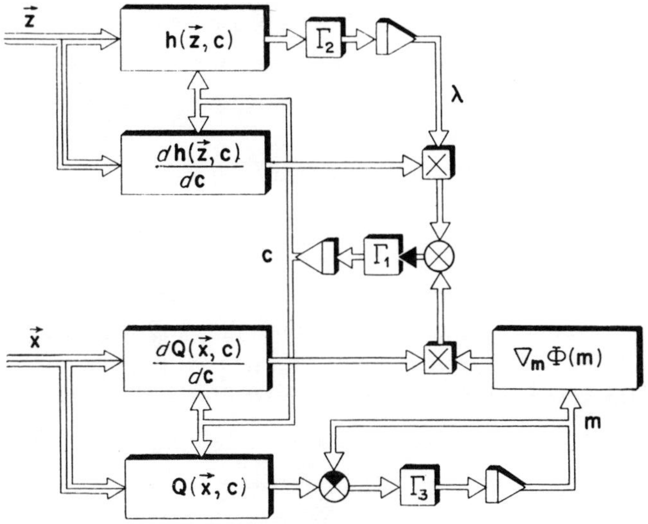

FIG. 2.9

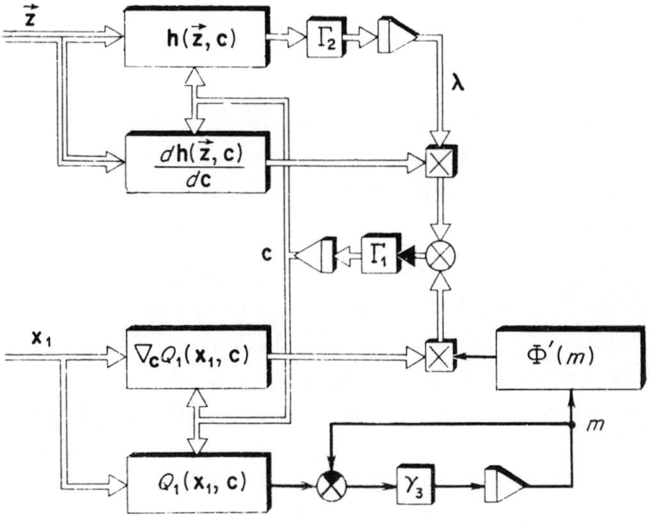

FIG. 2.10

Continuous algorithms:

$$\frac{d\mathbf{c}(t)}{dt} = -\Gamma_1(t)\left[\Phi'(\mathbf{m}(t))\,\nabla_{\mathbf{c}} Q_1(\mathbf{x}_1(t), \mathbf{c}(t)) + \left(\frac{d\mathbf{h}(\mathbf{z}(t), \mathbf{c}(t))}{d\mathbf{c}}\right)^{\mathrm{T}} \boldsymbol{\lambda}(t)\right], \tag{2.83}$$

$$d\boldsymbol{\lambda}(t)/dt = \Gamma_2(t)\mathbf{h}(\vec{\mathbf{z}}(t), \mathbf{c}(t)), \tag{2.84}$$

$$d\mathbf{m}(t)/dt = -\gamma_3(t)[m(t) - Q_1(\mathbf{x}_1(t), \mathbf{c}(t))]. \tag{2.85}$$

The block diagram representing these algorithms is shown in Fig. 2.10.

If $\Phi(m)$ is a linear function, Algorithms (2.80), (2.81), (2.83), and (2.84) are transformed into simple algorithms that correspond to the simplest goal of learning in the presence of constraints.

2.11 Conclusion

The algorithms of learning, with which we became familiar in this chapter, guarantee the attainment of the corresponding goal of learning when the conditions of the stability criteria are satisfied. Since the goal of learning is reached in time, the learning system that realizes these algorithms is an asymptotically optimal system. The same goal of learning can be reached by various algorithms of learning—simple or modified, with simultaneous or alternative action.

Comments

2.2 The algorithmic approach is described at greater length in the book by the author [1] in Chapter 1. A sufficiently complete bibliography is also given there. Various iterative methods for solving operator equations are considered in the interesting book by Krasnoselskii *et al.* [1].

2.3 Discrete and continuous algorithms of learning are also described in the author's paper [1] and book [1] in Chapter 1. Hybrid algorithms were introduced in the author's paper [2]. The publications by Ventner [1], Krasulina [2], and Fabian [1–3] are devoted to the development of the classical stochastic approximation method. See also the book by Wasan [1]. The works by Kacprzynski [1–3], which consider slightly different algorithms of learning, are also very interesting. We have limited our discussion to the single stage discrete algorithms of learning and the continuous algorithms of the first order.

Multistage algorithms and algorithms of a higher order are described in the book by the author [1] in Chapter 1 and in the works by Brusin [1, 2].

An interesting monograph by Albert and Gardner [1] is devoted to the questions of solving nonlinear regression equations of the type

$$\mathsf{M}\{Y_n\} = F_n(c)$$

using the stochastic approximation method. This book also contains a good description of the methods for investigating the convergence of various iterative algorithms. The search algorithms for multiextremal problems corresponding to many goals of learning were studied by Veisbord and Yudin [1, 2], and Krasulina [1].

2.4 Exact formulations of the concept of convergence of the type (2.12)–(2.13) are given in the books by Loève [1], Middleton [1] in Chapter 4, and Hasminskii [1]. The last book is especially recommended to those who are interested in the problems of stochastic stability.

The modification of the definition of convergence expressed by (2.16) is due to Litvakov [1].

2.5 Recently, a number of publications appeared which are devoted to the convergence of discrete algorithms. The most prominent one is the fundamental work by Braverman and Rozonoer. These results are repeated in the work by Braverman and Litvakov [1]. The proof of the criterion of convergence for discrete algorithms presented here can be found in the work by Devyaterikov *et al.* [1]. Closely related to the same questions are the works by Ermolyev [1], Ermolyev and Nekrilova [1, 2], Ermolyev and Shor [1], and Shor [1], in which the method of generalized stochastic algorithms is developed. Also see the book by Polyak [2].

Classical results obtained by Gladishev [1] represent a conceptual basis for numerous works concerned with the convergence of discrete algorithms. This fact is clearly illustrated in the paper by Morozan [1].

For continuous algorithms, the conditions of convergence are given only for random processes with finite increments. Many theorems on the convergence of various continuous algorithms were obtained by Sakrison [1], Hasminskii [1], and Csibi [1].

It would be very interesting to find general conditions of convergence under sufficiently broad assumptions about stationary processes.

2.6 Special cases of modified algorithms, the simplest modified algorithms of simultaneous action were considered by Nikolic and Fu [1], and also by Blaydon [1] in Chapter 6. The simplest linear algorithms of repetitive action were considered by Chien and Fu [1] and the author [4]. The statement that modified algorithms converge faster than ordinary algorithms (Nikolic and Fu [1]) is incorrect (see the works by the author [2] in Chapter 6, and Chien and Fu [1]).

2.7 Generalized algorithms were considered by the author [4] but unfortunately, complete conditions for convergence of generalized algorithms of learning have not been obtained. The question is related to the constraints imposed on the function $\Phi(\,\cdot\,)$.

2.9–2.10 The conditions for applying algorithms in the presence of constraints is investigated relatively little. The conditions for deterministic continuous algorithms under both equality and inequality constraints are given in the book by Arrow *et al.* [1] and in a more formal way in the work by Polyak [1].

REFERENCES

Albert, A. E.
[1] Nonlinear regression and stochastic approximation. *IEEE Internat. Conv. Rec.* **15**, No. 3 (1967).

Albert, A. E., and Gardner, L. A.
[1] "Stochastic Approximation and Nonlinear Regression." MIT Press, Cambridge, Massachusetts, 1967.

Arrow, K. J., Hurwicz, L., and Uzava, H.
[1] "Studies in Linear and Non-Linear Programming." Stanford Univ. Press, Stanford, California, 1958.

Braverman, E. M., and Litvakov, B. M.
[1] Convergence of algorithms of learning and adaptation. *Congr. IFAC, 4th, Warszawa, July 16–21, 1969.*

Brusin, V. A.
[1] A generalized problem of stochastic approximation. *Izv. Vysš. Učebn. Zaved. Radiofizika* **12**, No. 3 (1969) (in Russian).
[2] A generalization of the problem of stochastic approximation. *Avtomat. i Telemeh.* No. 3 (1969).

Butz, A. R.
[1] Relative saddle point technique. *SIAM J. Appl. Math.* **15**, No. 3 (1967).

Chien, Y. T., and Fu, K. S.
[1] On Bayesian learning and stochastic approximation. *IEEE Trans. System. Sci. Cybernetics* **SSC-2**, No. 1 (1967).

Csibi, S.
[1] On continuous stochastic approximation. *Proc. Colloq. Information Theory, 1967.* Bolyai Math. Soc. Debrecen, Hungary.

Devyaterikov, I. P., Kaplinskii, A. I., and Tsypkin, Ya. Z.
[1] On the convergence of the algorithms of learning. *Avtomat. i Telemeh.* No. 10 (1969).
Ermolyev, Yu. M.
[1] The methods of solving non-linear extremal problems. *Kibernetika (Kiev)* No. 4 (1966).
[2] On the method of generalized stochastic gradients and stochastic quasi-Feyer series. *Kibernetika (Kiev)* No. 2 (1969).
Ermolyev, Yu. M., and Nekrilova, Z. V.
[1] On certain methods of stochastic approximation. *Kibernetika (Kiev)* No. 6 (1966).
[2] The method of stochastic gradients and its application. *Semin. Theory of Optimal Decisions, 1st, Kiev, 1967.*
Ermolyev, Yu. M., and Shor, N. Z.
[1] The method of random search for a two-stage problem of stochastic programming and its generalization. *Kibernetika (Kiev)* No. 1 (1968).
Fabian, V.
[1] Stochastic approximation methods. *Czechoslovak Math. J.* **10** (85), No. 1 (1960).
[2] Pregled deterministickych a stochastikych approximacnich method pro minimalizaci funkci. *Kybernetica (Kiev)* **1**, 6 (1965).
[3] Stochastic approximation of minima with improved asymptotic speed. *Ann. Math. Statist.* **38**, No. 1 (1967).
[4] Stochastic approximation of constrained minima. *Trans. Conf. Information Theory, Statist. Design Functions, Random Process, 4th, Prague, 1965.* Academia, Prague, 1967.
Fu, K. S., and Nikolic, Z. J.
[1] On some reinforcement techniques and their relations to the stochastic approximation. *IEEE Trans. Automatic Control* **AC-11**, No. 4 (1966).
Gikhman, I. I., and Skorohod, A. V.
[1] "Stochastic Differential Equations." Naukova Dumka, 1968.
Gladishev, E. G.
[1] On stochastic approximation. *Teor. Verojatnost. i Primenen.* **10**, No. 2 (1965).
Hasminskii, R. Z.
[1] "Stability of Differential Equations with Randomly Disturbed Parameters." Nauka, Moscow, 1969 (in Russian).
Kacprzynski, B.
[1] Sekwencyjna methoda poszukiwania ekstremum. *Arch. Automat. i Telemech.* **11**, No. 2 (1966).
[2] O pewnej metodzie rozwiazywonia rownania regresji, *Arch. Automat. i Telemech.* **13**, No. 2 (1968).
[3] O pewnej metodzie sekwencyjnego poszukiwania ekstremum funkcji regresji klasy $\lim_m I$. *Arch. Automat. i Telemech.* **14**, No. 1 (1969).
Krasnoselskii, M. A., Vainiko, G. M., Zabreyko, P. P., Rutitskii, Ya. B., and Stecenko, V. Ya.
[1] "Approximate Solutions of the Operator Equations." Nauka, Moscow, 1969.
Krasulina, T. B.
[1] On Robbins–Monro procedure in the case of several roots. *Teor. Verojatnost. i Primenen.* **12**, No. 2 (1967).

[2] On application of stochastic approximation algorithms to the problems of automatic control in the presence of strong disturbances. *Avtomat. i Telemeh.* No. 5 (1969).

Litvakov, B. M.

[1] On the convergence of recursive algorithms of learning in pattern recognition. *Avtomat. i Telemeh.* No. 1 (1968).

Loève, M.

[1] "Probability Theory," 3rd ed. Van Nostrand–Reinhold, Princeton, New Jersey, 1963.

Loginov, N. V.

[1] Stochastic approximation methods. *Avtomat. i Telemeh.* No. 4 (1966).

Morozan, T.

[1] Sur l'approximation stochastique. *C. R. Acad. Sci. Paris, Ser. A-B* **264**, No. 13 (1967).

Nikolic, Z. J., and Fu, K. S.

[1] A mathematical model of learning in an unknown random environment. *Proc. Nat. Electron. Conf.* **22** (1966).

Polyak, B. T.

[1] On certain dual methods of solving the problems of conditional extremum. The questions of accuracy and effectiveness of algorithms, *Trudy Symp., Kiev, 1969*, **4** (in Russian).

[2] Minimization of discontinuous functionals. *Z. Vyčisl. Mat. i Mat. Fiz.* **9**, No. 3 (1969).

Sakrison, D. J.

[1] A continuous Kiefer–Wolfowitz procedure for random processes. *Ann. Math. Stat.* **35**. No. 2 (1964).

Shor, N. Z.

[1] On convergence of the generalized algorithm. *Kybernetika* (*Prague*), No. 3 (1968)

Tsypkin, Ya. Z.

[1] Optimization, adaptation and learning in automatic systems. *In* "Computer and Information Sciences, II (J. T. Tou, ed.). Academic Press, New York, 1967.

[2] Optimal hybrid algorithms of adaptation and learning. *Avtomat. i Telemeh.* No. 8 (1968).

[3] Generalized algorithms of learning. *Avtomat. i Telemeh.* No. 1 (1970).

[4] Learning control systems. *Avtomat. i Telemeh.* No. 4 (1970).

Veisbord, E. M., and Yudin, D. B.

[1] Stochastic approximation for multiextremal problems in Hilbert space. *Dokl. Akad. Nauk SSSR* **181**, No. 5 (1968).

[2] Multiextremal stochastic approximation. *Izv. Akad. Nauk SSSR Tehn. Kibernet.* No. 5 (1968).

Ventner, T. M.

[1] An extension of the Robbins–Monro procedure. *Ann. Math. Statist.* **38**, No. 1 (1967).

Wasan, M. T.

[1] "Stochastic Approximation." Cambridge Univ. Press, London and New York, 1969.

Chapter III

Algorithms of Optimal Learning

There are many different opinions, but hardly anyone knows the truth.

HESIOD

3.1 Introduction

Any learning system that satisfies the conditions of the convergence criterion can reach the goal of learning, but the criterion of convergence establishes very broad boundaries of convergence. This creates then a natural desire to select within these boundaries such parameters of the algorithms for which the learning proceeds in a certain best sense. Therefore, we face the problem of finding the algorithms that are optimal from a certain given viewpoint.

Learning systems in which simple algorithms of learning are used, as we mentioned earlier, are asymptotically optimal systems. On the other hand, learning systems in which algorithms of optimal learning are employed, are optimal learning systems. In this chapter, the performance indices of learning will be considered, the methods of obtaining quasi-optimal, optimal, and suboptimal learning are given, and their properties and characteristics are explained.

Algorithms of optimal learning are very complex and only in certain rare cases can they be completely realized. Therefore, their role is to establish those limits that can be achieved in the course of building more complex learning systems.

3.2 Performance Indices of Learning

In order to evaluate the quality of learning, it is necessary to introduce a certain measure—a functional that at each instant estimates the *distance* between the current state and the optimal state, that is, the state that corresponds to the goal of learning. An algorithm of learning can then be considered to be an algorithm of optimal learning if the "distance" is minimal at each instant.

Such a measure can be used as the performance index of learning. One of the most convenient performance indices of learning is perhaps the variance of the estimate of the optimal vector $\mathbf{c}^*$ at each instant:

$$V^2[n] = \mathsf{M}\{\| \mathbf{c}[n] - \mathbf{c}^* \|^2\}, \tag{3.1}$$

for discrete algorithms of learning, and

$$V^2(t) = \mathsf{M}\{\| \mathbf{c}(t) - \mathbf{c}^* \|^2\}, \tag{3.2}$$

for continuous or hybrid algorithms.

However, when *a priori* information is sufficiently small, the performance indices of learning (3.1) and (3.2) can be applied effectively only to the linear algorithms of learning.

Is it then possible to find such a performance index of learning that can be applied to the nonlinear algorithms of learning and, in the case of linear algorithms, that would lead to the algorithms that can follow from the performance indices (3.1) and (3.2)? It appears that this is possible. Such a performance index can be an estimate $\hat{J}(\mathbf{c})$ of the original performance index $J(\mathbf{c})$ that defines with its minimum the goal of learning, that is, an estimate of the functional

$$J(\mathbf{c}) = \int_X Q(\mathbf{x}, \mathbf{c})p(\mathbf{x})\, d\mathbf{x}. \tag{3.3}$$

This estimate can be obtained in the following way: Let us designate by $\mathbf{x}[m]$ or $\mathbf{x}(\tau)$ the observed samples. The empirical estimate of the probability density function $p(\mathbf{x})$ can then be given in the form

$$\hat{p}(\mathbf{x}) = n^{-1} \sum_{m=1}^{n} \delta(\mathbf{x} - \mathbf{x}[m]) \tag{3.4}$$

for discrete data, and

$$\hat{p}(\mathbf{x}) = t^{-1} \int_0^t \delta(\mathbf{x} - \mathbf{x}(\tau))\, d\tau \tag{3.5}$$

for continuous data.

In Eqs. (3.4) and (3.5), $\delta(\mathbf{x})$ represents a multidimensional δ-function that has these properties:

$$\delta(\mathbf{x}-\mathbf{x}^0)=\begin{cases}0 & \text{when}\quad \mathbf{x}\neq\mathbf{x}^0\\ \infty & \text{when}\quad \mathbf{x}=\mathbf{x}^0\end{cases} \tag{3.6}$$

and

$$\int_X f(\mathbf{x})\delta(\mathbf{x}-\mathbf{x}^0)\,d\mathbf{x}=f(\mathbf{x}^0). \tag{3.7}$$

The estimate of the functional (3.3) is equal to

$$\hat{J}(\mathbf{c})=\int_X Q(\mathbf{x},\mathbf{c})\hat{p}(\mathbf{x})\,d\mathbf{x}. \tag{3.8}$$

By substituting $\hat{p}(\mathbf{x})$ from Eq. (3.4) and again from Eq. (3.5) into (3.8) and by considering Eq. (3.7), we obtain

$$\hat{J}(\mathbf{c}[n])=n^{-1}\sum_{m=1}^{n}Q(\mathbf{x}[m],\mathbf{c}[n]) \tag{3.9}$$

for discrete data, and

$$\hat{J}(\mathbf{c}(t))=t^{-1}\int_0^t Q(\mathbf{x}(\tau),\mathbf{c}(t))\,d\tau \tag{3.10}$$

for continuous data. The functionals (3.9) and (3.10) can be considered to be the performance indices of learning.

3.3 Generalized Performance Indices of Learning

When linear algorithms of optimal learning are not desired to minimize simultaneously different performance indices, for instance, (3.1) and (3.9), it is convenient to use the performance indices of learning that, unlike (3.9) and (3.10), do not need infinite memory $\mathbf{x}[m]$, $\mathbf{x}(\tau)$; $\mathbf{c}[n]$, $\mathbf{c}(t)$. The functional

$$\hat{J}_N(\mathbf{c}[n])=[N(n)+1]^{-1}\sum_{m=n-N(n)}^{n}Q(\mathbf{x}[m],\mathbf{c}[n]) \tag{3.11}$$

or

$$\hat{J}_T(\mathbf{c}(t))=[T(t)]^{-1}\int_{t-T(t)}^{t}Q(\mathbf{x}(\tau),\mathbf{c}(t))\,d\tau \tag{3.12}$$

can serve as such performance indices. These are the generalized performance indices. In the special case when $N(n)=n$ and $T(t)=t$, they become our well-known performance indices (3.9) and (3.10).

It is self-evident that the algorithms of optimal learning become necessary when the time interval for observing the samples $\mathbf{x}[n]$ or $\mathbf{x}(t)$ is finite, and when the best estimate of the vector $\mathbf{c}$ must be found with respect to the selected performance index.

3.4 Discrete Algorithms of Quasi-Optimal Learning

Let us write the discrete algorithm in this form:

$$\mathbf{c}[n] = \mathbf{c}[n-1] - \mathfrak{A}\boldsymbol{\gamma}[n]\,\nabla_{\mathbf{c}} Q(\mathbf{x}[n], \mathbf{c}[n-1]), \tag{3.13}$$

where $\mathfrak{A}$ is the operator that transforms the vector $\boldsymbol{\gamma}$ into a diagonal matrix, that is,

$$\mathfrak{A}\boldsymbol{\gamma} = \begin{pmatrix} \gamma_1 & 0 & \cdots & 0 \\ 0 & \gamma_2 & \cdots & 0 \\ \vdots & \vdots & & \vdots \\ 0 & 0 & \cdots & \gamma_N \end{pmatrix}. \tag{3.14}$$

Using $\mathbf{c}[n]$ from (3.13) in the performance index of learning (3.9), we obtain

$$\hat{J}(\mathbf{c}[n]) = n^{-1} \sum_{m=1}^{n} Q(\mathbf{x}[m], \mathbf{c}[n-1] - \mathfrak{A}\boldsymbol{\gamma}[n]\,\nabla_{\mathbf{c}} Q(\mathbf{x}[n], \mathbf{c}[n-1])). \tag{3.15}$$

We shall now search for the values of the vector $\boldsymbol{\gamma}[n]$ which minimize this functional for any current value n. By computing the gradient (3.15) with respect to $\boldsymbol{\gamma}$, we obtain the condition of optimality

$$\begin{aligned} \nabla_{\gamma}\hat{J}(\mathbf{c}[n]) &= -\mathfrak{A}\,\nabla_{\mathbf{c}} Q(\mathbf{x}[n], \mathbf{c}[n-1])n^{-1} \sum_{m=1}^{n} \nabla Q(\mathbf{x}[m], \mathbf{c}[n-1] \\ &\qquad - \mathfrak{A}\boldsymbol{\gamma}[n]\,\nabla_{\mathbf{c}} Q(\mathbf{x}[n], \mathbf{c}[n-1])) \\ &= 0, \qquad n = 1, 2, \ldots, \end{aligned} \tag{3.16}$$

or

$$\begin{aligned} &\sum_{m=1}^{n} \nabla_{\mathbf{c}} Q(\mathbf{x}[m], \mathbf{c}[n-1] - \mathfrak{A}\boldsymbol{\gamma}[n]\,\nabla_{\mathbf{c}} Q(\mathbf{x}[n], \mathbf{c}[n-1])) \\ &\qquad = 0, \qquad n = 1, 2, \ldots. \end{aligned} \tag{3.17}$$

Due to Algorithm (3.13), this equation is equivalent to

$$\sum_{m=1}^{n} \nabla_{\mathbf{c}} Q(\mathbf{x}[m], \mathbf{c}[n]) = 0, \qquad n = 1, 2, \ldots. \tag{3.18}$$

It follows from (3.17) and (3.18) that the minimum of the performance index is simultaneously reached using $\boldsymbol{\gamma}[n]$ and $\mathbf{c}[n]$.

In general, condition (3.17) is nonlinear with respect to $\mathbf{c}$ and $\boldsymbol{\gamma}$, and an explicit expression for $\boldsymbol{\gamma}_{\text{opt}}[n]$ cannot be obtained from (3.17). Therefore, the only solution is to find an approximate quasioptimal expression for $\boldsymbol{\gamma}_{\text{opt}}[n]$. In order to accomplish this, we assume that the norm of $\boldsymbol{\gamma}[n]$ is sufficiently small, that is,

$$\| \boldsymbol{\gamma}[n] \| \ll 1. \tag{3.19}$$

Due to Algorithm (3.13), this is equivalent to the condition that the norm of the first difference $\nabla\mathbf{c}[n-1] = \mathbf{c}[n] - \mathbf{c}[n-1]$ is also sufficiently small, that is,

$$\| \nabla\mathbf{c}[n-1] \| \ll 1. \tag{3.20}$$

By considering the inequality (3.19) or (3.20), which is equivalent, the condition (3.17) can be replaced by an approximate condition

$$\sum_{m=1}^{n} \nabla_{\mathbf{c}} Q(\mathbf{x}[m], \mathbf{c}[n-1]) - \left[\sum_{m=1}^{n} \nabla_{\mathbf{c}}^2 Q(\mathbf{x}[m], \mathbf{c}[n-1])\right] \mathfrak{A}\boldsymbol{\gamma}[n] \nabla_{\mathbf{c}} Q(\mathbf{x}[n], \mathbf{c}[n-1]) \approx 0, \tag{3.21}$$

where

$$\nabla_{\mathbf{c}}^2 Q(\mathbf{x}, \mathbf{c}) = \left(\frac{\partial Q(\mathbf{x}, \mathbf{c})}{\partial c_\nu\, \partial c_\mu}\right), \qquad \nu, \mu = 1, 2, \ldots, N, \tag{3.22}$$

is a matrix of second derivatives of the stochastic functional $Q(\mathbf{x}, \mathbf{c})$. Since at each step we have to satisfy the condition (3.18) and thus the condition

$$\sum_{m=1}^{n-1} \nabla_{\mathbf{c}} Q(\mathbf{x}[m], \mathbf{c}[n-1]) = 0 \tag{3.23}$$

by multiplying (3.21) from the left by the inverse matrix

$$H[n] = \left[\sum_{m=1}^{n} \nabla_{\mathbf{c}}^2 Q(\mathbf{x}[m], \mathbf{c}[n-1])\right]^{-1}, \tag{3.24}$$

we obtain the condition

$$H[n] \nabla_{\mathbf{c}} Q(\mathbf{x}[n], \mathbf{c}[n-1]) \approx \mathfrak{A}\gamma_{\text{k opt}}[n] \nabla_{\mathbf{c}} Q(\mathbf{x}[n], \mathbf{c}[n-1]). \tag{3.25}$$

If we also consider the property of the operator $\mathfrak{A}$,

$$\mathfrak{A}\boldsymbol{\gamma}[n] \cdot \nabla_{\mathbf{c}} Q(\mathbf{x}[n], \mathbf{c}[n-1]) = \mathfrak{A}\, \nabla_{\mathbf{c}} Q(\mathbf{x}[n], \mathbf{c}[n-1])\boldsymbol{\gamma}[n], \tag{3.26}$$

we easily obtain from (3.25)

$$\gamma_{\mathrm{k\,opt}}[n] \approx [\mathfrak{A}\, \nabla_{\mathbf{c}} Q(\mathbf{x}[n], \mathbf{c}[n-1])]^{-1} H[n]\, \nabla_{\mathbf{c}} Q(\mathbf{x}[n], \mathbf{c}[n-1]). \tag{3.27}$$

Therefore, Algorithm (3.13) is written in the form

$$\mathbf{c}[n] = \mathbf{c}[n-1] - \mathfrak{A}\gamma_{\mathrm{k\,opt}}[n]\, \nabla_{\mathbf{c}} Q(\mathbf{x}[n], \mathbf{c}[n-1]), \tag{3.28}$$

or, using (3.25),

$$\mathbf{c}[n] = \mathbf{c}[n-1] - H[n]\, \nabla_{\mathbf{c}} Q(\mathbf{x}[n], \mathbf{c}[n-1]). \tag{3.29}$$

Let us emphasize once more that Algorithms (3.28) and (3.29) are correct only when the condition (3.19) or (3.20) is satisfied, and that these algorithms are not optimal but quasioptimal.

3.5 Linear Discrete Algorithms of Optimal Learning: I

In the case when $\nabla_{\mathbf{c}} Q(\mathbf{x}, \mathbf{c})$ is a linear function of $\mathbf{c}$, we can obtain strictly optimal algorithms. For instance, let

$$Q(\mathbf{x}, \mathbf{c}) = \tfrac{1}{2}(y - \mathbf{c}^{\mathrm{T}} \boldsymbol{\varphi}(\mathbf{x}))^2, \tag{3.30}$$

where y and $\mathbf{x}$ are the observed processes, $\boldsymbol{\varphi}(\mathbf{x})$ is a known vector function, and $\mathbf{c}$ is an unknown vector of parameters. The discrete algorithm (3.13) then takes the form

$$\mathbf{c}[n] = \mathbf{c}[n-1] + \mathfrak{A}\gamma[n](y[n] - \mathbf{c}^{\mathrm{T}}[n-1]\boldsymbol{\varphi}(\mathbf{x}[n]))\boldsymbol{\varphi}(\mathbf{x}[n]). \tag{3.31}$$

For such a linear discrete algorithm, the substitution (3.17) by (3.21), which is in general an approximate one, becomes exact, and this means that the relationships (3.25) and (3.27) are also exact. In the case of $Q(\mathbf{x}, \mathbf{c})$ defined by (3.30), we obtain

$$H[n] = K[n] = \left[\sum_{m=1}^{n} \boldsymbol{\varphi}(\mathbf{x}[m])\boldsymbol{\varphi}^{\mathrm{T}}(\mathbf{x}[m])\right]^{-1}. \tag{3.32}$$

From (3.25) and (3.27) we obtain the equations

$$\mathfrak{A}\gamma[n]\boldsymbol{\varphi}(\mathbf{x}[n]) = K[n]\boldsymbol{\varphi}(\mathbf{x}[n]) \tag{3.33}$$

and

$$\gamma_{\mathrm{opt}}[n] = [\mathfrak{A}\boldsymbol{\varphi}(\mathbf{x}[n])]^{-1} K[n]\boldsymbol{\varphi}(\mathbf{x}[n]). \tag{3.34}$$

On the basis of Eq. (3.33), the linear algorithm of optimal learning (3.31) can finally be written in the form

$$\mathbf{c}[n] = \mathbf{c}[n-1] + K[n](y[n] - \mathbf{c}^{\mathrm{T}}[n-1]\boldsymbol{\varphi}(\mathbf{x}[n]))\boldsymbol{\varphi}(\mathbf{x}[n]). \qquad (3.35)$$

Algorithm (3.35) is a recursive form of the least-squares method.

The computation of the matrix $K[n]$ at each stage is not a very pleasant procedure. This procedure can be simplified if it is also accomplished with the help of a recursive formula. For this purpose we mention the relationship

$$K^{-1}[n] = K^{-1}[n-1] + \boldsymbol{\varphi}(x[n])\boldsymbol{\varphi}^{\mathrm{T}}(x[n]). \qquad (3.36)$$

that follows from (3.32).

Then, using the well-known matrix identity

$$(A + BCB^{\mathrm{T}})^{-1} = A^{-1} - A^{-1}B(C^{-1} + B^{\mathrm{T}}A^{-1}B)^{-1}B^{\mathrm{T}}A$$

and setting

$$A = K^{-1}[n], \qquad B = I\boldsymbol{\varphi}(\mathbf{x}[n]), \qquad C = I, \qquad (3.37)$$

we obtain

$$K[n] = K[n-1] - \frac{[K[n-1]\boldsymbol{\varphi}(\mathbf{x}[n])][K[n-1]\boldsymbol{\varphi}(\mathbf{x}[n])]^{\mathrm{T}}}{1 + \boldsymbol{\varphi}^{\mathrm{T}}(\mathbf{x}[n])K[n-1]\boldsymbol{\varphi}(\mathbf{x}[n])}. \qquad (3.38)$$

Algorithms (3.35) and (3.38) thus provide the solution of the problem. The block diagram of the system realizing this algorithm is shown in Fig. 3.1.

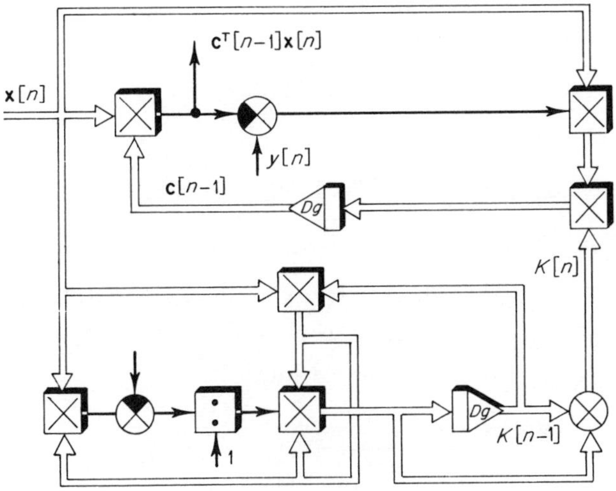

FIG. 3.1

3.6 Linear Discrete Algorithms of Optimal Learning: II

The linear discrete algorithm of optimal learning (3.35) minimizes the estimate $\hat{J}(\mathbf{c}[n])$ given by (3.9) at each step. We shall show that this algorithm also at each step minimizes the variance of the optimal vector (3.1). In order to simplify the notation, we introduce the following symbols:

$$\mathbf{c}[n] - \mathbf{c}^* = \boldsymbol{\eta}[n] \tag{3.39}$$

and

$$y[n] - \mathbf{c}^{*\mathrm{T}}\boldsymbol{\varphi}(\mathbf{x}[n]) = y[n] - \boldsymbol{\varphi}^{\mathrm{T}}(\mathbf{x}[n])\mathbf{c}^* = \xi[n]. \tag{3.40}$$

$\xi[n]$ is an independent sequence with the mean equal to zero, and the variance equal to σ^2, that is,

$$\mathsf{M}\{\xi\} = 0, \qquad \mathsf{M}\{\xi^2\} = \sigma^2. \tag{3.41}$$

Linear algorithm (3.31) is then written in the form

$$\mathbf{c}[n] = \mathbf{c}[n-1] + \boldsymbol{\alpha}[n](y[n] - \boldsymbol{\varphi}^{\mathrm{T}}(\mathbf{x}[n])\mathbf{c}[n-1]), \tag{3.42}$$

where

$$\boldsymbol{\alpha}[n] = \mathfrak{A}\boldsymbol{\gamma}[n]\boldsymbol{\varphi}(\mathbf{x}[n]). \tag{3.43}$$

We shall find such a vector $\boldsymbol{\alpha}[n]$ for which the variance of the estimate (3.31) is minimized.

From (3.42), using the notations (3.39) and (3.40), we obtain

$$\boldsymbol{\eta}[n] = \boldsymbol{\eta}[n-1] + \boldsymbol{\alpha}[n](\xi[n] - \boldsymbol{\varphi}^{\mathrm{T}}(\mathbf{x}[n])\boldsymbol{\eta}[n-1]). \tag{3.44}$$

The minimizing functional

$$V^2[n] = \mathsf{M}\{\| \boldsymbol{\eta}[n] \|^2\} \tag{3.45}$$

represents nothing else but a quantity proportional to the trace of the matrix

$$G[n] = \sigma^{-2}\mathsf{M}\{\boldsymbol{\eta}[n]\boldsymbol{\eta}^{\mathrm{T}}[n]\}, \qquad n = 1, 2, \ldots. \tag{3.46}$$

By setting Eq. (3.44) into (3.46), we obtain

$$\begin{aligned} G[n] = G[n-1] &- \frac{[G[n-1]\boldsymbol{\varphi}(\mathbf{x}[n])][G(n-1]\boldsymbol{\varphi}(\mathbf{x}[n])]^{\mathrm{T}}}{1 + \boldsymbol{\varphi}^{\mathrm{T}}(\mathbf{x}[n])G[n-1]\boldsymbol{\varphi}(\mathbf{x}[n])} \\ &+ (1 + \boldsymbol{\varphi}^{\mathrm{T}}(\mathbf{x}[n])G[n-1]\boldsymbol{\varphi}(\mathbf{x}[n])) \\ &\times \left(\boldsymbol{\alpha}[n] - \frac{G[n-1]\boldsymbol{\varphi}(\mathbf{x}[n])}{1 + \boldsymbol{\varphi}^{\mathrm{T}}(\mathbf{x}[n])G[n-1]\boldsymbol{\varphi}(\mathbf{x}[n])}\right) \\ &\times \left(\boldsymbol{\alpha}[n] - \frac{G[n-1]\boldsymbol{\varphi}(\mathbf{x}[n])}{1 + \boldsymbol{\varphi}^{\mathrm{T}}(\mathbf{x}[n])G[n-1]\boldsymbol{\varphi}(\mathbf{x}[n])}\right)^{\mathrm{T}}. \end{aligned} \tag{3.47}$$

The expression for the trace of the matrix $G[n]$ is then

$$\operatorname{tr} G[n] = \operatorname{tr} G[n-1] - \frac{\boldsymbol{\varphi}(\mathbf{x}[n])G[n-1]\boldsymbol{\varphi}(\mathbf{x}[n])}{1+\boldsymbol{\varphi}^{\mathrm{T}}(\mathbf{x}[n])G[n-1]\boldsymbol{\varphi}(\mathbf{x}[n])}$$
$$+(1+\boldsymbol{\varphi}^{\mathrm{T}}(\mathbf{x}[n])G[n-1]\boldsymbol{\varphi}(\mathbf{x}[n]))$$
$$\times\left\| \boldsymbol{\alpha}[n] - \frac{G[n-1]\boldsymbol{\varphi}(\mathbf{x}[n])}{1+\boldsymbol{\varphi}^{\mathrm{T}}(\mathbf{x}[n])G[n-1]\boldsymbol{\varphi}(\mathbf{x}[n])} \right\|^2. \tag{3.48}$$

It follows from this expression that the optimal value of the vector $\boldsymbol{\alpha}[n]$, which minimizes the functional (3.45), is equal to

$$\boldsymbol{\alpha}[n] = \frac{G[n-1]\boldsymbol{\varphi}(\mathbf{x}[n])}{1+\boldsymbol{\varphi}^{\mathrm{T}}(\mathbf{x}[n])G(n-1]\boldsymbol{\varphi}(\mathbf{x}[n])}. \tag{3.49}$$

For this value of $\boldsymbol{\alpha}[n]$ we obtain from (3.47)

$$G[n] = G[n-1] - \frac{[G[n-1]\boldsymbol{\varphi}(\mathbf{x}[n])][G[n-1]\boldsymbol{\varphi}(\mathbf{x}[n])]^{\mathrm{T}}}{1+\boldsymbol{\varphi}^{\mathrm{T}}(\mathbf{x}[n])G[n-1]\boldsymbol{\varphi}(\mathbf{x}[n])}. \tag{3.50}$$

Using this last relationship, we obtain

$$G[n]\boldsymbol{\varphi}(\mathbf{x}[n])$$
$$= G[n-1]\boldsymbol{\varphi}(\mathbf{x}[n])\left[1 - \frac{\boldsymbol{\varphi}^{\mathrm{T}}(\mathbf{x}[n])G[n-1]\boldsymbol{\varphi}(\mathbf{x}[n])}{1+\boldsymbol{\varphi}^{\mathrm{T}}(\mathbf{x}[n])G[n-1]\boldsymbol{\varphi}(\mathbf{x}[n])}\right], \tag{3.51}$$

or, by equating it with (3.49),

$$G[n]\boldsymbol{\varphi}(\mathbf{x}[n]) = \frac{G[n-1]\boldsymbol{\varphi}(\mathbf{x}[n])}{1+\boldsymbol{\varphi}^{\mathrm{T}}(\mathbf{x}[n])G[n-1]\boldsymbol{\varphi}(\mathbf{x}[n])} = \boldsymbol{\alpha}[n]. \tag{3.52}$$

Therefore, we obtain the algorithm of optimal learning

$$\mathbf{c}[n] = \mathbf{c}[n-1] + G[n](y[n] - \mathbf{c}^{\mathrm{T}}[n-1]\boldsymbol{\varphi}(\mathbf{x}[n]))\boldsymbol{\varphi}(\mathbf{x}[n]), \tag{3.53}$$

where $G[n]$ is defined by the recursive equation (3.50).

By comparing (3.50) with (3.38), we conclude that for $G[n_0] = K[n_0]$ the matrices $K[n]$ and $G[n]$ are identical, and thus Algorithms (3.35) and (3.53) are identical.

Therefore, linear algorithms (3.35) or (3.53) can be called "double" optimal.

3.7 Discussion

It may seem that the algorithms (3.35) and (3.38), or their equivalent algorithms (3.53) and (3.50), provide a complete solution to the problem of algorithms of optimal learning. However, under more careful considerations, this conclusion is not completely correct. The fact is that the matrix $K[n]$, as follows from its definition (3.32), exists only for $n \geq N$, where N is the dimension of the vector $\mathbf{c}$. This can be expected, since for $n < N$ the number of equations that define the components of the vector $\mathbf{c}$ is smaller than the number of unknowns, and the matrix $K^{-1}[n]$ is degenerate. Thus, the algorithms of optimal learning (3.35) and (3.38), strictly speaking, can be used only for $n \geq N$ after the matrix $K[n]$ is found.

Therefore, after a sufficient number of samples $\mathbf{x}[m]$, $m = 1, 2, \ldots, N$, is collected, and the matrix $\sum_{m=1}^{N} \boldsymbol{\varphi}(\mathbf{x}[m])\boldsymbol{\varphi}^{\mathrm{T}}(\mathbf{x}[m])$ is inverted, we can apply the algorithms of optimal learning.

The matrix inversion is characterized by cumbersome computations. Such difficulties can be avoided if we ask for suboptimal learning. In that case, we assign an arbitrary initial positive definite matrix $K_0[0]$, and use the algorithms (3.38) to determine $K[n]$, for $n > 0$. This is then used in the basic algorithm of learning (3.35). It is clear that in this case the performance index of learning depends on the choice of the initial matrix $K_0[0]$. If, however, the minimal eigenvalue of the matrix $\sum_{m=1}^{N} \boldsymbol{\varphi}(\mathbf{x}[m])\boldsymbol{\varphi}^{\mathrm{T}}(\mathbf{x}[m])$, for $n \to \infty$, diverges to infinity, we then obtain an estimate $\mathbf{c}[n]$ that converges to the optimal $\mathbf{c}^*$ for any initial $\mathbf{c}[0]$ and initial matrix $K_0[0]$.

3.8 The Simplest Linear Discrete Algorithms of Optimal Learning

Let

$$Q(x, c) = \tfrac{1}{2}(\varphi(x) - c)^2, \tag{3.54}$$

where x is the observed process, $\varphi(x)$ is a known function, and c is an unknown parameter. In this case the discrete algorithm (3.13) has the simple form

$$c[n] = c[n-1] + \gamma[n](\varphi(x[n]) - c[n-1]). \tag{3.55}$$

The corresponding modified algorithm of alternative actions, as it follows from (2.33), can be written in the following form:

$$c[N(n)] = c[N(n-1)] + \gamma[n][\Delta N(n-1)]^{-1} \sum_{m=N(n-1)+1}^{N(n)} [\varphi(x[m]) - c[N(n-1)]], \tag{3.56}$$

where $N(n)$ is the total number of discrete samples observed up to the nth estimate, $\Delta N(n) = N(n) - N(n-1)$ is the number of samples observed between the nth and $(n-1)$th estimate. We shall find the optimal value $\gamma[n]$ for which the variance of the estimate

$$V^2[N(n)] = \mathsf{M}\{(c[N(n)] - c^*)^2\} \tag{3.57}$$

is minimal at each step $n = 1, 2, \ldots$.

By introducing the notations

$$c[N(n)] - c^* = \eta[N(n)], \tag{3.58}$$

$$\varphi(x[m]) - c^* = \xi[\Lambda], \tag{3.59}$$

where $\xi[m]$ is assumed to be an independent sequence such that

$$\mathsf{M}\{\xi\} = 0, \qquad \mathsf{M}\{\xi^2\} = \sigma^2, \tag{3.60}$$

we write (3.56) in the form

$$\eta[N(n)] = (1 - \gamma[n])\eta[N(n-1)] + \gamma[n][\Delta N(n-1)]^{-1} \sum_{m=N(n-1)+1}^{N(n)} \xi[m]. \tag{3.61}$$

We could have obtained the same result, that is, $\gamma_{\text{opt}}[n]$, from the results in Section 3.6 by direct substitution of the corresponding symbols. However, we prefer the direct approach. We first square (3.61) and, by setting $\eta^2[N(n)]$ into (3.57), we obtain

$$V^2[N(n)] = (1 - \gamma[n])^2 V^2[N(n-1)] + \gamma^2[n][\sigma^2/\Delta N(n-1)]. \tag{3.62}$$

By equating the derivative of (3.62) with respect to $\gamma[n]$ to zero, we find

$$\gamma[n] = \frac{V^2[N(n-1)]}{V^2[N(n-1)] + [\sigma^2/\Delta N(n-1)]}. \tag{3.63}$$

By substituting this $\gamma[n]$ into (3.62), we get

$$V^2[N(n)] = \frac{[\sigma^2/\Delta N(n-1)]V^2[N(n-1)]}{V^2[N(n-1)] + [\sigma^2/\Delta N(n-1)]}. \tag{3.64}$$

From (3.63) and (3.64), we finally have

$$\gamma_{\text{opt}}[n] = \frac{\Delta N(n-1)}{N(n) + \{\sigma^2/V^2[N(0)]\}}, \tag{3.65}$$

$$V^2_{\min}[N(n)] = \frac{\sigma^2}{N(n) + \{\sigma^2/V^2[N(0)]\}}. \tag{3.66}$$

If *a priori* information about the initial variance does not exist, $V^2[N(0)]$ is infinite, and

$$\gamma_{\text{opt}}[n] = \Delta N(n-1)/N(n), \tag{3.67}$$

$$V^2_{\min}[N(n)] = \sigma^2/N(n). \tag{3.68}$$

TABLE 3.1

	$\Delta N(n-1)$	$N(n)$	Algorithm	$\gamma_{\text{opt}}[n]$
1	1	n	$c[n] = \mathbf{c}[n-1] - \gamma[n](c[n-1] - \boldsymbol{\varphi}(x[n]))$	$1/n$
2	k_0	$k_0 n$	$c[k_0 n] = c[k_0(n-1)] - \gamma[n]\left(c[k_0(n-1)] - \frac{1}{k_0 n} \sum_{m=k_0(n-1)+1}^{k_0 n} \boldsymbol{\varphi}(x[m])\right)$	$1/n$
3	n	$n(n+1)/2$	$c[n(n+1)/2] = c[(n-1)n/2] - \gamma[n]\left(c[(n-1)n/2] - \frac{2}{n(n+1)} \sum_{m=[n(n-1)/2]+1}^{n(n+1)/2} \boldsymbol{\varphi}(x[m])\right)$	$2/(n+1)$

It is important to notice that $V^2_{\min}[N(n)]$ does not depend on the number of samples in the groups, that is, on $\Delta N(n-1)$, but only on the total number of samples $N(n)$. This invariance of the general algorithm of optimal learning with respect to the variation of the number of samples in the groups is extremely important in a number of problems since it permits us to perform estimation less frequently than using the simplest algorithms, and without sacrificing the accuracy of estimation. Certain special cases of these algorithms are given in Table 3.1.

3.9 More on Discrete Linear Algorithms of Optimal Learning

Let us consider a special case of the general performance index (3.11) for $N(n) = 0$:

$$\hat{J}_0(\mathbf{c}[n]) = Q(\mathbf{x}[n], \mathbf{c}[n]). \tag{3.69}$$

For the quadratic functional (3.30)

$$\begin{aligned}\hat{J}_0(\mathbf{c}[n]) &= \tfrac{1}{2}(y[n] - \mathbf{c}^{\mathrm{T}}[n]\boldsymbol{\varphi}(\mathbf{x}[n])^2) \\ &= \tfrac{1}{2}(y[n] - \boldsymbol{\varphi}^{\mathrm{T}}(\mathbf{x}[n])\mathbf{c}[n])^2.\end{aligned} \tag{3.70}$$

Considering Algorithm (3.31), we write (3.69) in the form

$$\hat{J}_0(\mathbf{c}[n]) = \tfrac{1}{2}(y[n] - \boldsymbol{\varphi}^{\mathrm{T}}(\mathbf{x}[n])\mathbf{c}[n-1])^2(1-\boldsymbol{\varphi}^{\mathrm{T}}(\mathbf{x}[n]\mathfrak{A}\boldsymbol{\gamma}[n]\boldsymbol{\varphi}(\mathbf{x}[n]))^2. \tag{3.71}$$

This functional has the minimum equal to zero when

$$\boldsymbol{\varphi}^{\mathrm{T}}(\mathbf{x}[n])\mathfrak{A}\boldsymbol{\gamma}[n]\boldsymbol{\varphi}(\mathbf{x}[n]) = 1. \tag{3.72}$$

By setting

$$\mathfrak{A}\boldsymbol{\gamma}[n] = I\boldsymbol{\gamma}[n], \tag{3.73}$$

we obtain from (3.72)

$$\boldsymbol{\gamma}[n] = \{\boldsymbol{\varphi}^{\mathrm{T}}(\mathbf{x}[n])\boldsymbol{\varphi}(\mathbf{x}[n])\}^{-1} \tag{3.74}$$

and therefore the algorithm of optimal learning has the very simple form

$$\mathbf{c}[n] = \mathbf{c}[n-1] + \frac{(y[n] - \mathbf{c}^{\mathrm{T}}[n-1]\boldsymbol{\varphi}(\mathbf{x}[n]))}{\boldsymbol{\varphi}^{\mathrm{T}}(\mathbf{x}[n])\boldsymbol{\varphi}(\mathbf{x}[n])}\boldsymbol{\varphi}(\mathbf{x}[n]). \tag{3.75}$$

This algorithm corresponds to the so-called algorithm of Kaczmarz. We should also notice that $\boldsymbol{\gamma}[n]$ in (3.74) does not satisfy the criterion of convergence (2.21). Therefore, Algorithm (3.75) converges only when $\alpha = \beta = 0$, that is, when there is no noise.

However, this algorithm can be used even when noise exists if, starting from a certain $n \geq n_0$, the obtained vectors $\mathbf{c}[n]$ are averaged.

3.10 Continuous and Hybrid Algorithms of Optimal Learning

Let us consider the continuous algorithm

$$d\mathbf{c}(t)/dt = -\Gamma(t)\,\nabla_{\mathbf{c}}Q(\mathbf{x}(t), \mathbf{c}(t)), \tag{3.76}$$

where $\Gamma(t)$ is an unknown matrix. We shall search for such a matrix that minimizes the performance index of learning (3.10) at each instant. The condition of the minimum is obtained by equating the gradient of the functional (3.10) to zero, that is,

$$\int_0^t \nabla_{\mathbf{c}} Q(\mathbf{x}(\tau), \mathbf{c}(t))\, d\tau = 0. \tag{3.77}$$

In order to determine the sought optimal matrix $\Gamma(t) = \Gamma_{\text{opt}}(t)$, we write (3.77) in the equivalent form

$$(d/dt) \int_0^t \nabla_{\mathbf{c}} Q(\mathbf{x}(\tau), \mathbf{c}(t))\, d\tau = 0. \tag{3.78}$$

By performing differentiation and then substituting $d\mathbf{c}(t)/dt$ according to Algorithm (3.76), we obtain

$$\nabla_{\mathbf{c}} Q(\mathbf{x}(t), \mathbf{c}(t)) - \left[\int_0^t \nabla_{\mathbf{c}}^2 Q(\mathbf{x}(\tau), \mathbf{c}(t))\, d\tau\right] \Gamma(t)\, \nabla_{\mathbf{c}} Q(\mathbf{x}(t), \mathbf{c}(t)) = 0. \tag{3.79}$$

From this, we find

$$\Gamma_{\text{opt}}(t) = \left[\int_0^t \nabla_{\mathbf{c}}^2 Q(\mathbf{x}(\tau), \mathbf{c}(t))\, d\tau\right]^{-1}. \tag{3.80}$$

Therefore, we obtain the algorithm of optimal learning

$$d\mathbf{c}(t)/dt = -\Gamma_{\text{opt}}(t)\, \nabla_{\mathbf{c}} Q(\mathbf{x}(t), \mathbf{c}(t)). \tag{3.81}$$

If we differentiate both sides of (3.80) with respect to t, we obtain the differential equation

$$d\Gamma_{\text{opt}}(t)/dt = -\Gamma_{\text{opt}}(t)\left[\nabla_{\mathbf{c}}^2 Q(\mathbf{x}(t), \mathbf{c}(t)) + \int_0^t \nabla_{\mathbf{c}}^3 Q(\mathbf{x}(\tau), \mathbf{c}(t))\, d\tau\, \frac{d\mathbf{c}(t)}{dt}\right] \Gamma_{\text{opt}}(t). \tag{3.82}$$

It is frequently more convenient to realize the optimal matrix $\Gamma_{\text{opt}}(t)$ in the form of the differential equation (3.82), since in that case there is no need to invert the matrix at each instant t as is required by Expression (3.80). The algorithm of optimal learning is then defined by two differential equations (3.81) and (3.82).

If in these equations the continuous process is replaced by stepwise $\mathbf{x}[t]$ (2.9), we obtain the hybrid algorithms of optimal learning

$$d\mathbf{c}(t)/dt = -\Gamma_{\text{opt}}(t)\nabla_{\mathbf{c}} Q(\mathbf{x}[t], \mathbf{c}(t)), \tag{3.83}$$

$$d\Gamma_{\text{opt}}(t)/dt = -\Gamma_{\text{opt}}\Big[\nabla_{\mathbf{c}}^2 Q(\mathbf{x}[t], \mathbf{c}(t)) + \int_0^t \nabla_{\mathbf{c}}^3 Q(\mathbf{x}[\tau], \mathbf{c}(t))\, d\tau \, \frac{d\mathbf{c}(t)}{dt}\Big]\Gamma_{\text{opt}}(t). \tag{3.84}$$

Unlike discrete algorithms, which in the best case can only be quasioptimal, the continuous and hybrid algorithms can in principle be strictly optimal. However, it should be noticed that the realization of optimal continuous and hybrid algorithms in the general case is faced with a series of difficulties. One of the difficulties is caused by the necessity to compute the integral $\int_0^t \nabla_{\mathbf{c}}^3 Q(\mathbf{x}(\tau), \mathbf{c}(t))\, d\tau$ in Algorithm (3.82). In this integral, the integration is performed according to the "local" time τ, and the actual time t is a parameter.

In order to obtain $\mathbf{x}(\tau)$, it is necessary first to remember the process $\mathbf{x}(\tau)$, for $0 \leq \tau \leq t$, and then, after the required transformations that are speci-

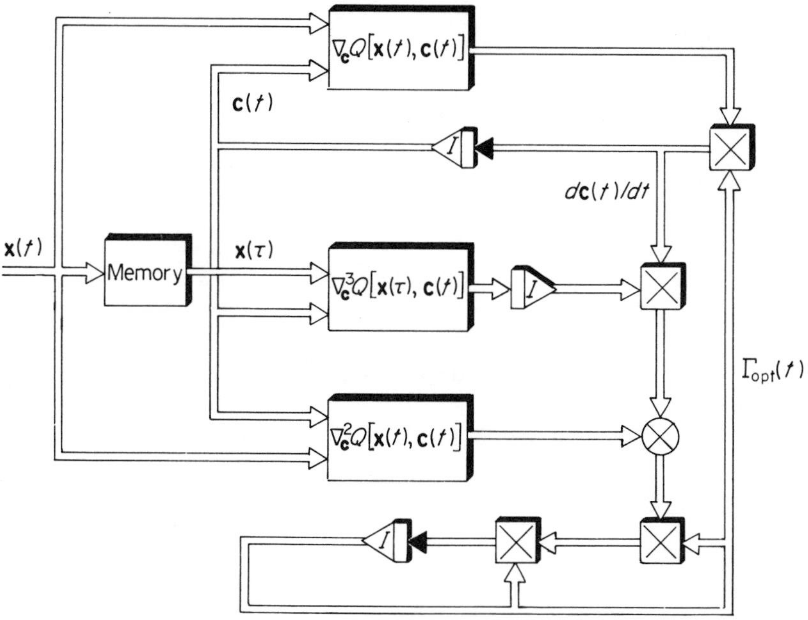

FIG. 3.2

fied by the expression $\nabla_{\mathbf{c}}^3 Q(\mathbf{x}(\tau), \mathbf{c}(t))$, the integration with respect to τ is performed for current t. The difficulties of this last operation are obvious. For the quadratic functional, $\nabla_{\mathbf{c}}^3 Q(\mathbf{x}(\tau), \mathbf{c}(t)) = 0$, and this difficulty disappears. We shall say more in Section 3.14 about other difficulties in the realization of optimal algorithms of learning.

All these conditions prevent us from presenting an exact block diagram of the system that realizes continuous and hybrid algorithms of optimal learning. We limit ourselves to a certain symbolic block diagram corresponding to the algorithm of optimal learning without describing in detail the functions of the blocks that are designated for computation of the mentioned integral. Such a symbolic block diagram corresponding to the continuous algorithm of optimal learning is shown in Fig. 3.2.

3.11 Special Cases

Let us consider now the special forms of the continuous algorithms of optimal learning, which correspond to the cases where $\Gamma(t)$ is a diagonal matrix with different elements

$$\Gamma(t) = \begin{pmatrix} \gamma_1(t) & 0 & \cdots & 0 \\ 0 & \gamma_2(t) & \cdots & 0 \\ \vdots & \vdots & & \vdots \\ 0 & 0 & \cdots & \gamma_N(t) \end{pmatrix} = \mathfrak{A}\boldsymbol{\gamma}(t) \tag{3.85}$$

or identical elements

$$\Gamma(t) = \begin{pmatrix} \gamma(t) & 0 & \cdots & 0 \\ 0 & \gamma(t) & \cdots & 0 \\ \vdots & \vdots & & \vdots \\ 0 & 0 & \cdots & \gamma(t) \end{pmatrix} = I\gamma(t). \tag{3.86}$$

By substituting $\Gamma(t)$ from (3.85) into (3.79), we obtain

$$\nabla_{\mathbf{c}} Q(\mathbf{x}(t), \mathbf{c}(t)) - \Gamma_{\mathrm{opt}}^{-1}(t)\mathfrak{A}\boldsymbol{\gamma}(t)\, \nabla_{\mathbf{c}} Q(\mathbf{x}(t), \mathbf{c}(t)) = 0, \tag{3.87}$$

where $\Gamma_{\mathrm{opt}}(t)$ is defined by Eq. (3.80). By multiplying both sides of (3.87) by $\Gamma_{\mathrm{opt}}(t)$, we find

$$\Gamma_{\mathrm{opt}}(t)\, \nabla_{\mathbf{c}} Q(\mathbf{x}(t), \mathbf{c}(t)) = \mathfrak{A}\boldsymbol{\gamma}(t)\, \nabla_{\mathbf{c}} Q(\mathbf{x}(t), \mathbf{c}(t)), \tag{3.88}$$

from which, using the obvious relationship

$$\mathcal{Q}\boldsymbol{\gamma}(t)\,\nabla_{\mathbf{c}}Q(\mathbf{x}(t),\mathbf{c}(t)) = \mathcal{Q}\,\nabla_{\mathbf{c}}Q(\mathbf{x}(t),\mathbf{c}(t))\boldsymbol{\gamma}(t), \tag{3.89}$$

we easily obtain

$$\boldsymbol{\gamma}_{\text{opt}}(t) = [\mathcal{Q}\,\nabla_{\mathbf{c}}Q(\mathbf{x}(t),\mathbf{c}(t))]^{-1}\,\Gamma_{\text{opt}}(t)\,\nabla_{\mathbf{c}}Q(\mathbf{x}(t),\mathbf{c}(t)). \tag{3.90}$$

Similarly, by setting $\Gamma(t)$ from (3.86) into (3.79), we obtain

$$\nabla_{\mathbf{c}}Q(\mathbf{x}(t),\mathbf{c}(t)) - \gamma(t)\Gamma_{\text{opt}}^{-1}(t)\,\nabla_{\mathbf{c}}Q(\mathbf{x}(t),\mathbf{c}(t)) = 0. \tag{3.91}$$

If $\gamma(t)$ is a scalar, the condition (3.91) cannot be used directly since it corresponds to a system of N equations with respect to one unknown. In order to obtain one equation with respect to $\gamma(t)$, we multiply both sides of Eq. (3.91) by the transpose $\nabla_{\mathbf{c}}{}^{\mathrm{T}}Q(\mathbf{x}(t),\mathbf{c}(t))$ and obtain

$$\gamma_{\text{opt}}(t) = \frac{\nabla_{\mathbf{c}}{}^{\mathrm{T}}Q(\mathbf{x}(t),\mathbf{c}(t))\,\nabla_{\mathbf{c}}Q(\mathbf{x}(t),\mathbf{c}(t))}{\nabla_{\mathbf{c}}{}^{\mathrm{T}}Q(\mathbf{x}(t),\mathbf{c}(t))\Gamma_{\text{opt}}^{-1}(t)\,\nabla_{\mathbf{c}}Q(\mathbf{x}(t),\mathbf{c}(t))}. \tag{3.92}$$

Although $\gamma_{\text{opt}}(t)$ is now a scalar, we must still know $\Gamma_{\text{opt}}^{-1}(t)$. However, the need for computing the inverse no longer exists.

We must mention that the presented method for obtaining $\gamma_{\text{opt}}(t)$ very much resembles the method of steepest descent. Therefore, in the algorithms of optimal learning, $\Gamma(t)$ can be a complete matrix or a diagonal matrix either with different or identical elements. In the latter case, the matrix is simply replaced by a scalar. As it follows from the relationship (3.88), the algorithms with complete and diagonal matrices are equivalent and thus provide the same minimal value of the performance index of learning. In the case when $\Gamma = I\gamma$, naturally, the minimum value of the performance index of learning is greater than in the preceding case.

3.12 More on Continuous Algorithms of Optimal Learning

In order to generalize the functional (3.12), instead of (3.78) we obtain the condition of the minimum in the form

$$(d/dt)\int_{t-T(t)}^{t} \nabla_{\mathbf{c}}Q(\mathbf{x}(\tau),\mathbf{c}(t))\,dt = 0. \tag{3.93}$$

Using the algorithm

$$d\mathbf{c}/dt = -\Gamma(t)\,\nabla_{\mathbf{c}}Q(\mathbf{x}(t),\mathbf{c}(t)), \tag{3.94}$$

we obtain

$$\nabla_{\mathbf{c}} Q(\mathbf{x}(t), \mathbf{c}(t)) - \nabla_{\mathbf{c}} Q(\mathbf{x}(t - T(t)), \mathbf{c}(t))[1 - T'(t)] \\ - \int_{t-T(t)}^{t} \nabla_{\mathbf{c}}^2 Q(\mathbf{x}(\tau), \mathbf{c}(t))\, d\tau \cdot \Gamma(t)\, \nabla_{\mathbf{c}} Q(\mathbf{x}(t), \mathbf{c}(t)) = 0, \tag{3.95}$$

or

$$\Gamma(t)\, \nabla_{\mathbf{c}} Q(\mathbf{x}(t), \mathbf{c}(t)) = \Gamma_{T,\mathrm{opt}}(t)[\nabla_{\mathbf{c}} Q(\mathbf{x}(t), \mathbf{c}(t)) \\ - \nabla_{\mathbf{c}} Q(\mathbf{x}(t - T(t)), \mathbf{c}(t))[1 - T'(t)]], \tag{3.96}$$

where

$$\Gamma_{T,\mathrm{opt}}(t) = \left[\int_{t-T(t)}^{t} \nabla_{\mathbf{c}}^2 Q(\mathbf{x}(\tau), \mathbf{c}(t))\, d\tau\right]^{-1}. \tag{3.97}$$

Taking (3.96) into consideration, we write Algorithm (3.94) in this form:

$$d\mathbf{c}(t)/dt = -\Gamma_{T,\mathrm{opt}}(t)[\nabla_{\mathbf{c}} Q(\mathbf{x}(t), \mathbf{c}(t)) \\ - \nabla_{\mathbf{c}} Q(\mathbf{x}(t - T(t)), \mathbf{c}(t))[1 - T'(t)]]. \tag{3.98}$$

By differentiating (3.97) with respect to t, we obtain the equation

$$d\Gamma_{T,\mathrm{opt}}(t)/dt = -\Gamma_{T,\mathrm{opt}}(t)[\nabla_{\mathbf{c}}^2 Q(\mathbf{x}(t), \mathbf{c}(t)) \\ - \nabla_{\mathbf{c}}^2 Q(\mathbf{x}(t - T(t)), \mathbf{c}(t))[1 - T'(t)] \\ + \int_{t-T(t)}^{t} \nabla_{\mathbf{c}}^3 Q(\mathbf{x}(\tau), \mathbf{c}(t))\, d\tau\, \frac{d\mathbf{c}(t)}{dt}\right]\Gamma_{T,\mathrm{opt}}(t). \tag{3.99}$$

By setting $T(t) = T$ in (3.98), and this means $T'(t) = 0$, we obtain

$$d\mathbf{c}(t)/dt = -\Gamma_{T,\mathrm{opt}}(t)[\nabla_{\mathbf{c}} Q(\mathbf{x}(t), \mathbf{c}(t)) - \nabla_{\mathbf{c}} Q(\mathbf{x}(t - T), \mathbf{c}(t))]. \tag{3.100}$$

By setting $T(t) = t$ in (3.98) and (3.99), and this means $T'(t) = 1$, we obtain the preceding algorithms of optimal learning (3.81) and (3.82).

3.13 The Limiting Case

Let us consider the limiting case of the continuous algorithm of optimal learning (3.100) when $T \to 0$ for the quadratic functional

$$Q(\mathbf{x}, \mathbf{c}) = \tfrac{1}{2}(y - \mathbf{c}^{\mathrm{T}}\boldsymbol{\varphi}(\mathbf{x}))^2. \tag{3.101}$$

By writing Algorithm (3.100) in the form

$$d\mathbf{c}(t)/dt = T\Gamma_{T,\mathrm{opt}}(t)T^{-1}[(y(t) - \mathbf{c}^{\mathrm{T}}(t)\boldsymbol{\varphi}(\mathbf{x}(t)))\boldsymbol{\varphi}(\mathbf{x}(t)) \\ - (y(t - T) - \mathbf{c}^{\mathrm{T}}(t)\boldsymbol{\varphi}(\mathbf{x}(t - T)))\boldsymbol{\varphi}(\mathbf{x}(t - T))] \tag{3.102}$$

and noticing that

$$\lim_{T\to 0} T\Gamma_{T,\mathrm{opt}}(t) = \lim_{T\to 0}\left[T^{-1}\int_{t-T}^{t} \boldsymbol{\varphi}(\mathbf{x}(\tau))\boldsymbol{\varphi}^{\mathrm{T}}(\mathbf{x}(\tau))\, d\tau\right]^{-1}$$
$$= [\boldsymbol{\varphi}(\mathbf{x}(t))\boldsymbol{\varphi}^{\mathrm{T}}(\mathbf{x}(t))]^{-1} \tag{3.103}$$

and

$$\lim_{T\to 0} T^{-1}[(y(t) - \mathbf{c}^{\mathrm{T}}(t)\boldsymbol{\varphi}(\mathbf{x}(t)))\boldsymbol{\varphi}(\mathbf{x}(t)) - (y(t-T)$$
$$-\mathbf{c}^{\mathrm{T}}(t)\boldsymbol{\varphi}(\mathbf{x}(t-T)))\boldsymbol{\varphi}(\mathbf{x}(t-\tau))]$$
$$= \left(\frac{dy(t)}{dt} - \mathbf{c}^{\mathrm{T}}\frac{d\boldsymbol{\varphi}(\mathbf{x}(t))}{dt}\right)\boldsymbol{\varphi}(\mathbf{x}(t)), \tag{3.104}$$

we obtain

$$d\mathbf{c}(t)/dt = [\boldsymbol{\varphi}(\mathbf{x}(t))\boldsymbol{\varphi}^{\mathrm{T}}(\mathbf{x}(t))]^{-1}$$
$$\times\left(\frac{dy(t)}{dt} - \mathbf{c}^{\mathrm{T}}(t)\frac{d\boldsymbol{\varphi}(\mathbf{x}(t))}{dt}\right)\boldsymbol{\varphi}(\mathbf{x}(t)). \tag{3.105}$$

But since the matrix $[\boldsymbol{\varphi}(\mathbf{x}(t))\boldsymbol{\varphi}^{\mathrm{T}}(\mathbf{x}(t))]$ is always singular, its inverse matrix (3.103) does not exist, and the limiting algorithm does not have any meaning. However, let us assume that there exists a certain inverse matrix $H(t)$, still unknown, for which

$$\frac{d\mathbf{c}(t)}{dt} = H(t)\left(\frac{dy(t)}{dt} - \mathbf{c}^{\mathrm{T}}(t)\frac{d\boldsymbol{\varphi}(\mathbf{x}(t))}{dt}\right)\boldsymbol{\varphi}(\mathbf{x}(t)). \tag{3.106}$$

In order to find this matrix, we use the limit of the condition (3.93) for $Q(\mathbf{x}, \mathbf{c})$ defined by (3.101), or, more accurately, by the limit of the condition

$$(d/dt)T^{-1}\int_{t-T}^{T} (y(\tau) - \mathbf{c}^{\mathrm{T}}(t)\boldsymbol{\varphi}(\mathbf{x}(\tau)))\boldsymbol{\varphi}(\mathbf{x}(\tau))\, d\tau = 0. \tag{3.107}$$

When $T \to 0$, we obtain

$$(d/dt)(y(t) - \mathbf{c}^{\mathrm{T}}(t)\boldsymbol{\varphi}(\mathbf{x}(t)))\boldsymbol{\varphi}(\mathbf{x}(t)) = 0. \tag{3.108}$$

Considering that for any t

$$y(t) - \mathbf{c}^{\mathrm{T}}(t)\boldsymbol{\varphi}(\mathbf{x}(t)) = 0, \tag{3.109}$$

after substitution of $d\mathbf{c}(t)/dt$ from (3.108) into (3.106), we obtain

$$\left(\frac{dy(t)}{dt} - \mathbf{c}^{\mathrm{T}}(t)\frac{d\boldsymbol{\varphi}(\mathbf{x}(t))}{dt}\right)(1 - [H(t)\boldsymbol{\varphi}(\mathbf{x}(t))]^{\mathrm{T}}\boldsymbol{\varphi}(\mathbf{x}(t))) = 0. \tag{3.110}$$

This equality is satisfied for

$$H = I\gamma(t), \tag{3.111}$$

where

$$\gamma(t) = [\boldsymbol{\varphi}^{\mathrm{T}}(\mathbf{x}(t))\boldsymbol{\varphi}(\mathbf{x}(t))]^{-1}. \tag{3.112}$$

Therefore, we arrive at the continuous algorithm of the form

$$\begin{aligned} d\mathbf{c}(t)/dt = {} & [\boldsymbol{\varphi}^{\mathrm{T}}(\mathbf{x}(t))\boldsymbol{\varphi}(\mathbf{x}(t))]^{-1} \\ & \times\left(\frac{dy(t)}{dt} - \mathbf{c}^{\mathrm{T}}(t)\,\frac{d\boldsymbol{\varphi}(\mathbf{x}(t))}{dt}\right)\boldsymbol{\varphi}(\mathbf{x}(t)). \end{aligned} \tag{3.113}$$

This algorithm is actually the limiting case of the discrete algorithm of Kaczmarz (3.75). It is interesting to notice that the continuous algorithms qualitatively differ from the discrete algorithm. In the continuous algorithms, the observed variables are replaced by their derivatives.

3.14 Discussion

Generally speaking, the continuous algorithms of optimal learning (3.81) and (3.82) are nonlinear differential equations that are not completely defined. In order to define these equations completely, we have to specify the initial conditions $\mathbf{c}(t_0)$ for (3.81) and $\Gamma(t_0)$ for (3.82), where t_0 is a positive quantity as small as desired. When $t_0 = 0$, as can be easily seen, $\Gamma(0)$ does not exist.

The initial conditions are not arbitrary. According to (3.77), $\mathbf{c}(t_0) = \mathbf{c}_*(t_0)$ is determined by the solution of the equation

$$\int_0^{t_0} \nabla_{\mathbf{c}} Q(\mathbf{x}(\tau), \mathbf{c}_*(t_0))\, d\tau = 0, \tag{3.114}$$

and according to (3.80), $\Gamma(t_0) = \Gamma_*(t_0)$ is obtained by matrix inverting

$$\Gamma_*(t_0) = \left[\int_0^{t_0} \nabla_{\mathbf{c}} Q(\mathbf{x}(\tau), \mathbf{c}_*(t_0))\, d\tau\right]^{-1}. \tag{3.115}$$

It follows from this that the continuous algorithms are actually algorithms of optimal learning if we can exactly solve Eq. (3.114) in order to find the vector $\mathbf{c}_*(t)$, and then, using this vector $\mathbf{c}_*(t)$, perform the matrix inversion and obtain $\Gamma_*(t_0)$.

This matrix inversion, although an unpleasant operation, can be accomplished. Regarding the solution of Eq. (3.114), this is actually the basic problem that will be solved with the help of the algorithms of optimal learning. Obviously, an explicit solution of this problem is only possible in special cases, namely when Eq. (3.114) is linear with respect to $\mathbf{c}_*(t)$. Therefore, the realization of similar algorithms of optimal learning is confronted by insurmountable difficulties. The answer to this situation lies in selecting an arbitrary initial condition $\mathbf{c}(t_0)$ and an arbitrary initial positive definite matrix $\Gamma(t_0)$ instead of computing exact initial values $\mathbf{c}_*(t_0)$ and $\Gamma_*(t_0)$. In that case, naturally learning cannot be optimal in the previous sense. For such arbitrary initial values $\mathbf{c}(t_0)$, the minimum of the functional

$$\hat{J}(\mathbf{c}(t), \mathbf{c}(t_0), \Gamma(t_0)) = t^{-1}\left\{\int_0^t Q(\mathbf{x}(\tau), \mathbf{c}(t))\, d\tau + \mathbf{r}^{\mathrm{T}}\mathbf{c} + \frac{\mathbf{c}^{\mathrm{T}}G\mathbf{c}}{2}\right\}, \tag{3.116}$$

where $\mathbf{r}$ is a vector, and G is a positive definite symmetric matrix that depends on $\mathbf{c}(t_0)$ and $\Gamma(t_0)$. When $\mathbf{c}(t_0) = \mathbf{c}_*(t_0)$ and $\Gamma(t_0) = \Gamma_*(t_0)$ defined by (3.114) and (3.115), all components of the vector $\mathbf{r}$ and all the elements of matrix G are equal to zero. The functional (3.116) converges to the well-known performance index

$$\hat{J}(\mathbf{c}(t)) = t^{-1}\int_0^t Q(\mathbf{x}(\tau), \mathbf{c}(t))\, d\tau. \tag{3.117}$$

It is appropriate to call the algorithms of learning (3.81) and (3.82), with arbitrary initial conditions $\mathbf{c}(t)$ and $\Gamma(t)$, the algorithms of suboptimal learning.

3.15 Algorithms of Learning with Repetition

The role and the importance of the algorithms of optimal learning is clearly apparent in the cases when a stationary (discrete or continuous) process $\mathbf{x}$ has finite duration, and when it is necessary, after finishing with the observations, to determine the exact value of the vector $\mathbf{c}$. The algorithms of optimal and suboptimal learning can cope with this problem, but not in a simple fashion. These algorithms of learning are complicated; they need the computation of $\Gamma_{\text{opt}}(t)$, which is connected with the difficult operation of matrix inversion. Can simpler algorithms, either continuous or discrete, for instance,

$$d\mathbf{c}(t)/dt = -[a_0/(t+1)]\, \nabla_{\mathbf{c}} Q(\mathbf{x}(t), \mathbf{c}(t)) \tag{3.118}$$

and

$$\mathbf{c}[n] = \mathbf{c}[n-1] - (a_0/n)\, \nabla_{\mathbf{c}} Q(\mathbf{x}[n], \mathbf{c}[n-1]), \tag{3.119}$$

that guarantee the convergence of $\mathbf{c}(t)$ or $\mathbf{c}[n]$ to the optimal vector $\mathbf{c}^*$ be used when infinitely long observations of the processes $\mathbf{x}(t)$ or $\mathbf{x}[n]$ exist? It appears that this is possible if we use the idea expressed in the well-known proverb, "repetition is the mother of learning."

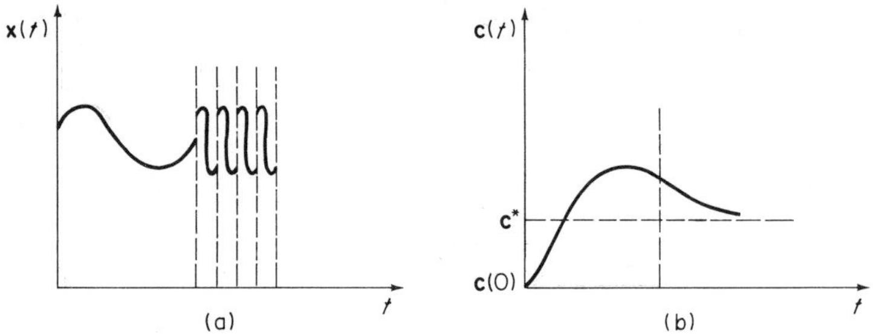

FIG. 3.3

Generally speaking, when the processes of duration T_0 are only observed, the estimates $\mathbf{c}(t)$ obtained with the help of Algorithm (3.118) for $t = T_0$ will be far from the estimates that can be obtained at the same instant using optimal algorithms considered earlier. However, if periodically, in the accelerated time, we repeat this process (Fig. 3.3a), after a sufficient number of cycles, the simplest algorithm determines an estimate that is close to one given by the optimal algorithm (Fig. 3.3b). Such algorithms of learning with repetition can be written in the form

$$d\mathbf{c}(t)/dt = -[a_0/(t+1)]\, \nabla_{\mathbf{c}} Q(\mathbf{x}(t), \mathbf{c}(t)), \qquad 0 \le t < T_0, \tag{3.120}$$

$$d\mathbf{c}(t)/dt = -[a_0/(t+1)]\, \nabla_{\mathbf{c}} Q(\tilde{\mathbf{x}}(\alpha t), \mathbf{c}(t)), \qquad T_0 \le t, \tag{3.121}$$

where $\tilde{\mathbf{x}}(t)$ is the periodic continuation of $\mathbf{x}(t)$, and $\tilde{\mathbf{x}}(\alpha t)$, $\alpha \gg 1$, is a periodic continuation of $\mathbf{x}(t)$ in the accelerated time. Of course, in this case it is necessary to increase the time with respect to T_0 in order to obtain an estimate $\mathbf{c}(t)$ that is close to the optimal one.

For discrete data, we can avoid the described loss in time for $n \ge N_0$ if we use the intervals of time between the arrival of samples to repeat the samples that have arrived so far (Fig. 3.4). The discrete algorithm which realizes described operations, can be written in the following form:

$$\mathbf{c}[n, m] = \mathbf{c}[n, m-1] - (a_0/m)\, \nabla_{\mathbf{c}} Q(\tilde{\mathbf{x}}[n, m], \mathbf{c}[n, m-1]), \tag{3.122}$$

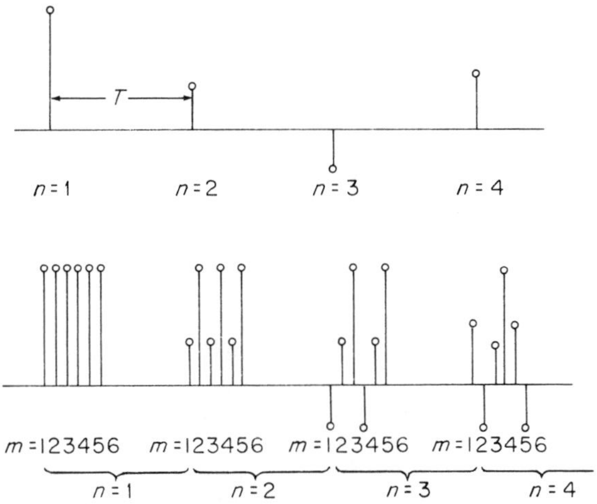

FIG. 3.4

where m takes integer values for every fixed n. Actually, Algorithm (3.122) corresponds to the repetitious application of the simple discrete algorithm (3.118) for an ever increasing number of samples $\mathbf{x}[n, m]$.

3.16 Conclusion

We have considered possible ways of constructing algorithms of optimal learning that do not simply reach the goal of learning, but reach it in an optimal fashion. It was shown that, in general, the discrete algorithms can only be quasi-optimal. On the other hand, linear discrete algorithms are "double" optimal.

Regarding continuous and hybrid algorithms, there are no constrains characteristic of the discrete algorithms. Hybrid algorithms in principle can provide optimal estimates using discrete data in the cases where the discrete algorithms are only quasi-optimal.

Unfortunately, the application of the algorithms of optimal learning is confronted with enormous difficulties, which are connected to the necessity of computing an initial value of the estimate and the matrix parameters in the algorithm. Therefore, the role of the algorithms of optimal learning should not be overemphasized. They cannot be used in practice. However, they are important since they indicate the limiting possibilities of learning. Regarding the applications, we have to be satisfied with the algorithms of suboptimal learning which do not require the computation of the initial value of the estimate and the matrix of the parameters in the algorithm.

In a number of cases it is advisable to apply the algorithms of learning with repetition in obtaining optimal estimates. After considering the goals of learning, the algorithms of learning, and evaluating the methods of obtaining algorithms of optimal learning, we can finally approach the formulation and the solution of the problems connected with the design of learning systems.

Comments

3.1 The causes for different approaches to the construction of discrete algorithms of optimal learning were discussed by Stratonovich [1–3], Repin and Tartakovskii [1], and the author [1]. In the last paper and this chapter, the form of the algorithm is given, and the parameters of the algorithm which minimize a certain performance index are sought. In the other works mentioned above, both the form of the algorithm and its parameters are sought on the basis of statistical decision theory. Very frequently both approaches lead to the identical results.

3.2 It would be very interesting to learn if more reasonable performance indices of learning exist.

In essence, the functional (3.9) is also obtained by Stratonovich [1], showing that for exponential distributions

$$\mathsf{M}\{Q(x, c)[x[1], x[2], \ldots, x[n]\} = n^{-1} \sum_{m=1}^{n} Q(x[m], c[n]).$$

3.4 These same results, using a slightly different approach, were obtained by Stratonovich [1]. However, he does not emphasize the fact that discrete algorithms in general may be only quasi-optimal.

3.5 The presented results are closely related to the well-known Kalman's method [1]. In order to emphasize this, it is appropriate to call $K[n]$ Kalman's matrix. See also the work by Hutorovskii [1].

3.6 The conclusions here are due to Albert and Gardner [1] in Chapter 2. In their book, the reader can find many interesting and useful conclusions related to the stochastic approximation and nonlinear regression.

3.7 We hope the reader has understood that the question about algorithms of optimal learning is not as simple as it may appear by reading the mentioned works on optimal algorithms. This theme also was not exhausted here.

The reader interested in linear optimal algorithms is advised to read the works by Fagin [1], Albert and Sittler [1], Albert and Gardner [1] in Chapter 2. In the works by Stratonovich [1–3], Repin and Tartakovskii [1], and the author [1] which are devoted to the algorithms of optimal learning, the questions related to the use of algorithms when $\mathbf{c}[0] = \mathbf{c}^*$, and to the removal of necessity for inversion of the initial matrix were not considered. The application of the so-called pseudomatrices obviates many difficulties. See the book by Lee [1]. In the case of nonlinear algorithms of quasi-optimal learning, there is a question of their convergence, which with the exception of Albert and Gardner, no one has yet considered.

3.8 The idea of finding optimal $\gamma[n]$ for the simplest linear algorithms can be found in the work of Dvoretsky [1]. It was used by Nikolic and Fu [1] in Chapter 2, and also by the author [1]. The algorithm No. 3, given in Table 3.1, was obtained by Chien and Fu [1] in Chapter 2.

3.9 The algorithm of Kaczmarz is described in the original work [1] and in the book by Raibman and Chadeev [1]. Lelashvili [1–3] has broadly used the algorithm of Kaczmarz in the identification problems, and also for interpretation and generalization of these algorithms.

3.10 Optimal continuous and hybrid algorithms were considered in the works of the author [1, 2] and [1] in Chapter 2.

3.13 Until recently, it was assumed that the discrete algorithm of Kaczmarz and its continuous analog are similar to each other. See the book by Raibman and Chadeev [1] where the analog algorithm of Kaczmarz is given in the form

$$\frac{d\mathbf{c}(t)}{dt} = \frac{\boldsymbol{\varphi}(\mathbf{x}(t))}{\boldsymbol{\varphi}^{\mathrm{T}}(\mathbf{x}(t))\boldsymbol{\varphi}(\mathbf{x}(t))}\,(y - \mathbf{c}^{\mathrm{T}}(t)\boldsymbol{\varphi}(\mathbf{x}(t))).$$

Actually this is not so. This fact was discovered by E. D. Avedyan.

3.14 These questions were clarified in the conversations with M. A. Krasnoselskii and P. P. Zabreyko.

Similar proofs, related to the algorithms of suboptimal learning are presented in the article by Zabreyko, Krasnoselskii, and the author (Section 3.1).

3.15 The use of periodically repeating data for linear algorithms was introduced by Litvakov [1]. The device which realizes the optimal algorithm described at the end of Section 3.12, was first described by the author and Medvedev [1].

REFERENCES

Albert, A. E., and Sittler, R. W.

[1] A method for computing least squares estimators that keep up with the data. SIAM *J. Appl. Math.* **3**, No. 3 (1965).

Dvoretsky, A.

[1] On stochastic approximation. *Proc. Symp. Math. Statist. Probability, 3rd, Berkeley, 1956*, **1**.

Fagin, S. L.

[1] Recursive linear regression theory, optimal filter theory and error analysis of optimal systems. *IEEE Internat. Conv. Rec.* 1 (1964).

Hutorovskii, Z. N.

[1] Structure of an optimal unbiased estimation of linear filtering of discrete data. *In* "Analysis and Synthesis of Automatic Control Systems." Nauka, Moscow, 1968 (in Russian).

Kaczmarz, S.

[1] Angenäherte Auflösung von Systemen Linearen Gleichungen. *Bull. Internat. Acad. Polon. Sci. Lett. Cl. Sci. Math. Nat. A* (1937).

Kalman, R.

[1] New approach to the linear filtering and prediction problems. *J. Basic Eng.* **83**, No. 1 (1961).

Lee, C. K.

[1] "Optimal Estimation, Identification and Control." MIT Press, Cambridge, Massachusetts, 1964.

Lelashvili, S. G.

[1] Application of an iterative algorithm to the analysis of multivariable control systems. *In* "Schemes of Automatic Control." Tbilisi, 1965 (in Russian).

[2] Certain questions regarding the synthesis of the models of multivariable plants. *In* "Automatic Control." Tbilisi, 1967 (in Russian).

[3] Statistical modeling of identification of adaptive models. *In* "Automatic Control." Tbilisi, 1967 (in Russian).

Litvakov, B. M.

[1] An iterative method based on a finite number of observations for approximation of functions. *Avtomat. i Telemeh.* No. 4 (1966).

Raibman, N. S., and Chadeev, V. M.

[1] "Adaptive Models." Sovyetskoe Radio, Moscow, 1967.

Repin, V. G., and Tartakovskii, G. P.

[1] Adaptation of the communication and information systems and statistical decision theory. *Avtomat. i Telemeh.* No. 3 (1968).

Stratonovich, R. L.

[1] Is there a theory of synthesis for optimal adaptive, learning, self-learning, and self-organizing systems? *Avtomat. i Telemeh.* No. 1 (1968).

[2] Optimal algorithms of recognition. *Avtomat. i Telemeh.* No. 2 (1968).

[3] Effectiveness of the methods of mathematical statistics in the problems of synthesis of algorithms for restoration of unknown functions. *Izv. Akad. Nauk SSSR Tehn. Kibernet.* No. 1 (1969).

Tsypkin, Ya. Z.

[1] Is there indeed a theory of synthesis of optimal adaptive systems? *Avtomat. i Telemeh.* No. 1 (1968).

[2] "Über Optimale Lern—und Adaptations Algorithmen," Vol. 12, No. 1. Messen, Steuern, Regelung, 1969.

Tsypkin, Ya. Z., and Medvedev, I. L.

[1] An adaptive computer. Pat. No. 249773 and No. 1242010, May 23, 1968 (in Russian).

Zabreyko, P. P., Krasnoselskii, M. A., and Tsypkin, Ya. Z.

[1] On algorithms of optimal learning. *Avtomat. i Telemeh.* No. 9 (1970).

Chapter IV

Elements of Statistical Decision Theory

A certain lady claims that, after tasting a cup of tea with milk, she can say which is first poured into the cup—milk or tea. This lady states that even if she sometimes makes mistakes, she is more often right than wrong.

R. FISHER

4.1 Introduction

Many problems of modern science and engineering are reduced to the recognition or, if it is convenient, to the classification of observed situations, events, and patterns. The prominent examples are the industrial and medical diagnostics, detection of useful situations, signals, and so forth. The classification of observed situations is accomplished by various recognition systems on the basis of a certain decision rule. The methods for defining decision rules depend on the volume of *a priori* information. In the case of sufficient *a priori* information, these decision rules are obtained on the basis of statistical decision theory. Learning becomes necessary when *a priori* information is insufficient and so small that the results of statistical decision theory cannot be used directly. But before we consider this case, it is necessary to become familiar with the basic classical results of statistical decision theory. In this chapter, the presentation of the statistical decision theory differs slightly from the traditional one. This is done with the purpose of covering all possible results—the classical results and those connected with the design of learning systems.

4.2 Average Risk

In order to obtain a decision rule, we must first formulate a performance index of recognition or classification. The decision rule has to be formulated in such a way that the performance index reaches an extremum.

Let us assume that a situation $\mathbf{x}$ occurs randomly, and that each situation belongs to one of M initially unknown classes X_k^0 ($k = 1, 2, \ldots, M$). We shall designate by X the space of situations. This space is partitioned into M regions X_k ($k = 1, 2, \ldots, M$). In order to describe the concept of "best" partition, we also introduce the loss function

$$F_{km}(\mathbf{x}, \vec{\mathbf{c}}), \qquad k, m = 1, 2, \ldots, M, \tag{4.1}$$

where

$$\vec{\mathbf{c}} = (\mathbf{c}_1, \mathbf{c}_2, \ldots, \mathbf{c}_M) \tag{4.2}$$

is the component vector of the parameters.

The loss function (4.1) characterizes the losses that occur when a situation from class X_k^0 is classified into X_m^0, or, in other words, when a situation from class X_k^0 falls into the region X_m. The loss functions form the cost matrix

$$\begin{pmatrix} F_{11}(\mathbf{x}, \vec{\mathbf{c}}) & F_{12}(\mathbf{x}, \vec{\mathbf{c}}) & \cdots & F_{1M}(\mathbf{x}, \vec{\mathbf{c}}) \\ F_{21}(\mathbf{x}, \vec{\mathbf{c}}) & F_{22}(\mathbf{x}, \vec{\mathbf{c}}) & \cdots & F_{2M}(\mathbf{x}, \vec{\mathbf{c}}) \\ \vdots & \vdots & & \vdots \\ F_{M1}(\mathbf{x}, \vec{\mathbf{c}}) & F_{M2}(\mathbf{x}, \vec{\mathbf{c}}) & \cdots & F_{MM}(\mathbf{x}, \vec{\mathbf{c}}) \end{pmatrix}. \tag{4.3}$$

The main diagonal of the matrix contains the losses related to the correct decisions, and the off-diagonal terms are the losses due to incorrect decisions. If $F_{mm}(\mathbf{x}, \vec{\mathbf{c}}) < 0$ ($m = 1, 2, \ldots, M$), such negative losses can be considered as gains due to correct decisions.

The situation $\mathbf{x}$ of each class X_k^0 is characterized by the conditional probability density $p(\mathbf{x}/k) = p_k(\mathbf{x})$ and *a priori* probability P_k. Therefore, the performance of recognition or classification can be evaluated by the average risk

$$R = \sum_{k=1}^{M} \sum_{m=1}^{M} \int_{X_m} F_{km}(\mathbf{x}, \vec{\mathbf{c}}) P_k p_k(\mathbf{x})\, d\mathbf{x}. \tag{4.4}$$

The average risk is a functional of the boundaries Λ_{km} between the regions X_k and X_m, and of the component vector $\vec{\mathbf{c}}$. It should be noticed that the (4.4) differs from a usual one in which the loss functions are considered

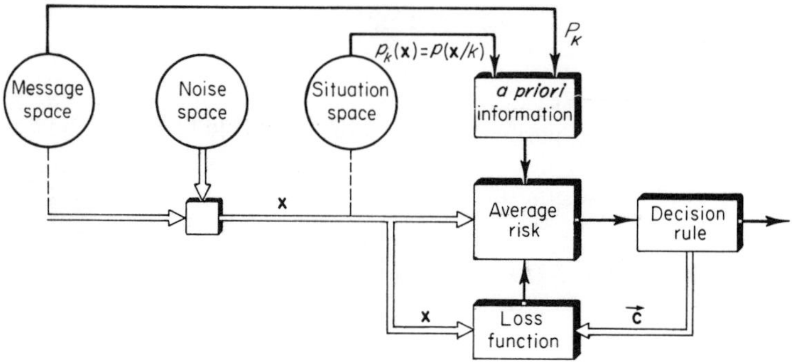

FIG. 4.1

to be constant. The loss function is considered here to depend on the situations $\mathbf{x}$, and which is very important, on the component vector $\vec{\mathbf{c}}$. As already mentioned, the decision rules, which define the boundaries Λ_{km} between the regions X_k and X_m, are found by minimizing the average risk. The general symbolic scheme of obtaining decision rules is shown in Fig. 4.1.

4.3 Conditions for the Minimum of the Average Risk

Let us first find the conditions for minimizing the average risk R (Eq. (4.4)). When the parameter vector $\vec{\mathbf{c}}$ is fixed, the minimum is defined over the boundary Λ_{km} between the regions X_k and X_m. Such an approach is only a slight generalization of the approach used in statistical decision theory. However, since we face more difficult problems, we shall consider that the loss functions are only known up to the parameter vector $\vec{\mathbf{c}}$. Simultaneously with the determination of the boundaries between the regions, we shall also search for the optimal value of the parameter vector. For this purpose we introduce the characteristic function

$$\theta_m(\mathbf{x}, \vec{\mathbf{c}}) = \begin{cases} 1 & \text{if} \quad \mathbf{x} \in X_m \\ 0 & \text{if} \quad \mathbf{x} \bar{\in} X_m . \end{cases} \tag{4.5}$$

The expression of the average risk, (4.4), can then be written in a "parametric form"

$$R(\vec{\mathbf{c}}) = \sum_{k=1}^{M} \sum_{m=1}^{M} \int_X \theta_m(\mathbf{x}, \vec{\mathbf{c}}) F_{km}(\mathbf{x}, \vec{\mathbf{c}}) P_k p_k(\mathbf{x}) \, d\mathbf{x}. \tag{4.6}$$

$R(\vec{\mathbf{c}})$, in the end, depends only on the parameter vector $\vec{\mathbf{c}}$. The boundaries between the regions are then defined by the characteristic functions $\theta(\mathbf{x}, \vec{\mathbf{c}})$ that depend on $\vec{\mathbf{c}}$. Therefore, the condition for obtaining the minimum of the average risk is obtained by equating the gradient of R with respect to $\vec{\mathbf{c}}$ with zero, that is,

$$\nabla_{\vec{\mathbf{c}}} R(\vec{\mathbf{c}}) = \sum_{k=1}^{M} \sum_{m=1}^{M} \int_X \theta_m(\mathbf{x}, \vec{\mathbf{c}}) \nabla_{\vec{\mathbf{c}}} F_{km}(\mathbf{x}, \vec{\mathbf{c}}) P_k p_k(\mathbf{x}) \, d\mathbf{x} + \sum_{k=1}^{M} \sum_{m=1}^{M} \int_X \nabla_{\vec{\mathbf{c}}} \theta_m(\mathbf{x}, \vec{\mathbf{c}}) F_{km}(\mathbf{x}, \vec{\mathbf{c}}) P_k p_k(\mathbf{x}) \, d\mathbf{x} = 0. \tag{4.7}$$

The first term in the expression represents the sensitivity of the loss function, and the second the sensitivity of the characteristic functions with respect to $\vec{\mathbf{c}}$.

Considering that the characteristic functions (4.5), which define the boundaries A_{km} between the regions, are such that for each fixed $\vec{\mathbf{c}}$ they provide the minimum of the average risk, we conclude that their sensitivity must be equal to zero, that is,

$$\nabla_{\vec{\mathbf{c}}} R_1 = \sum_{k=1}^{M} \sum_{m=1}^{M} \int_X \nabla_{\vec{\mathbf{c}}} \theta_m(\mathbf{x}, \vec{\mathbf{c}}) F_{km}(\mathbf{x}, \vec{\mathbf{c}}) P_k p_k(\mathbf{x}) \, d\mathbf{x} = 0. \tag{4.8}$$

Therefore, it follows from (4.7) that

$$\nabla_{\vec{\mathbf{c}}} R_2 = \sum_{k=1}^{M} \sum_{m=1}^{M} \int_X \theta_m(\mathbf{x}, \vec{\mathbf{c}}) \nabla_{\vec{\mathbf{c}}} F_{km}(\mathbf{x}, \vec{\mathbf{c}}) P_k p_k(\mathbf{x}) \, d\mathbf{x} = 0. \tag{4.9}$$

Since $\nabla_{\mathbf{c}} \theta_m(\mathbf{x}, \vec{\mathbf{c}})$ is a multidimensional δ-function that is equal to zero everywhere except for the points that lie on the boundary A_{km} between the regions X_k and X_m, we have

$$\nabla_{\vec{\mathbf{c}}} R_1 = \sum_{k=1}^{M} \int_{A_{sm}} [F_{ks}(\mathbf{x}, \vec{\mathbf{c}}) - F_{km}(\mathbf{x}, \vec{\mathbf{c}})] P_k p_k(\mathbf{x}) \, d\mathbf{x} = 0 \tag{4.10}$$

or, since this equality must be valid for every $\vec{\mathbf{c}}$,

$$f_{sm}(\mathbf{x}, \vec{\mathbf{c}}) = \sum_{k=1}^{M} [F_{ks}(\mathbf{x}, \vec{\mathbf{c}}) - F_{km}(\mathbf{x}, \vec{\mathbf{c}})] P_k p_k(\mathbf{x}) = 0. \tag{4.11}$$

Conditions (4.9) and (4.11) are the necessary conditions for minimizing average risk.

Equation (4.11) defines the surface that separates the regions X_s and X_m. The functions $f_{sm}(\mathbf{x}, \vec{\mathbf{c}})$ can be called the *discriminant functions*. The sign of the discriminant function permits us to distinguish the regions. Therefore, the decision rule can be formulated in the following way: $\mathbf{x} \in X_k$, that is, $\mathbf{x}$ is classified into X_k^0 when

$$f_{km}(\mathbf{x}, \vec{\mathbf{c}}) < 0, \qquad m = 1, 2, \ldots, M, \tag{4.12}$$

where in (4.11) $\vec{\mathbf{c}}$ is determined from the condition (4.9).

4.4 Binary Case

The binary case corresponds to the case of two classes. By setting $M = 2$ in (4.6), (4.9), and (4.11), we obtain the following expression for the average risk:

$$\begin{aligned} R = &\int_{X_1} F_{11}(\mathbf{x}, \vec{\mathbf{c}}) P_1 p_1(\mathbf{x})\, d\mathbf{x} + \int_{X_1} F_{21}(\mathbf{x}, \vec{\mathbf{c}}) P_2 p_2(\mathbf{x})\, d\mathbf{x} \\ &+ \int_{X_2} F_{12}(\mathbf{x}, \vec{\mathbf{c}}) P_1 p_1(\mathbf{x})\, d\mathbf{x} + \int_{X_2} F_{22}(\mathbf{x}, \vec{\mathbf{c}}) P_2 p_2(\mathbf{x})\, d\mathbf{x}, \end{aligned} \tag{4.13}$$

and the condition for the minimum of the average risk

$$\begin{aligned} \nabla_{\vec{\mathbf{c}}} R_1 = &\int_X [\theta_1(\mathbf{x}, \vec{\mathbf{c}}) \nabla_{\vec{\mathbf{c}}} F_{11}(\mathbf{x}, \vec{\mathbf{c}}) P_1 p_1(\mathbf{x}) + \theta_1(\mathbf{x}, \vec{\mathbf{c}}) \nabla_{\vec{\mathbf{c}}} F_{21}(\mathbf{x}, \vec{\mathbf{c}}) P_2 p_2(\mathbf{x})]\, d\mathbf{x} \\ &+ \int_X [\theta_2(\mathbf{x}, \vec{\mathbf{c}}) \nabla_{\vec{\mathbf{c}}} F_{12}(\mathbf{x}, \vec{\mathbf{c}}) P_1 p_1(\mathbf{x}) + \theta_2(\mathbf{x}, \vec{\mathbf{c}}) \nabla_{\vec{\mathbf{c}}} F_{22}(\mathbf{x}, \vec{\mathbf{c}}) P_2 p_2(\mathbf{x})]\, d\mathbf{x} \\ = &\ 0, \end{aligned} \tag{4.14}$$

and

$$\begin{aligned} f_{12}(\mathbf{x}, \vec{\mathbf{c}}) = &[F_{11}(\mathbf{x}, \vec{\mathbf{c}}) - F_{12}(\mathbf{x}, \vec{\mathbf{c}})] P_1 p_1(\mathbf{x}) \\ &+ [F_{21}(\mathbf{x}, \vec{\mathbf{c}}) - F_{22}(\mathbf{x}, \vec{\mathbf{c}})] P_2 p_2(\mathbf{x}) = 0. \end{aligned} \tag{4.15}$$

Optimal decision rule is then $\mathbf{x} \in X_1$, that is, $\mathbf{x}$ is classified into X_1^0 if

$$f_{12}(\mathbf{x}, \vec{\mathbf{c}}) < 0, \tag{4.16}$$

and $\mathbf{x} \in X_2$, that is, $\mathbf{x}$ is classified into X_2^0 if

$$f_{12}(\mathbf{x}, \vec{\mathbf{c}}) > 0. \tag{4.17}$$

The parameter vector $\vec{\mathbf{c}}$ of the decision rule (4.15) is determined from the condition (4.14).

The obtained decision rule differs from the usual decision rules of statistical decision theory since its loss functions are not constants but are specified up to a certain set of unknown parameters.

At first glance this does not appear natural, but when the problems of learning and self-learning are considered, this fact will be broadly used and we hope that the readers familiar with the classical statistical decision theory would also become used to this difference.

Furthermore, in order to preserve the clarity and completeness of presentation, we shall next consider the case of two classes, with constant loss functions.

4.5 Classical Bayes Approach

In the classical Bayes approach, the loss functions are considered constant, such that

$$\begin{aligned} F_{12}(\mathbf{x}, \vec{\mathbf{c}}) &= w_{12} > 0, \qquad F_{11}(\mathbf{x}, \vec{\mathbf{c}}) = w_{11} \leq 0, \\ F_{21}(\mathbf{x}, \vec{\mathbf{c}}) &= w_{21} > 0, \qquad F_{22}(\mathbf{x}, \vec{\mathbf{c}}) = w_{22} \leq 0. \end{aligned} \tag{4.18}$$

Then

$$\begin{aligned} R = {} & w_{11}P_1 \int_{X_1} p_1(\mathbf{x})\, d\mathbf{x} + w_{21}P_2 \int_{X_1} p_2(\mathbf{x})\, d\mathbf{x} \\ & + w_{12}P_1 \int_{X_2} p_1(\mathbf{x})\, d\mathbf{x} + w_{22}P_2 \int_{X_2} p_2(\mathbf{x})\, d\mathbf{x}. \end{aligned} \tag{4.19}$$

Here

$$\alpha = \int_{X_2} p_1(\mathbf{x})\, d\mathbf{x} \tag{4.20}$$

is the conditional error probability of the first kind;

$$\beta = \int_{X_1} p_2(\mathbf{x})\, d\mathbf{x} \tag{4.21}$$

is the conditional error probability of the second kind;

$$1 - \alpha = \int_{X_1} p_1(\mathbf{x})\, d\mathbf{x}, \qquad 1 - \beta = \int_{X_2} p_2(\mathbf{x})\, d\mathbf{x}, \tag{4.22}$$

is the conditional probability of correct decision. In selecting the constant loss functions (4.18), the condition (4.14) is also satisfied because

$$\nabla_{\vec{\mathbf{c}}} F_{km}(\mathbf{x}, \vec{\mathbf{c}}) \equiv 0. \tag{4.23}$$

From the condition (4.15) we obtain

$$f_{12}(\mathbf{x}, \vec{\mathbf{c}}) = (w_{11} - w_{12})P_1 p_1(\mathbf{x}) + (w_{21} - w_{22})P_2 p_2(\mathbf{x}) = 0, \qquad (4.24)$$

or

$$p_1(\mathbf{x})/p_2(\mathbf{x}) = [(w_{21} - w_{22})/(w_{12} - w_{11})](P_2/P_1). \qquad (4.25)$$

The left-hand side of (4.25)

$$l(x) = p_1(\mathbf{x})/p_2(\mathbf{x}) \qquad (4.26)$$

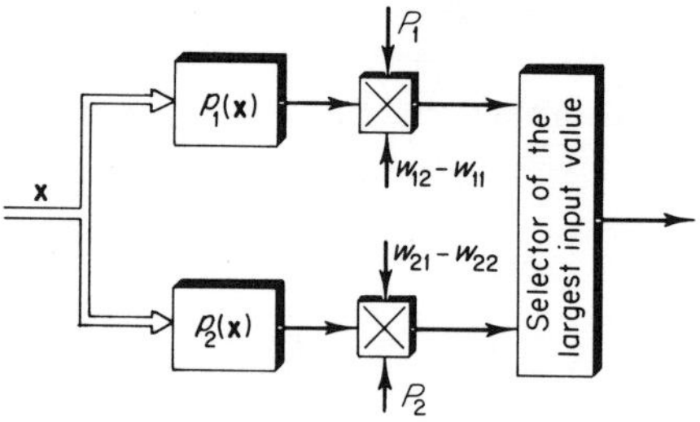

FIG. 4.2

is called the likelihood ratio. The right-hand side of (4.25)

$$h = [(w_{21} - w_{22})/(w_{12} - w_{11})](P_2/P_1) \qquad (4.27)$$

is the threshold.

The optimal decision rule, often called the Bayes rule, is reduced to the computation of the likelihood ratio (4.26), and to the comparison of the computed likelihood ratio with the threshold.

If

$$l(\mathbf{x}) > h, \qquad (4.28)$$

then $\mathbf{x}$ is classified into X_1^0.

If, on the other hand,

$$l(\mathbf{x}) < h, \qquad (4.29)$$

then $\mathbf{x}$ is classified into X_2^0.

The block diagram of the device that performs Bayes decision can have two forms. The first form (Fig. 4.2) is based on the inequalities (4.16)

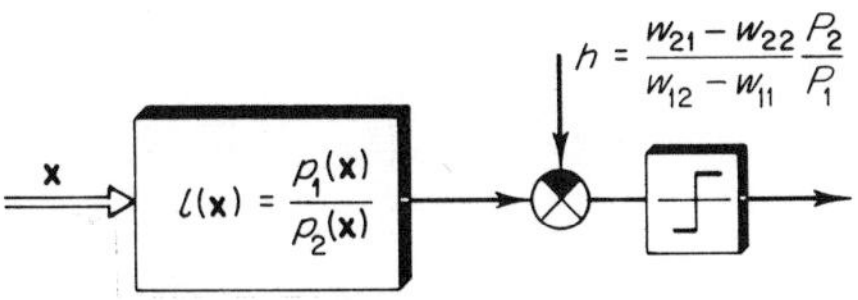

FIG. 4.3

and (4.17) obtained from (4.24), and the second form (Fig. 4.3) is based on the inequalities (4.28) and (4.29).

From these general decision rules and block diagrams, we can obtain various specific decision rules and their corresponding block diagrams.

4.6 Siegert–Kotelnikov Rule

The Siegert–Kotelnikov rule, often called the rule of an ideal observer, corresponds to the minimum of incorrect decisions.

By setting in (4.19)

$$w_{11} = w_{22} = 0, \qquad w_{12} = w_{21} = 1, \tag{4.30}$$

we obtain

$$R = P_2 \int_{X_1} p_2(\mathbf{x})\, d\mathbf{x} + P_1 \int_{X_2} p_1(\mathbf{x})\, d\mathbf{x}, \tag{4.31}$$

or, according to (4.20) and (4.21),

$$R = P_1\alpha + P_2\beta. \tag{4.32}$$

Using (4.30) in (4.27), we obtain an expression for the threshold

$$h = P_2/P_1. \tag{4.33}$$

Therefore, the Siegert–Kotelnikov rule minimizes the incorrect decisions (4.31) and differs from the general rule only by its threshold, which is equal to the ratio of *a priori* probabilities.

4.7 Maximum *A Posteriori* Probability Rule

According to Bayes formula, *a posteriori* probabilities that an observed situation $\mathbf{x}$ is classified into classes X_1^0 or X_2^0 are equal respectively to

$$P_1(\mathbf{x}) = P_1 p_1(\mathbf{x})/p(\mathbf{x}) \tag{4.34}$$

and

$$P_2(\mathbf{x}) = P_2 p_2(\mathbf{x})/p(\mathbf{x}), \tag{4.35}$$

where

$$p(\mathbf{x}) = P_1 p_1(\mathbf{x}) + P_2 p_2(\mathbf{x}) \tag{4.36}$$

is the joint probability density of the situations. The following decision rule is usually accepted.

The situation $\mathbf{x}$ is classified into X_1^0 if

$$P_1(\mathbf{x}) > P_2(\mathbf{x}), \tag{4.37}$$

and the situation $\mathbf{x}$ is classified into X_2^0 if

$$P_1(\mathbf{x}) < P_2(\mathbf{x}). \tag{4.38}$$

This is indeed the maximum *a posteriori* probability decision rule. The boundary corresponds to the equation

$$P_1(\mathbf{x}) = P_2(\mathbf{x}), \tag{4.39}$$

or, considering (4.34) and (4.35),

$$p_1(\mathbf{x})/p_2(\mathbf{x}) = P_2/P_1. \tag{4.40}$$

It follows that

$$h = P_2/P_1. \tag{4.41}$$

Therefore, the maximum *a posteriori* probability rule and the Siegert–Kotelnikov rule are identical.

We shall also mention that for $P_1 = P_2 = \frac{1}{2}$, that is, for the threshold

$$h = 1, \tag{4.42}$$

we obtain the maximum likelihood decision rule.

4.8 Mixed Decision Rule

The mixed decision rule corresponds to the maximum of the difference of conditional probability of correct decision and a quantity proportional to the conditional error probability of the first kind, that is,

$$(1 - \beta) - \lambda\alpha = \int_{X_2} p_2(\mathbf{x})\, d\mathbf{x} - \lambda \int_{X_2} p_1(\mathbf{x})\, d\mathbf{x} \tag{4.43}$$

or, which is equivalent to the minimum of

$$R_\lambda = \beta + \lambda\alpha = \int_{X_1} p_2(\mathbf{x})\, d\mathbf{x} + \lambda \int_{X_2} p_1(\mathbf{x})\, d\mathbf{x}, \tag{4.44}$$

where λ is a certain weighting coefficient.

By setting in (4.19)

$$w_{11} = w_{22} = 0, \qquad w_{12} = 2\lambda, \qquad w_{21} = 2, \\ P_1 = P_2 = \tfrac{1}{2}, \tag{4.45}$$

we immediately obtain an expression for the average risk that is identical to (4.44). Therefore, for the mixed decision rule, from (4.27) and (4.45) we find the threshold

$$h = \lambda^{-1}, \tag{4.46}$$

equal to the inverse of the weighting coefficient λ. By substituting the conditional probabilities in (4.44) with the total probabilities, we have

$$R_\lambda = P_2\beta + \lambda P_1\alpha. \tag{4.47}$$

In this case, the values

$$w_{11} = w_{22} = 0, \qquad w_{12} = \lambda, \qquad w_{21} = 1, \tag{4.48}$$

are used in the expression (4.27) of the threshold. This leads us to the following expression for the threshold:

$$h = \lambda^{-1}P_2/P_1. \tag{4.49}$$

Of course, for $\lambda = 1$, we obtain the Siegert–Kotelnikov rule and the maximum *a posteriori* probability rule.

4.9 Neyman–Pearson Rule

The Neyman–Pearson rule minimizes the conditional error probability of the second kind

$$\beta = \int_{X_1} p_2(\mathbf{x})\, d\mathbf{x} \tag{4.50}$$

when the conditional error probability of the first kind

$$\alpha = \int_{X_2} p_1(\mathbf{x})\, d\mathbf{x} = A = \text{const} \tag{4.51}$$

is given.

In order to solve this problem, we use the method of Lagrange multipliers. We form the functional

$$R_\lambda = \beta + \lambda\alpha = \int_{X_1} p_2(\mathbf{x})\, d\mathbf{x} + \lambda \int_{X_2} p_1(\mathbf{x})\, d\mathbf{x}. \tag{4.52}$$

This functional is identical to the functional in (4.44), but λ is now an unknown multiplier.

As before, we obtain an expression for the threshold

$$h = \lambda^{-1}. \tag{4.53}$$

The unknown multiplier, and thus the unknown threshold, can be found from the condition (4.51).

The problem of finding λ is simplified if we consider the one-dimensional variable $l(\mathbf{x})$ instead of multidimensional observations using

$$p_1(\mathbf{x})\, d\mathbf{x} = p_1(l)\, dl. \tag{4.54}$$

The condition (4.51) is then transformed into the condition

$$\alpha = \int_{l_0}^{\infty} p_1(l)\, dl = A = \text{const.} \tag{4.55}$$

It is now simple to conclude that

$$h = \lambda^{-1} = l_0, \tag{4.56}$$

where l_0 is determined from (4.55).

We can slightly modify the Neyman–Pearson rule if the total error probability of the second kind

$$P_2\beta = P_2 \int_{X_1} p_2(\mathbf{x})\, d\mathbf{x} \tag{4.57}$$

is minimized for a given level of total error probability of the first kind

$$P_1\alpha = P_1 \int_{X_2} p_1(\mathbf{x})\, d\mathbf{x} = A_1 = \text{const.} \tag{4.58}$$

In this case the functional (4.52) is replaced by

$$R_\lambda = P_2\beta + \lambda P_1\alpha = P_2 \int_{X_1} p_2(\mathbf{x})\, d\mathbf{x} + \lambda P_1 \int_{X_2} p_1(\mathbf{x})\, d\mathbf{x}. \tag{4.59}$$

Now, similarly to (4.49), the threshold will be equal to

$$h = \lambda^{-1}P_2/P_1, \tag{4.60}$$

and the unknown multiplier λ^{-1} becomes

$$\lambda^{-1} = l_1, \tag{4.61}$$

where l_1 is determined from the condition

$$P_1 \int_{l_1}^{\infty} p_1(l)\, dl = A_1 = \text{const.} \tag{4.62}$$

Therefore, we have again obtained a decision rule with a threshold.

4.10 Min–Max Decision Rule

If *a priori* probabilities

$$P_1 \qquad \text{and} \qquad P_2 = 1 - P_1 \tag{4.63}$$

are unknown, the decision rules considered above cannot be applied.

In such cases, the min–max decision rule, which minimizes the maximal possible risk, is recommended.

Let us consider the average risk (4.19) under the condition

$$w_{11} = w_{22} = 0. \tag{4.64}$$

Then, using (4.63) and the notations (4.20) and (4.21),

$$R = w_{21}(1 - P_1)\beta + w_{12}P_1\alpha, \tag{4.65}$$

we shall find such

$$P_1 = P_1^0, \tag{4.66}$$

for which R is maximized. By differentiating (4.65) with respect to P_1 and by equating the obtained derivative with zero, we obtain

$$w_{21}\beta = w_{12}\alpha. \tag{4.67}$$

This relationship represents the equality of the conditional average risks for the errors of the second and the first kind. If the conditional error probabilities α and β depend on the boundaries between the regions, then they also depend on *a priori* probability P_1. Therefore, generally speaking, (4.67) represents a transcendental equation with respect to P_1. By finding the root of Eq. (4.67), we obtain from (4.27) and (4.64) the threshold

$$h = (w_{21}/w_{12})(1 - P_1^0)/P_1^0. \tag{4.68}$$

Obviously, the actual average risk (4.65) with $P_1 \neq P_1^0$ will always be smaller than the average risk for P_1^0. The computation of the worst case is carried here under the most convenient condition. Thus, the min–max decision rule is a special Bayes rule for the least favorable *a priori* probabilities. The min–max decision rule gives a guaranteed estimate of the average risk. However, this overcautious estimate can be frequently far removed from the actual value.

Let us mention in the conclusion that for

$$w_{21} = w_{12} = 1 \tag{4.69}$$

it follows from (4.67) that

$$\beta = \alpha. \tag{4.70}$$

In this case the min–max decision rule simply provides the equality of the conditional error probabilities of the first and the second kind. The min–max decision rule is connected with certain computational difficulties caused by the necessity to solve the transcendental equation (4.67). But, even if this difficulty is crossed, we again obtain a decision rule with the threshold.

4.11 General Decision Rule

Thus far we have considered the decision rules that minimize the average risk given by a linear combination of the conditional error probabilities α and β. In general, the criterion can be an arbitrary function of conditional error probabilities, that is,

$$R_\Phi = \Phi(\alpha, \beta). \tag{4.71}$$

The decision rule must then guarantee the minimum of R_Φ. This minimum coincides with the minimum of the function $\Phi(\alpha, \beta)$ when α and β are varying in a certain region Y of the possible values of these parameters. The region Y consists of all points (pairs of α and β) that correspond to all possible partitions of the situation space X into the regions X_1 and X_2. If the function $\Phi(\alpha, \beta)$ has a minimum, and this minimum lies within Y, the values α^* and β^* corresponding to the minimum are determined by solving the following system of equations:

$$\partial\Phi(\alpha, \beta)/\partial\alpha = 0, \qquad \partial\Phi(\alpha, \beta)/\partial\beta = 0. \tag{4.72}$$

Of course, we assume that $\Phi(\alpha, \beta)$ is differentiable with respect to its arguments. Usually R_Φ is such that its minimum does not lie within the region Y. This means that the minimum of R_Φ coincides with the smallest value of $\Phi(\alpha, \beta)$ on the boundary L of the region Y. In order to find the boundary L, we fix the value $\alpha = \alpha_1$, and then find the corresponding minimum value $\beta = \beta_1$. The values α_1 and β_1 correspond to the points that lie on the boundary L. By continuing this process for different fixed values α $(0 < \alpha < 1)$, we obtain the boundary L.

As it was shown in Section 4.9, the problem of finding the minimum β under fixed value α is solved on the basis of the Neyman–Pearson rule. The selection of a particular solution depends on the threshold h, which in this case corresponds to the smallest value of $\Phi(\alpha, \beta)$. This smallest value of $\Phi(\alpha, \beta)$ can be found by computing α and β as the functions of h:

$$\alpha = \alpha(h), \qquad \beta = \beta(h), \tag{4.73}$$

and using them in (4.71),

$$R_\Phi = \Phi(\alpha(h), \beta(h)) = \Phi_1(h). \tag{4.74}$$

The final value $h = h_0$ is found from the condition

$$d\Phi_1(h)/dh = 0 \tag{4.75}$$

using deterministic iterative algorithms. By equating the likelihood ratio l with the optimal threshold h_0, we solve the problem of classifying a situation $\mathbf{x}$ into one of the regions. In a similar fashion, we can also solve the problem for the criterion

$$R_\Phi = \Phi(P_1\alpha, P_2\beta). \tag{4.76}$$

It should be obvious from the material presented that general decision rules require very tedious computations.

4.12 Discussion

All decision rules discussed thus far lead to the same decision procedure. The likelihood ratio $l(\mathbf{x})$ (4.26) is computed, and the situation $\mathbf{x}$ is classified into the class $X_1^0(X_2^0)$ when the likelihood ratio is smaller (greater) than a prespecified threshold that depends on the chosen decision rule. The general block diagram of the system that realizes all these rules is shown in Fig. 4.3. Similar systems for specific decision rules differ only by their thresholds h. For convenience, all decision rules considered above are listed in Table 4.1.

It is important to remember that the applications of these rules require sufficient *a priori* information. All decision rules assume that *a priori* probabilities P_1 and P_2 are given. In the maximum likelihood decision rule and in the Neyman–Pearson rule, they are simply considered to be equal. The least favorable *a priori* probabilities are assumed in the min–max decision rule. Of course, all these decision rules are far from being optimal if actual *a priori* probabilities are very different from the assumed ones.

The systems that minimize the average risk will be called Bayes systems.

TABLE 4.1

Decision Rule	Criterion of optimality	Threshold
Bayes	$\min(w_{12}P_1\alpha + w_{21}P_2\beta)$	$h = (w_{21}/w_{12})(P_2/P_1)$
Siegert–Kotelnikov	$\min(P_1\alpha + P_2\beta)$	$h = P_2/P_1$
Maximum *a posteriori* probability	$\max_k P_k p_k(\mathbf{x}) \quad (k = 1, 2)$	$h = P_2/P_1$
Maximum likelihood	$\max_k p_k(\mathbf{x}) \quad (k = 1, 2)$	$h = 1,\ P_1 = P_2 = \frac{1}{2}$
Mixed	$\max[(1 - \beta) - \lambda\alpha]$ or $\min(\beta + \lambda\alpha)$	$h = \lambda^{-1},\ P_1 = P_2 = \frac{1}{2}$
	$\max(P_2(1 - \beta) - \lambda P_1\alpha)$ or $\min(P_2\beta + \lambda P_1\alpha)$	$h = \lambda^{-1}P_2/P_1$
Neyman–Pearson	$\min \beta$ when $\alpha = \text{const}$	$h = \lambda^{-1},\ P_1 = P_2 = \frac{1}{2}$, $\int_{l_0}^{\infty} p_1(l)\, dl = \text{const}$
	$\min P_2\beta$ when $P_1\alpha = \text{const}$	$h = \lambda^{-1}P_2/P_1$, $P_1 \int_{l_1}^{\infty} p_1(l)\, dl = \text{const}$
Min–max	$\min_{P_1} \max(w_{12}P_1\alpha + w_{21}P_2\beta)$	$h = (w_{21}/w_{12})(1 - P_1^0/P_1^0)$, $w_{12}\alpha = w_{21}\beta$

4.13 Conclusion

Bayes systems form one class of optimal systems. Sufficient *a priori* information is needed for their realization.

If such *a priori* information is given, the problems of recognition and classification consist of computing and comparing the likelihood ratio and threshold. Minimization of different criteria of optimality is reduced to a corresponding change of thresholds. In this case, when *a priori* information is insufficient, almost all of these rules are inconvenient. These are several ways to overcome lack of *a priori* information. One which is very difficult consists of processing current information in order to determine necessary data. Another one consists of applying the min–max decision rule that guarantees the best decision under the worst conditions. If the conditions are actually close to the worst conditions, this approach provides an acceptable solution. In general, we obtain a decision system that has a larger margin of error than is desirable. One solution can be found in the applications of learning systems.

Comments

4.2 In the classical statistical decision theory, the loss function, and thus the average risk, do not depend on the situation $\mathbf{x}$ and the parameter vector $\mathbf{c}$. See the books by Gutkin [1], Wald [1], Levin [1], Middleton [1], Sisoev [1], Helstrom [1], and Falkovich [1]. For our purposes such generalization of the average risk is important.

4.3 These results can be obtained more rigorously, but also in a more involved manner, using the methods of variational calculus. Special cases of the conditions for the minimum of the average risk were obtained in the books mentioned in the comments for Section 4.2, and also in the book by Fel'dbaum [1] in Chapter 1 and in the work by Elmans [1].

4.5–4.10 The basic results of classical statistical decision theory in hypothesis testing (see Peterson *et al.* [1]) are presented here. We slightly alter the classical terminology.

4.11 The description of the general rule is borrowed from the book by Andreev [1] in Chapter 1.

4.12 Application of statistical decision theory to the problems of pattern recognition was presented in the book by Barabash *et al.* [1], and in the works of Gabisonia [1], Kovalevskii [1], and Loginov and Hurgin [1]. Important results in this approach were obtained by Pugachev [1–4]. Statistical decision theory was applied in the design of adaptive systems in the book by Sawaragi *et al.* [1].

REFERENCES

Barabash, Yu. L., Varskii, B. V., Zinovyev, V. T., Kirichenko, V. S., and Sapegin, V. F.

[1] "The Questions of the Statistical Theory of Pattern Recognition." Sovyetskoe Radio, Moscow, 1967 (in Russian).

Elmans, R. I.

[1] On optimization of pattern recognition in nonstationary noise. *Engrg. Cybernetics* No. 5 (1966).

Falkovich, S. E.

[1] "Reception of Radar Signals in the Fluctuating Noise." Sovyetskoe Radio, Moscow, 1961 (in Russian).

Gabisonia, B. V.

[1] Pattern recognition using the methods of statistical decision theory. *In* "Automatic Devices." Tbilisi, 1967 (in Russian).

Gutkin, L. S.

[1] "Theory of Optimal Methods of Reception under Fluctuating Disturbances." Gosenergoizdat, Moscow-Leningrad, 1961 (in Russian).

Helstrom, C. W.

[1] "Statistical Theory of Signal Detection." Pergamon, Oxford, 1960.

Kovalevskii, V. A.

[1] The problems of pattern recognition from the viewpoint of mathematical statistics. *In* "Reading Automata and Pattern Recognition," Naukova Dumka, Kiev, 1965 (in Russian).

Levin, B. L.

[1] "Theoretical Foundations of Statistical Communications," Vol. 2. Sovyetskoe Radio, Moscow, 1968 (in Russian).

Loginov, V. I., and Hurgin, Ya. I.

[1] Pattern recognition and mathematical statistics. *Proc. All-Union Conf. Automat. Control Eng. Cybernetics, 3rd,* **3**. Nauka, Moscow, 1967.

Middleton, D.

[1] "An Introduction to Statistical Communication Theory." McGraw-Hill, New York, 1960.

Peterson, W. W., Birdsall, T., and Fox, V. C.

[1] The theory of signal detectability. *Trans. PGIT-IRE* **4**, No. 2, 171 (1954).

Pugachev, V. S.

[1] Statistical problems of the theory of pattern recognition. *Proc. All-Union Conf. Automat. Control Eng. Cybernetics, 3rd,* **3**. Nauka, Moscow, 1967.

[2] Statistical theory of learning automatic systems. *Izv. Akad. Nauk SSSR Eng. Cybernetics* No. 6 (1967).

[3] Optimal algorithms of learning in the case of an unreliable teacher. *Dokl. Akad. Nauk SSSR* **172**, No. 5 (1967).

[4] Optimal learning systems. *Dokl. Akad. Nauk SSSR* **175**, No. 5 (1967).

Sawaragi, Y., Sunahara, Y., and Nakamizo, T.

[1] "Statistical Decision Theory in Adaptive Control Systems." Academic Press, New York, 1967.

Sisoev, L. P.

[1] "Parameter Estimation, Detection and Extraction of Signals." Nauka, Moscow, 1969 (in Russian).

Wald, A.

[1] "Statistical Decision Functions." Wiley, New York, 1950.

Chapter V

Learning Pattern Recognition Systems

There is something common in the orientations in a city and in any scientific area: from every given point we must be able to reach any other one.

G. PÓLYA and G. SZEGO

5.1 Introduction

Incomplete *a priori* information, which implies that neither the likelihood ratio nor *a priori* probabilities are known in advance, represents a serious barrier to the applications of the classical Bayes approach.

Learning systems, which after a certain training period can execute a decision rule and thus perform recognition or classification, are what is needed in such cases.

Lack of knowledge is overcome by learning. The smaller the *a priori* knowledge, the longer is the period necessary for learning. This is a natural cost of ignorance. As mentioned in Section 1.5, two forms of learning can be distinguished: learning with supervision (or with reinforcement) and learning without supervision (or without reinforcement), or briefly, self-learning. In this chapter, we consider learning with supervision.

Until recently, the decision rules based on insufficient *a priori* information have been obtained by considering independent and, at first glance, unrelated problems of learning. However, all existent and new decision rules, and their related algorithms can be obtained using the adaptive approach when the minimum of the average risk is selected to be the goal of learning. Such questions are considered in this chapter.

5.2 Goal of Learning

Let us select as the goal of learning the minimum of the average risk (4.4) that in its specific form provides the foundation for the statistical decision theory. But now we shall assume that *a priori* information is very small, that is, that we do not know *a priori* and conditional probabilities P_k and $p_k(\mathbf{x})$. Only the cost matrix (4.3) is available to us, and in many cases, this matrix is only known up to a certain parameter vector. Under these conditions, the goal of learning is the minimum of the average risk that is implicitely defined by

$$R = \sum_{k=1}^{M} \sum_{m=1}^{M} \int_{X_m} F_{km}(\mathbf{x}, \vec{\mathbf{c}}) P_k p_k(\mathbf{x}) \, d\mathbf{x}, \tag{5.1}$$

or by the implicitly defined conditions for the minimum of the average risk,

$$\sum_{k=1}^{M} \sum_{m=1}^{M} \int_{X_m} \nabla_{\vec{\mathbf{c}}} F_{km}(\mathbf{x}, \vec{\mathbf{c}}) P_k p_k(\mathbf{x}) \, d\mathbf{x} = 0 \tag{5.2}$$

and

$$f_{sm}(\mathbf{x}, \vec{\mathbf{c}}) = \sum_{k=1}^{M} [F_{ks}(\mathbf{x}, \vec{\mathbf{c}}) - F_{km}(\mathbf{x}, \vec{\mathbf{c}})] P_k p_k(\mathbf{x}) = 0, \qquad \mathbf{x} \in \Lambda_{sm}. \tag{5.3}$$

Condition (5.2) can be written even in a more compact form:

$$\mathsf{M}_{\mathbf{x}} \{\Phi(\mathbf{x}, \vec{\mathbf{c}})\} = 0, \tag{5.4}$$

where

$$\Phi(\mathbf{x}, \vec{\mathbf{c}}) = \nabla_{\vec{\mathbf{c}}} F_{km}(\mathbf{x}, \vec{\mathbf{c}}), \tag{5.5}$$

if $\mathbf{x}$, a situation from the class X_k^0, is classified into X_m^0. Therefore, the goal of learning consists of finding the decision rule from (5.4) and (5.3) on the basis of available observations.

5.3 Binary Case

For two pattern classes, $M = 2$, the expression of the average risk

$$R = \int_{X_1} F_{11}(\mathbf{x}, \vec{\mathbf{c}}) P_1 p_1(\mathbf{x}) \, d\mathbf{x} + \int_{X_1} F_{21}(\mathbf{x}, \vec{\mathbf{c}}) P_2 p_2(\mathbf{x}) \, d\mathbf{x}$$
$$+ \int_{X_2} F_{12}(\mathbf{x}, \vec{\mathbf{c}}) P_1 p_1(\mathbf{x}) \, d\mathbf{x} + \int_{X_2} F_{22}(\mathbf{x}, \vec{\mathbf{c}}) P_2 p_2(\mathbf{x}) \, d\mathbf{x} \tag{5.6}$$

follows from (5.1), and from (5.4) and (5.3) we obtain the condition for the minimum of the average risk that is written in the convenient form

$$\mathsf{M}_{\mathbf{x}}\{\Phi(\mathbf{x}, \vec{\mathbf{c}})\} = 0, \tag{5.7}$$

where

$$\Phi(\mathbf{x}, \vec{\mathbf{c}}) = \begin{cases} \nabla_{\vec{\mathbf{c}}} F_{11}(\mathbf{x}, \vec{\mathbf{c}}) & \text{when a situation from class } X_1^0 \text{ is placed into } X_1^0 \\ \nabla_{\vec{\mathbf{c}}} F_{21}(\mathbf{x}, \vec{\mathbf{c}}) & \text{when a situation from class } X_2^0 \text{ is placed into } X_1^0 \\ \nabla_{\vec{\mathbf{c}}} F_{12}(\mathbf{x}, \vec{\mathbf{c}}) & \text{when a situation from class } X_1^0 \text{ is placed into } X_2^0 \\ \nabla_{\vec{\mathbf{c}}} F_{22}(\mathbf{x}, \vec{\mathbf{c}}) & \text{when a situation from class } X_2^0 \text{ is placed into } X_2^0 \end{cases} \tag{5.8}$$

and

$$f_{12}(\mathbf{x}, \vec{\mathbf{c}}) = [F_{11}(\mathbf{x}, \vec{\mathbf{c}}) - F_{12}(\mathbf{x}, \vec{\mathbf{c}})]P_1 p_1(\mathbf{x}) + [F_{21}(\mathbf{x}, \vec{\mathbf{c}}) - F_{22}(\mathbf{x}, \vec{\mathbf{c}})]P_2 p_2(\mathbf{x}) = 0 \quad \text{when} \quad x \in \Lambda_{12}. \tag{5.9}$$

The goal of learning is reached if we are able to determine unknown parameter vector $\vec{\mathbf{c}}$ and the corresponding decision rule using the observed situations $\mathbf{x}$. We next consider various possibilities.

5.4 Traditional Adaptive Approach

The adaptive approach, based on the application of algorithms of learning, is broadly used in the design of learning pattern recognition systems. This approach will be called traditional.

Let us designate the discriminant function by

$$\hat{y} = f(\mathbf{x}, \mathbf{c}), \tag{5.10}$$

where $f(\mathbf{x}, \mathbf{c})$ is a function that is known up to the parameter vector $\mathbf{c} = (c_1, \ldots, c_N)$. The signs of the discriminant functions define the regions

$$X_1 = \{\mathbf{x} : f(\mathbf{x}, \mathbf{c}) < 0\}, \qquad X_2 = \{\mathbf{x} : f(\mathbf{x}, \mathbf{c}) > 0\}. \tag{5.11}$$

On the other hand, a teacher gives us the correct classification of each observed situation:

$$y = \begin{cases} -1 & \text{if } \mathbf{x} \text{ is classified into class } X_1^0 \\ +1 & \text{if } \mathbf{x} \text{ is classified into class } X_2^0. \end{cases} \tag{5.12}$$

Obviously, the decisions will be correct if

$$yf(\mathbf{x}, \mathbf{c}) > 0, \tag{5.13}$$

and incorrect if the opposite is true, that is,

$$yf(\mathbf{x}, \mathbf{c}) < 0. \tag{5.14}$$

As a penalty function, we select a certain convex function of the difference between y and $\hat{y}$, that is,

$$F(y - f(\mathbf{x}, \mathbf{c})). \tag{5.15}$$

We set

$$\begin{aligned} F_{11}(\mathbf{x}, \mathbf{c}) &= F(y - f(\mathbf{x}, \mathbf{c})) \quad \text{if} \quad y = -1, \\ F_{22}(\mathbf{x}, \mathbf{c}) &= F(y - f(\mathbf{x}, \mathbf{c})) \quad \text{if} \quad y = 1, \end{aligned} \quad \text{and} \quad yf(\mathbf{x}, \mathbf{c}) > 0, \tag{5.16}$$

and

$$\begin{aligned} F_{21}(\mathbf{x}, \mathbf{c}) &= F(y - f(\mathbf{x}, \mathbf{c})) \quad \text{if} \quad y = 1, \\ F_{12}(\mathbf{x}, \mathbf{c}) &= F(y - f(\mathbf{x}, \mathbf{c})) \quad \text{if} \quad y = -1, \end{aligned} \quad \text{and} \quad yf(\mathbf{x}, \mathbf{c}) < 0. \tag{5.17}$$

Then the average risk (5.6), and the first condition of the minimum (5.7) and (5.8) are written in the following form:

$$\begin{aligned} R &= \int_X F(y - f(\mathbf{x}, \mathbf{c}))p(\mathbf{x})\, d\mathbf{x} \\ &= \mathsf{M}_{\mathbf{x}}\{F(y - f(\mathbf{x}, \mathbf{c}))\} \end{aligned} \tag{5.18}$$

and

$$\begin{aligned} \nabla_{\mathbf{c}} R &= \int_X \nabla_{\mathbf{c}} F(y - f(\mathbf{x}, \mathbf{c}))p(\mathbf{x})\, d\mathbf{x} \\ &= \mathsf{M}_{\mathbf{x}}\{\nabla_{\mathbf{c}} F(y - f(\mathbf{x}, \mathbf{c}))\} \\ &= 0, \end{aligned} \tag{5.19}$$

where

$$p(\mathbf{x}) = P_1 p_1(\mathbf{x}) + P_2 p_2(\mathbf{x}) \tag{5.20}$$

is the mixture probability density.

The second condition (5.9) is not used now since the decision rule or the discriminant function (5.10) is introduced.

It is usually assumed that

$$f(\mathbf{x}, \mathbf{c}) = \mathbf{c}^{\mathrm{T}}\boldsymbol{\varphi}(\mathbf{x}) = \sum_{\nu=1}^{N} c_\nu \varphi_\nu(\mathbf{x}), \tag{5.21}$$

where $\varphi_\nu(\mathbf{x})$ $(\nu = 1, 2, \ldots, N)$ are linearly independent functions. By applying discrete (2.6) or hybrid (2.8) algorithms to (5.19), and by noticing that under the condition (5.21)

$$\nabla_{\mathbf{c}} F(y - f(\mathbf{x}, \mathbf{c})) = \nabla_{\mathbf{c}} F(y - \mathbf{c}^{\mathrm{T}}\boldsymbol{\varphi}(\mathbf{x})) = -F'(y - \mathbf{c}^{\mathrm{T}}\boldsymbol{\varphi}(\mathbf{x}))\boldsymbol{\varphi}(\mathbf{x}), \tag{5.22}$$

we obtain discrete algorithms

$$\mathbf{c}[n] = \mathbf{c}[n-1] + \Gamma[n]F'(y[n] - \mathbf{c}^{\mathrm{T}}[n-1]\boldsymbol{\varphi}(\mathbf{x}[n]))\boldsymbol{\varphi}(\mathbf{x}[n]) \tag{5.23}$$

or hybrid algorithms

$$d\mathbf{c}(t)/dt = \Gamma(t)F'(y(t) - \mathbf{c}^{\mathrm{T}}(t)\boldsymbol{\varphi}(\mathbf{x}[t]))\boldsymbol{\varphi}(\mathbf{x}[t]). \tag{5.24}$$

By selecting various convex functions, we obtain their corresponding algorithms of learning.

The block diagrams of learning systems that realize these algorithms of learning are shown in Fig. 5.1. For a specific choice of $F(\,\cdot\,)$ and $\boldsymbol{\varphi}(\mathbf{x})$, this block diagram represents Rosenblatt's perceptron.

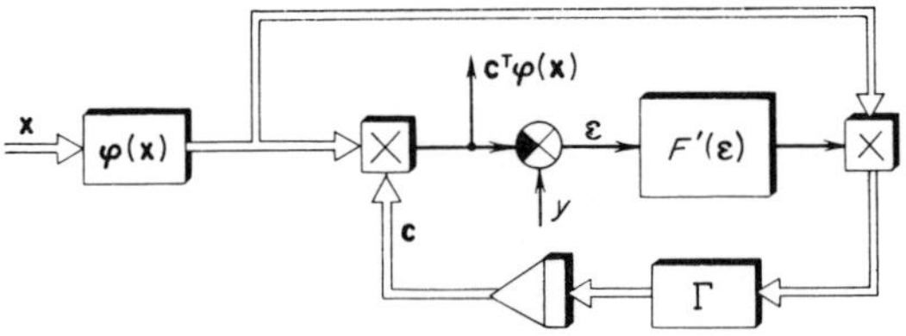

FIG. 5.1

If $\Gamma(t)$ in Algorithm (5.24) is chosen according to the differential equation

$$d\Gamma(t)/dt = -\Gamma(t)\Big[\nabla_{\mathbf{c}}^2 F(y(t) - \mathbf{c}^{\mathrm{T}}(t)\boldsymbol{\varphi}(\mathbf{x}[t])) + \int_0^t \nabla_{\mathbf{c}}^3 F(y(\tau) - \mathbf{c}^{\mathrm{T}}(t)\boldsymbol{\varphi}(\mathbf{x}[\tau]))\, d\tau \,\frac{d\mathbf{c}(t)}{dt}\Big]\Gamma(t), \tag{5.25}$$

we obtain algorithms of suboptimal learning. The difficulties in the realization of similar algorithms were discussed in Sections 3.10 and 3.14.

5.5 Adaptive Bayes Approach: I

As was shown in Sections 4.5–4.9, all known decision rules follow from the general decision rule (4.16) and (4.17), that is, they are defined by the sign of the function

$$f_{12}(\mathbf{x}, \mathbf{c}) = f_{12}(\mathbf{x}) = (w_{11} - w_{12})P_1 p_1(\mathbf{x}) + (w_{21} - w_{22})P_2 p_2(\mathbf{x}). \tag{5.26}$$

In the classical Bayes approach, this decision rule consists of comparing the likelihood ratio $l(\mathbf{x})$ (4.26) with the threshold $\mathbf{h}$ (4.27). Let us assume now that we do not know the likelihood ratio and *a priori* probabilities.

In order to determine the decision rule (5.26), we may decide to estimate the probabilities P_k and probability density functions $p_k(\mathbf{x})$. However, there is a simpler way based on direct estimation of the discriminant function instead of its components.

We shall approximate $f_{12}(\mathbf{x})$ by a system of linearly independent functions

$$\hat{f}_{12}(\mathbf{x}, \mathbf{c}) = \mathbf{c}^{\mathrm{T}}\boldsymbol{\varphi}(\mathbf{x}). \tag{5.27}$$

We ask that the error of approximation, defined by the functional

$$J(\mathbf{c}) = \int_X [f_{12}(\mathbf{x}) - \mathbf{c}^{\mathrm{T}}\boldsymbol{\varphi}(\mathbf{x})]^2 \, d\mathbf{x} \tag{5.28}$$

be minimal.

The condition of the minimum (5.28) has the form

$$\nabla J(\mathbf{c}) = -2 \int_X [f_{12}(\mathbf{x}) - \mathbf{c}^{\mathrm{T}}\boldsymbol{\varphi}(\mathbf{x})]\boldsymbol{\varphi}(\mathbf{x}) \, d\mathbf{x} = 0, \tag{5.29}$$

or

$$H\mathbf{c} - \int_X f_{12}(\mathbf{x})\boldsymbol{\varphi}(x) \, d\mathbf{x} = 0, \tag{5.30}$$

where

$$H = \int_X \boldsymbol{\varphi}(\mathbf{x})\boldsymbol{\varphi}^{\mathrm{T}}(\mathbf{x}) \, d\mathbf{x} \tag{5.31}$$

is an $N \times N$ matrix. By setting $f_{12}(\mathbf{x})$ from (5.26) into (5.30), we obtain

$$H\mathbf{c} - \int_X [(w_{11} - w_{12})P_1 p_1(\mathbf{x}) + (w_{21} - w_{22})P_2 p_2(\mathbf{x})]\boldsymbol{\varphi}(\mathbf{x}) \, d\mathbf{x} = 0 \tag{5.32}$$

or

$$H\mathbf{c} = \mathsf{M}_{\mathbf{x}}\{\Phi(\mathbf{x})\}, \tag{5.33}$$

where

$$\Phi(\mathbf{x}) = \begin{cases} (w_{11} - w_{12})\boldsymbol{\varphi}(\mathbf{x}) & \text{if } \mathbf{x} \text{ is a situation from class } X_1^0 \\ (w_{21} - w_{22})\boldsymbol{\varphi}(\mathbf{x}) & \text{if } \mathbf{x} \text{ is a situation from class } X_2^0. \end{cases} \tag{5.34}$$

Writing Eq. (5.33) in an equivalent form

$$\mathsf{M}_{\mathbf{x}}\{H\mathbf{c} - \Phi(\mathbf{x})\} = 0, \tag{5.35}$$

and by applying to it discrete algorithms of learning with

$$\Gamma[n] = \mathfrak{A}\gamma[n], \tag{5.36}$$

we obtain

$$\mathbf{c}[n] = \mathbf{c}[n-1] - \Gamma[n][H\mathbf{c}[n-1] - (w_{11} - w_{12})\boldsymbol{\varphi}(\mathbf{x}[n])] \tag{5.37}$$

if $\mathbf{x}$ is a situation from class X_1^0, and

$$\mathbf{c}[n] = \mathbf{c}[n-1] - \Gamma[n][H\mathbf{c}[n-1] - (w_{21} - w_{22})\boldsymbol{\varphi}(\mathbf{x}[n])] \tag{5.38}$$

if $\mathbf{x}$ is a situation from class X_2^0.

The block diagram of the learning system that realizes this algorithm is shown in Fig. 5.2.

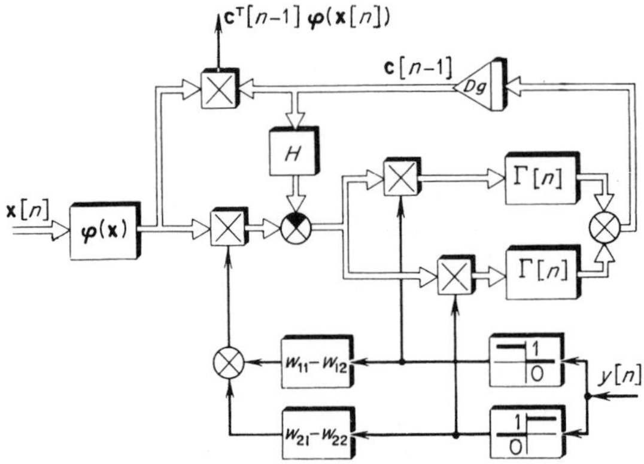

FIG. 5.2

Let us assume that the components of the vector function $\boldsymbol{\varphi}(\mathbf{x})$ are orthonormal. Then

$$H\mathbf{c} = I\mathbf{c} = \mathbf{c}. \tag{5.39}$$

If we also select

$$\Gamma[n] = In^{-1}, \tag{5.40}$$

we obtain the algorithm of optimal learning that provides the minimum variance estimate at each instant:

$$\mathbf{c}[n] = \mathbf{c}[n-1] - n^{-1}[\mathbf{c}[n-1] - (w_{11} - w_{12})\boldsymbol{\varphi}(\mathbf{x}[n])] \tag{5.41}$$

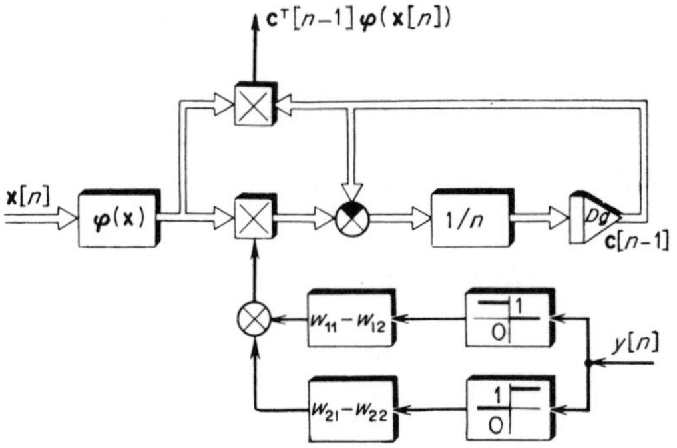

FIG. 5.3

if $\mathbf{x}$ is a situation from class $X_1{}^0$, and

$$\mathbf{c}[n] = \mathbf{c}[n-1] - n^{-1}[\mathbf{c}[n-1] - (w_{21} - w_{22})\boldsymbol{\varphi}(\mathbf{x}[n])] \tag{5.42}$$

if $\mathbf{x}$ is a situation from class $X_2{}^0$.

Therefore, we obtain a learning Bayes system that at each step applies optimal decision rule.

The block diagram of the learning Bayes system is shown in Fig. 5.3.

5.6 Adaptive Bayes Approach: II

Instead of the discriminant function $f_{12}(\mathbf{x})$ (5.26), let us consider its equivalent

$$\tilde{f}_{12}(\mathbf{x}) = \frac{f_{12}(\mathbf{x})}{p(\mathbf{x})} = \frac{(w_{11} - w_{12})P_1p_1(\mathbf{x}) + (w_{21} - w_{22})P_2p_2(\mathbf{x})}{P_1p_1(\mathbf{x}) + P_2p_2(\mathbf{x})} \tag{5.43}$$

and approximate it, as before, by $\hat{f}_{12}(\mathbf{x}, \mathbf{c})$ (5.27). But instead of the functional (5.28), we select

$$\begin{aligned} J(\mathbf{c}) &= \int_X [\tilde{f}_{12}(\mathbf{x}) - \mathbf{c}^{\mathrm{T}}\boldsymbol{\varphi}(\mathbf{x})]^2 p(\mathbf{x})\, d\mathbf{x} \\ &= \mathsf{M}\{(\tilde{f}_{12}(\mathbf{x}) - \mathbf{c}^{\mathrm{T}}\boldsymbol{\varphi}(\mathbf{x}))^2\}. \end{aligned} \tag{5.44}$$

The condition of the minimum of this functional has the form

$$\nabla J(\mathbf{c}) = -2\int_X [\tilde{f}_{12}(\mathbf{x}) - \mathbf{c}^{\mathrm{T}}\boldsymbol{\varphi}(\mathbf{x})]p(\mathbf{x})\boldsymbol{\varphi}(\mathbf{x})\, d\mathbf{x} = 0. \tag{5.45}$$

By setting $\tilde{f}_{12}(\mathbf{x})$ from (5.43) into (5.45), we obtain

$$\int_X \{[(w_{12} - w_{11}) + \mathbf{c}^T \boldsymbol{\varphi}(\mathbf{x})]\boldsymbol{\varphi}(\mathbf{x}) P_1 p_1(\mathbf{x}) + [(w_{22} - w_{21}) + \mathbf{c}^T \boldsymbol{\varphi}(\mathbf{x})]\boldsymbol{\varphi}(\mathbf{x}) P_2 p_2(\mathbf{x})\}\, d\mathbf{x} = 0. \tag{5.46}$$

Like (5.33), the expression (5.46) can be written in the form

$$\mathsf{M}_{\mathbf{x}}\{\Phi(\mathbf{x}, \mathbf{c})\} = 0, \tag{5.47}$$

where

$$\Phi(\mathbf{x}, \mathbf{c}) = \begin{cases} [(w_{12} - w_{11}) + \mathbf{c}^T \boldsymbol{\varphi}(\mathbf{x})]\boldsymbol{\varphi}(\mathbf{x}) & \text{if } \mathbf{x} \text{ is a situation from } X_1^0 \\ [(w_{22} - w_{21}) + \mathbf{c}^T \boldsymbol{\varphi}(\mathbf{x})]\boldsymbol{\varphi}(\mathbf{x}) & \text{if } \mathbf{x} \text{ is a situation from } X_2^0. \end{cases} \tag{5.48}$$

By applying discrete algorithms of learning to (5.47), we obtain

$$\mathbf{c}[n] = \mathbf{c}[n-1] + \Gamma[n][(w_{11} - w_{12}) - \mathbf{c}^T[n-1]\boldsymbol{\varphi}(\mathbf{x}[n])]\boldsymbol{\varphi}(\mathbf{x}[n]) \tag{5.49}$$

if $\mathbf{x}[n]$ is a situation from class X_1^0, and

$$\mathbf{c}[n] = \mathbf{c}[n-1] + \Gamma[n][(w_{21} - w_{22}) - \mathbf{c}^T[n-1]\boldsymbol{\varphi}(\mathbf{x}[n])]\boldsymbol{\varphi}(\mathbf{x}[n]) \tag{5.50}$$

if $\mathbf{x}[n]$ is a situation from class X_2^0.

The block diagram of the learning system that realizes these algorithms is shown in Fig. 5.4.

If the matrix $\Gamma[n]$ is optimal, that is,

$$\Gamma[n] = K[n] = \left[\sum_{m=1}^{n} \boldsymbol{\varphi}(\mathbf{x}[m])\boldsymbol{\varphi}^T(\mathbf{x}[m])\right]^{-1}, \tag{5.51}$$

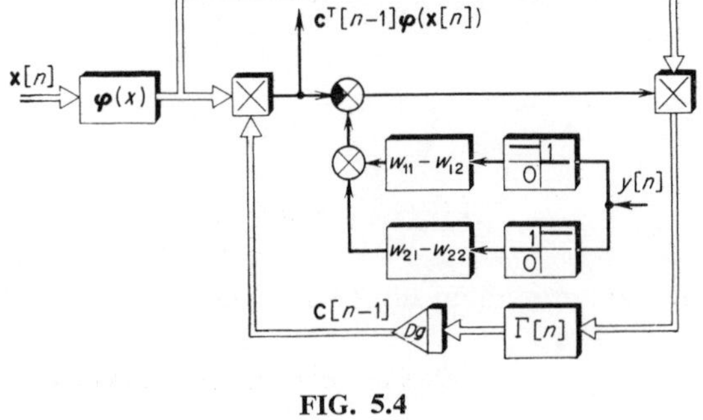

FIG. 5.4

or if Algorithms (5.49) and (5.50) are used with the recursive relations (3.38) that define the optimal matrix

$$K[n] = K[n-1] - \frac{[K[n-1]\boldsymbol{\varphi}(\mathbf{x}[n])][K[n-1]\boldsymbol{\varphi}(\mathbf{x}[n])]^{\mathrm{T}}}{1 + \boldsymbol{\varphi}^{\mathrm{T}}(\mathbf{x}[n])K[n-1]\boldsymbol{\varphi}(\mathbf{x}[n])}, \qquad (5.52)$$

we obtain the algorithm of suboptimal learning.

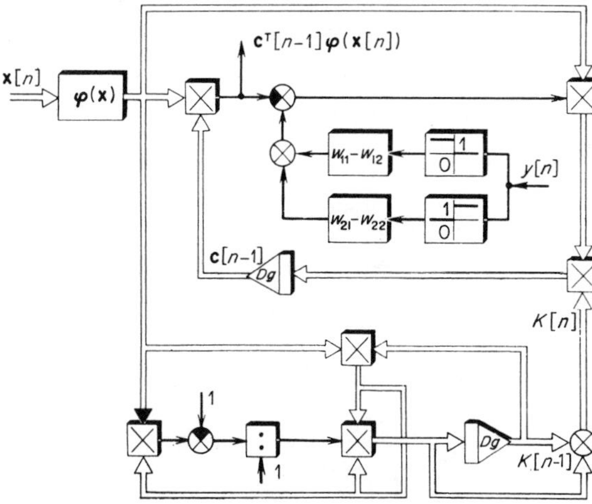

FIG. 5.5

The block diagram of Bayes learning system is given in Fig. 5.5.

Let us now consider various specific cases of learning that are based on classical decision rules.

5.7 Learning to Apply the Siegert–Kotelnikov Rule

In order to obtain the algorithms of learning systems of this type, we have (in accordance with the results of Section 4.6) to set

$$w_{11} = w_{22} = 0, \qquad w_{12} = w_{21} = 1, \qquad (5.53)$$

in Algorithms (5.41) and (5.42).

We then obtain

$$\mathbf{c}[n] = \mathbf{c}[n-1] - n^{-1}(\mathbf{c}[n-1] + \boldsymbol{\varphi}(\mathbf{x}[n])) \qquad (5.54)$$

if $\mathbf{x}[n]$ is a situation from class X_1^0 and

$$\mathbf{c}[n] = \mathbf{c}[n-1] - n^{-1}(\mathbf{c}[n-1] - \boldsymbol{\varphi}[n])) \tag{5.55}$$

if $\mathbf{x}[n]$ is a situation from class X_2^0.

Using the classifications provided by the "teacher" (5.12), these algorithms can be written in the form

$$\mathbf{c}[n] = \mathbf{c}[n-1] - n^{-1}(\mathbf{c}[n-1] - y[n]\boldsymbol{\varphi}(\mathbf{x}[n])). \tag{5.56}$$

The block diagram of the learning system representing this algorithm is shown in Fig. 5.6. This system can be called the Siegert–Kotelnikov learning system.

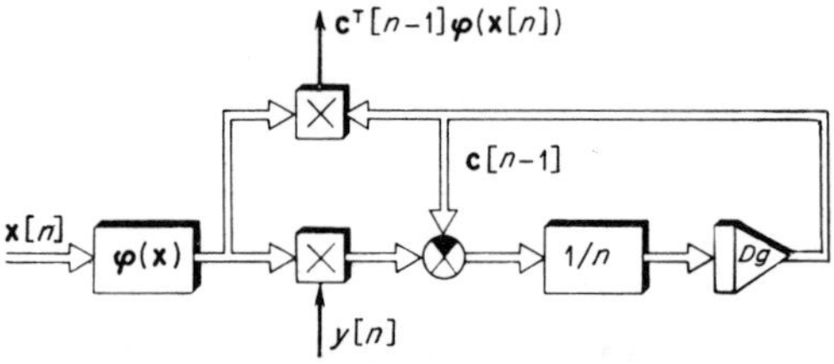

FIG. 5.6

Similarly, from (5.49) and (5.50), using (5.53), we obtain

$$\mathbf{c}[n] = \mathbf{c}[n-1] + \Gamma[n](-1 - \mathbf{c}^{\mathrm{T}}[n-1]\boldsymbol{\varphi}(\mathbf{x}[n]))\boldsymbol{\varphi}(\mathbf{x}[n]) \tag{5.57}$$

if $\mathbf{x}[n]$ is a situation from class X_1^0,

$$\mathbf{c}[n] = \mathbf{c}[n-1] + \Gamma[n](1 - \mathbf{c}^{\mathrm{T}}[n-1]\boldsymbol{\varphi}(\mathbf{x}[n]))\boldsymbol{\varphi}(\mathbf{x}[n]) \tag{5.58}$$

if $\mathbf{x}[n]$ is a situation from class X_2^0, or, using (5.12), we obtain

$$\mathbf{c}[n] = \mathbf{c}[n-1] + \Gamma[n](y[n] - \mathbf{c}^{\mathrm{T}}[n-1]\boldsymbol{\varphi}(\mathbf{x}[n]))\boldsymbol{\varphi}(\mathbf{x}[n]), \tag{5.59}$$

where $\Gamma[n]$ is defined by (5.51).

This algorithms is identical to Algorithm (5.23) if in the latter case the loss function $F(\cdot)$ is a quadratic function. The block diagram of the learning system in this case is identical to the block diagram of the perceptron given in Fig. 5.1. Naturally, these systems can learn with equal success the maximum *a posteriori* probability rule since, as was shown in Section 4.7, this rule is identical to the Siegert–Kotelnikov decision rule.

5.8 Learning to Apply the Mixed Decision Rule

According to the results of Section 4.8, we obtain the algorithms of learning systems of this type by setting

$$w_{11} = w_{22} = 0, \qquad w_{12} = \lambda, \qquad w_{21} = 1, \tag{5.60}$$

in Algorithms (5.41) and (5.42). We then obtain

$$\mathbf{c}[n] = \mathbf{c}[n-1] - n^{-1}(\mathbf{c}[n-1] + \lambda\boldsymbol{\varphi}(\mathbf{x}[n])), \tag{5.61}$$

if $\mathbf{x}[n]$ is a situation from class X_1^0,

$$\mathbf{c}[n] = \mathbf{c}[n-1] - n^{-1}(\mathbf{c}[n-1] - \boldsymbol{\varphi}(\mathbf{x}[n])), \tag{5.62}$$

if $\mathbf{x}[n]$ is a situation from class X_2^0.

The block diagram of the system representing these algorithms is shown in Fig. 5.7.

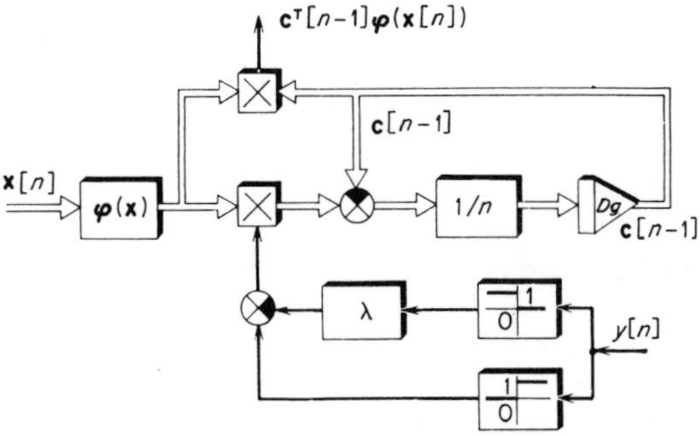

FIG. 5.7

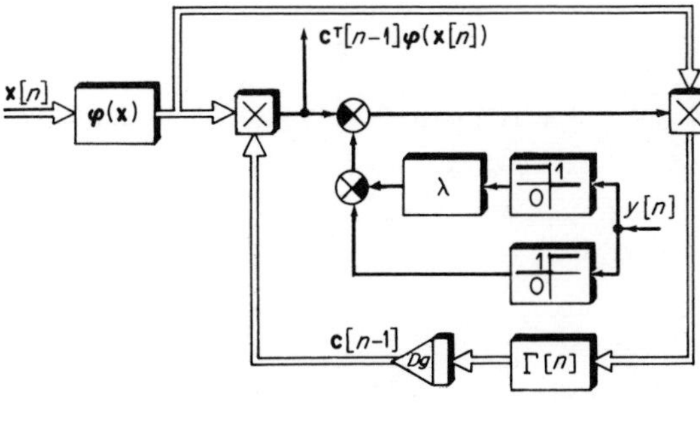

FIG. 5.8

Similarly, from (5.49) and (5.50), using (5.60), we obtain

$$\mathbf{c}[n] = \mathbf{c}[n-1] + \Gamma[n](-\lambda - \mathbf{c}^{\mathrm{T}}[n-1]\boldsymbol{\varphi}(\mathbf{x}[n]))\boldsymbol{\varphi}(\mathbf{x}[n]) \tag{5.63}$$

if $\mathbf{x}[n]$ is a situation from class X_1^0, and

$$\mathbf{c}[n] = \mathbf{c}[n-1] + \Gamma[n](1 - \mathbf{c}^{\mathrm{T}}[n-1]\boldsymbol{\varphi}(\mathbf{x}[n]))\boldsymbol{\varphi}[\mathbf{x}[n]) \tag{5.64}$$

if $\mathbf{x}[n]$ is a situation from class X_2^0, where $\Gamma[n]$ is defined by Eq. (5.51). The block diagram of this learning is shown in Fig. 5.8.

5.9 Learning to Apply the Neyman–Pearson Rule

Algorithms of learning systems of this type can be obtained by using the results of the preceding section, and additional algorithms for obtaining λ from the condition (4.58):

$$P_1 \int_{X_2} p_1(\mathbf{x})\, d\mathbf{x} = A_1. \tag{5.65}$$

In this case we have

$$\mathbf{c}[n] = \mathbf{c}[n-1] - n^{-1}(\mathbf{c}[n-1] + \lambda[n-1]\boldsymbol{\varphi}(\mathbf{x}[n]))$$

if $\mathbf{x}[n]$ is a situation from class X_1^0, and

$$\mathbf{c}[n] = \mathbf{c}[n-1] - n^{-1}(\mathbf{c}[n-1] - \boldsymbol{\varphi}(\mathbf{x}[n])) \tag{5.66}$$

if $\mathbf{x}[n]$ is a situation from class X_2^0.

Considering that Eq. (5.65) can be written in the form

$$\mathsf{M}_{\mathbf{x}}\{\theta(\mathbf{x})\} = 0,$$

where

$$\theta(\mathbf{x}) = \begin{cases} 1 - A & \text{if } \mathbf{x} \text{ is a situation from } X_2^0 \text{ and } \mathbf{c}^{\mathrm{T}}\boldsymbol{\varphi}(\mathbf{x}) < 0 \\ -A & \text{otherwise,} \end{cases} \tag{5.67}$$

we obtain the algorithm for finding λ:

$$\begin{aligned} \lambda[n] &= \lambda[n-1] - n^{-1}(1-A), \quad \text{if } \mathbf{c}^{\mathrm{T}}[n]\boldsymbol{\varphi}(x[n]) < 0 \\ &\qquad \text{and } \mathbf{x}[n] \text{ is a situation from } X_2^0, \\ \lambda[n] &= \lambda[n-1] + n^{-1}A \quad \text{otherwise.} \end{aligned} \tag{5.68}$$

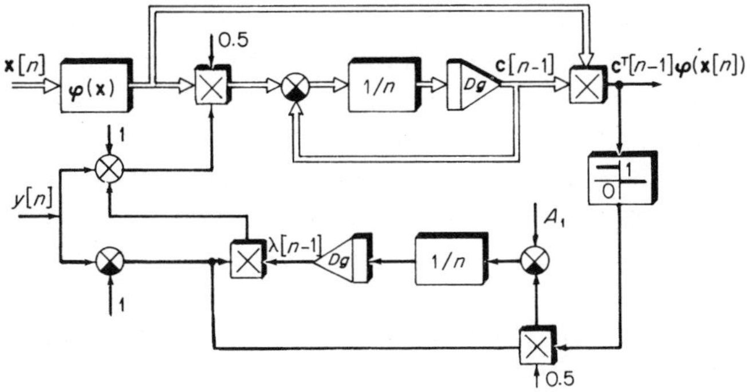

FIG. 5.9

The decision rule has the form

$$\begin{aligned} \mathbf{x}[n] \in X_1^0 \quad &\text{if} \quad \mathbf{c}^T[n-1]\boldsymbol{\varphi}(\mathbf{x}[n]) < 0, \\ \mathbf{x}[n] \in X_2^0 \quad &\text{if} \quad \mathbf{c}^T[n-1]\boldsymbol{\varphi}(\mathbf{x}[n]) > 0. \end{aligned} \tag{5.69}$$

The learning system representing these algorithms is shown in Fig. 5.9. This system can be called the Neyman–Pearson learning system.

5.10 Is It Necessary to Learn the Min–Max Decision Rule?

The min–max decision rule, as follows from the results of Section 4.10, corresponds to the discriminant function

$$f_{12}(\mathbf{x}) = w_{21}P_2^0 p_2(\mathbf{x}) - w_{12}P_1^0 p_1(\mathbf{x}), \tag{5.70}$$

where $P_1^0 = 1 - P_2^0$ must be found from the condition

$$w_{21}\beta = w_{12}\alpha. \tag{5.71}$$

Algorithms for learning this decision rule can in principle be constructed. For this purpose, as before, we approximate the decision rule by

$$\hat{f}_{12}(\mathbf{x}, \mathbf{c}) = \mathbf{c}^T\boldsymbol{\varphi}(\mathbf{x}) \tag{5.72}$$

and form the functional

$$J(\mathbf{c}) = \int_X [w_{21}(1 - P_1^0)p_2(\mathbf{x}) - w_{12}P_1^0 p_1(\mathbf{x}) - \mathbf{c}^T\boldsymbol{\varphi}(\mathbf{x})]^2 \, d\mathbf{x}. \tag{5.73}$$

We then have to minimize this functional, where P_1^0 is defined by (5.71). But we are not going to do this, since any difficulties caused by unknown *a priori* probabilities are removed by learning. Indeed, the observed situations, used in the learning systems of various decision rules, although indirectly, contain the information not only about probability density functions, but also about *a priori* probabilities. Therefore, we do not have any need to learn this conservative min–max decision rule that provides a large margin of error.

But regardless of this negative answer, persistent readers may, if they so desire, derive the algorithms for learning the min–max decision rule.

5.11 Learning to Apply the General Decision Rule

Let us consider the general criterion (4.71)

$$R_0 = \Phi(P_1\alpha, P_2\beta) = \Phi\left(P_1 \int_{X_2} p_1(\mathbf{x})\, d\mathbf{x}, P_2 \int_{X_1} p_2(\mathbf{x})\, d\mathbf{x}\right). \tag{5.74}$$

Using the characteristic function

$$\theta(\mathbf{x}) = \begin{cases} 1 & \text{if } \mathbf{x} \in X_2^0 \\ 0 & \text{if } \mathbf{x} \in X_1^0, \end{cases} \tag{5.75}$$

we write (5.74) in the form

$$R_\Phi = \Phi\left(P_1 \int_X \theta(\mathbf{x}) p_1(\mathbf{x})\, d\mathbf{x}, P_2 \int_X (1 - \theta(\mathbf{x})) p_2(\mathbf{x})\, d\mathbf{x}\right). \tag{5.76}$$

The conditions of the extremum on the boundary A between the regions X_1^0 and X_2^0 can be found using the approach described in Section 4.3:

$$\begin{aligned} f_{12}(m_1, m_2, x) &= \Phi'_{m_2}(m_1, m_2) P_2 p_2(\mathbf{x}) - \Phi'_{m_1}(m_1, m_2) P_1 p_1(\mathbf{x}) \\ &= 0 \qquad \text{for all} \quad \mathbf{x} \in A, \end{aligned} \tag{5.77}$$

where

$$m_1 = P_1 \int_{X_2} p_1(\mathbf{x})\, d\mathbf{x}, \qquad m_2 = P_2 \int_{X_1} p_2(\mathbf{x})\, d\mathbf{x}. \tag{5.78}$$

In order to determine the decision rule, we approximate $f_{12}(m_1, m_2, \mathbf{x})$ using

$$\hat{f}_{12}(\mathbf{x}, \mathbf{c}) = \mathbf{c}^{\mathrm{T}} \boldsymbol{\varphi}(\mathbf{x}). \tag{5.79}$$

Forming the functional of the type (5.28), and minimizing it with the constraint (5.78), we obtain a system of equations with respect to **c**, m_1, and m_2:

$$\mathbf{c} = \int_X [\Phi'_{m_2}(m_1, m_2)P_2 p_2(\mathbf{x}) - \Phi'_{m_1}(m_1, m_2)P_1 p_1(\mathbf{x})]\boldsymbol{\varphi}(\mathbf{x})\, d\mathbf{x},$$
$$m_1 = P_1 \int_{X_2} p_1(\mathbf{x})\, d\mathbf{x}, \qquad m_2 = P_2 \int_{X_1} p_2(\mathbf{x})\, d\mathbf{x}. \tag{5.80}$$

This provides the following algorithms of learning:

$$\mathbf{c}[n] = \mathbf{c}[n-1] - \gamma[n][\mathbf{c}[n-1] + \boldsymbol{\varphi}(\mathbf{x}[n])\Phi'_{m_1}(m_1[n-1], m_2[n-1])] \tag{5.81}$$

if $\mathbf{x}[n]$ is a situation from class $X_1{}^0$,

$$\mathbf{c}[n] = \mathbf{c}[n-1] - \gamma[n][\mathbf{c}[n-1] - \boldsymbol{\varphi}(\mathbf{x}[n])\Phi'_{m_2}(m_1[n-1], m_2(n-1])] \tag{5.82}$$

if $\mathbf{x}[n]$ is a situation from class $X_2{}^0$,

$$m_1[n] = m_1[n-1] - \gamma[n][m_1[n-1] - 1] \tag{5.83}$$

if $\mathbf{x}[n]$ is a situation from class $X_1{}^0$, and

$$\mathbf{c}^{\mathrm{T}}[n-1]\boldsymbol{\varphi}(\mathbf{x}[n]) > 0 \tag{5.84}$$

in other cases;

$$m_2[n] = m_2[n-1] - \gamma[n][m_2[n-1] - 1], \tag{5.85}$$

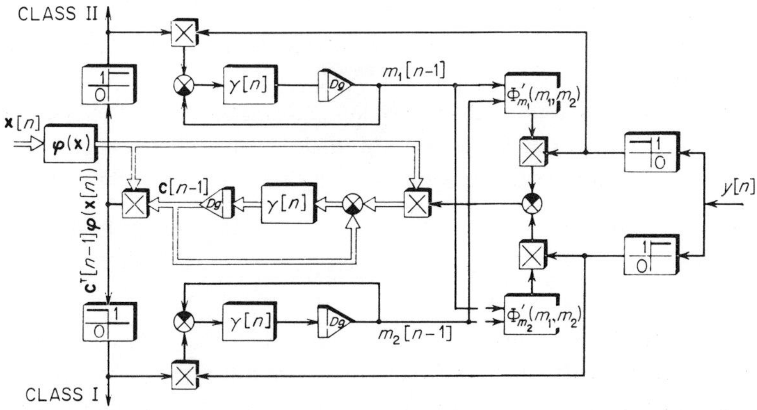

FIG. 5.10

if $\mathbf{x}[n]$ is a situation from class X_2^0, and

$$\begin{gathered} \mathbf{c}^{\mathrm{T}}[n-1]\boldsymbol{\varphi}(\mathbf{x}[n]) < 0, \\ m_2[n] = m_2[n-1] - \gamma[n]m_2[n-1] \end{gathered} \tag{5.86}$$

in the other cases. These algorithms are only different forms of the general algorithms of learning (Sections 2.7 and 2.8). The block diagram realizing algorithms (5.81)–(5.86) is shown in Fig. 5.10.

5.12 Discussion

The classical Bayes approach and its resulting decision rules lead to the comparison of the likelihood ratio with the thresholds that depend on the decision rules. They require sufficient *a priori* information.

The adaptive Bayes approach implies approximation of the discriminant function by a certain finite series of linearly independent functions, and it frees us from the heavy load of *a priori* information.

Unlike the traditional adaptive approach that minimizes the functional defining the goal of learning, the adaptive Bayes approach minimizes the difference between the correct but unknown discriminant functions and its approximation that is specified by us.

By selecting optimal algorithms of learning, we become capable of learning in the best sense, observing not an infinite but a finite number of situations.

For convenience, these algorithms for learning various decision rules are listed in Table 5.1. Naturally, this table does not contain the maximum *a posteriori* probability rule, maximum likelihood rule, and min–max rule, in which *a priori* probabilities $P_1 = P_2 = \frac{1}{2}$ or $P_1 = P_1^0$ and $P_2 = 1 - P_1^0$ are specified in advance. The adaptive approach does not need such stringent requirements.

Learning systems that realize optimal algorithms can be called Bayes systems. If the algorithms are not optimal, such systems can be called asymptotically adaptive Bayes systems.

5.13 Conclusion

The adaptive Bayes approach imposes a certain modification in the viewpoint of statistical decision theory. If *a priori* information is sufficiently complete, then Bayes rules should be used. When *a priori* information about the probabilities is not present, Bayes rules cannot be used, and one has to

TABLE 5.1

Decision rule	Criterion of optimality	Algorithms and decision Rule
Bayes	$\min_{\mathbf{c}} \int_X [(w_{11} - w_{12})P_1 p_1(\mathbf{x}) + (w_{21} - w_{22})P_2 p_2(\mathbf{x}) - \mathbf{c}^T \boldsymbol{\varphi}(\mathbf{x})]^2 \, d\mathbf{x}$	$\mathbf{c}[n] = \mathbf{c}[n-1] - n^{-1}[\mathbf{c}[n-1] - (w_{11} - w_{12})\boldsymbol{\varphi}(\mathbf{x}[n])]$ if $\mathbf{x}[n] \in X_1^0$; $\mathbf{c}[n] = \mathbf{c}[n-1] - n^{-1}[\mathbf{c}[n-1] - (w_{21} - w_{22})\boldsymbol{\varphi}(\mathbf{x}[n])]$ if $\mathbf{x}[n] \in X_2^0$; $\hat{f}_{12}(\mathbf{x}, \mathbf{c}) = \mathbf{c}^T \boldsymbol{\varphi}(\mathbf{x})$
Siegert–Kotelnikov	$\min_{\mathbf{c}} \int_X [P_2 p_2(\mathbf{x}) - P_1 p_1(\mathbf{x}) - \mathbf{c}^T \boldsymbol{\varphi}(\mathbf{x})]^2 \, d\mathbf{x}$	$\mathbf{c}[n] = \mathbf{c}[n-1] - n^{-1}[\mathbf{c}[n-1] - y[n]\boldsymbol{\varphi}(\mathbf{x}[n])]$; $y[n] = \begin{cases} -1 & \text{when } \mathbf{x}[n] \in X_1^0; \\ 1 & \text{when } \mathbf{x}[n] \in X_2^0; \end{cases}$ $\hat{f}_{12}(\mathbf{x}, \mathbf{c}) = \mathbf{c}^T \boldsymbol{\varphi}(\mathbf{x})$
Mixed decision	$\min_{\mathbf{c}} \int_X [\lambda P_2 p_2(\mathbf{x}) - P_1 p_1(\mathbf{x}) - \mathbf{c}^T \boldsymbol{\varphi}(\mathbf{x})]^2 \, d\mathbf{x}$	$\mathbf{c}[n] = \mathbf{c}[n-1] - n^{-1}[\mathbf{c}[n-1] + \lambda \boldsymbol{\varphi}(\mathbf{x}[n])]$ if $\mathbf{x}[n] \in X_1^0$; $\mathbf{c}[n] = \mathbf{c}[n-1] - n^{-1}[\mathbf{c}[n-1] - \boldsymbol{\varphi}(\mathbf{x}[n])]$ if $\mathbf{x}[n] \in X_2^0$; $\hat{f}(\mathbf{x}, \mathbf{c}) = \mathbf{c}^T \boldsymbol{\varphi}(\mathbf{x})$
Neyman–Pearson	$\min_{\mathbf{c}} \int_X [\lambda P_2 p_2(\mathbf{x}) + P_1 p_1(\mathbf{x}) - \mathbf{c}^T \boldsymbol{\varphi}(\mathbf{x})]^2 \, d\mathbf{x}$, $P_2 \int_{X_1} p_2(\mathbf{x}) \, d\mathbf{x} = A$	$\mathbf{c}[n] = \mathbf{c}[n-1] - n^{-1}[\mathbf{c}[n-1] + \lambda[n-1]\boldsymbol{\varphi}(\mathbf{x}[n])]$ if $\mathbf{x}[n] \in X_2^0$; $\mathbf{c}[n] = \mathbf{c}[n-1] - n^{-1}[\mathbf{c}[n-1] - \boldsymbol{\varphi}(\mathbf{x}[n])]$ if $\mathbf{x}[n] \in X_1^0$ and $\lambda[n] = \lambda[n-1] - n^{-1}(1 - A)$ for $\mathbf{c}^T[n]\boldsymbol{\varphi}(\mathbf{x}[n]) < 0$ and $\mathbf{x}[n] \in X_2^0$, $\lambda[n] = \lambda[n-1] + n^{-1}A$ otherwise; $\hat{f}_{12}(\mathbf{x}, \mathbf{c}) = \mathbf{c}^T \boldsymbol{\varphi}(\mathbf{x})$

use the min–max decision rule. If conditional probability density functions are also unknown, that is, if the likelihood ratio is unknown, we can do nothing else but first estimate likelihood ratio using one of the available approaches.

When the *a priori* information mentioned above does not exist, the adaptive approach can be used to train a system to apply Bayes decision rules without first estimating likelihood functions or relying on the min–max rule. This learning is based on the corresponding algorithms of learning that successively generate an estimate of the discriminant function. For unknown *a priori* information, we pay by spending time in learning. But in this case we are free from the hypothesis regarding *a priori* information which may be quite far from reality.

The traditional adaptive approach is a special case of the adaptive Bayes approach. Therefore, the Bayes approach represents the foundation of learning pattern recognition systems and learning models. This fact is important because it announces the end of an era of search for various functionals and comparisons of their corresponding algorithms.

It is now clear that the minimum of the average risk is the most general goal of learning, covering all the problems known thus far.

Comments

5.2 Until very recently, the number of goals of learning and their corresponding algorithms was extremely large. This can be seen in the bibliography of the book by the author [1] in Chapter 1 where it can be seen that all these goals of learning are only special cases of the minimum of average risk. This is also confirmed in the paper by Tsypkin *et al.* [1].

5.3 The special case with $F_{11}(x, c) = F_{22}(x, c) = 0$ was considered by Amari [1].

5.4 The traditional adaptive approach was described in detail by the author [1] of Chapter 1. We also recommend the following survey articles on the same subjects: Bertaux [1], Vasilyev [1], Fu [1], Zagoruyko [1], Nagy [1, 2], and Ho and Agravala [1].

The traditional adaptive approach includes the potential function method, the method of generalized portraits and the stochastic approximation method, which were used in the solution of pattern recognition problems. The potential function method, which was the topic of many publications by Aizerman, Braverman, and Rozonoer, is excellently presented in their monograph [1]. The method of generalized portrait was described by Vaprik *et al.* [1]. In our opinion, there are no significant differences among these three methods except perhaps their name and origin. Nevertheless, we highly recommend to the reader a comment by Aizerman [1], who has an opposite viewpoint.

Among the publications which came after 1966, we mention the works by Yakubovich [1], and Yau and Schumpert [1].

Search algorithms of learning in pattern recognition were applied by Bialasiewicz [1] and Leonov [1, 2].

In particular, the problems of pattern recognition were treated in the books by Sebestyen [1], Nillson [1], and in the collection of papers edited by Turbovich [1].

5.5 About the adaptive Bayes approach, see also the paper by the author and Kelmans [1]. Other possibilities in the construction of learning algorithms based on the Bayes formula were suggested by Lainiotis [1].

5.6 Very similar algorithms were obtained by Pitt and Womack [1] and Patterson *et al.* [1]. See also Wolverton and Wagner [1].

5.7 It is interesting to notice that the linear algorithms obtained by the potential function method are equivalent to Algorithms (5.59) for learning the Siegert–Kotelnikov decision rule or the rule of an ideal observed.

5.9 Also see the work by Esposito *et al.* [1].

REFERENCES

Aizerman, M. A.
[1] A comment on two problems related to pattern recognition. *Avtomat. i Telemeh.* No. 4 (1969).

Aizerman, M. A., Braverman, E. I., and Rozonoer, L. T.
[1] "Potential Function Method in the Problems of Machine Learning." Nauka, Moscow, 1970 (in Russian).

Amari, S.
[1] A theory of adaptive pattern classifiers. *IEEE Trans. Electronic Computers* **EC-16**, No. 3 (1967).
[2] A theory of pattern recognition. *J. Soc. Instrument and Control Eng.* **7**, No. 3 (1968).

Bertaux, D.
[1] La reconnaissance des formes problemes. Methodes et Resultats. *Automatisme* **12**, No. 6 (1967).

Bialasiewicz, J.
[1] O methodach redukcji danych opartych na procesach uczenia w zastosowanin do syntesu klassificatorow optimalnych. *Arch. Avtomat. i Telemech.* **13**, No. 4 (1968).

Esposito, R., Middleton, D., and Mullen, J. A.
[1] Some properties of adaptive Neyman–Pearson detectors. *Internat. J. Electronics* **20**, No. 1 (1966).

Fu, K. S.
[1] On learning techniques in engineering cybernetics systems (*Proc. Internat. Congr. Cybernetics, 5th*) *Cybernetica* **10**, No. 3 (1967).
[2] A class of learning control systems based on statistical decision theory. *Internat. IFAC Symp. Self-Organizing System, 2nd, London, 1967.*

Ho, Y. C., and Agravala, A. K.
[1] On pattern classification algorithms. Introduction and survey. *IEEE Trans. Automatic Control* **AC-13**, No. 6 (1969).

Lainiotis, D. G.
[1] A nonlinear adaptive estimation recursive algoritm. *IEEE Trans. Automatic Control* **AC-13**, No. 2 (1968).

Leonov, Yu. P.
[1] Classification and statistical testing of hypotheses. *Avtomat. i Telemeh.* No. 12 (1966).
[2] Classification and statistical testing of hypotheses, Part II. *Avtomat. i Telemeh.* No. 5 (1968).

Nagy, G.
[1] State of the art in pattern recognition. *Proc. IEEE* **56**, No. 5 (1968).
[2] Classification algorithms in pattern recognition. *IEEE Trans. Audio Electroacoustics* **AU-16**, No. 2 (1968).

Nillson, N. J.
[1] "Learning Machines." McGraw Hill, New York, 1965.

Patterson, J. D., Wagner, T. J., and Womack, B. F.
[1] A performance criterion for adaptive pattern classification systems. *IEEE Trans. Automatic Control* **AC-12**, No. 2 (1967).

Pitt, J. M., and Womack, B. F.
[1] A sequentialization of the Patterson classifier. *Proc. IEEE* **54**, No. 12 (1966).

Sebestyen, G. S.
[1] "Decision-Making Processes in Pattern Recognition." Macmillan, New York, 1962.

Tsypkin, Ya. Z., and Kelmans, G. K.
[1] Adaptive Bayes approach. *Problems of Information Transmission* **10**, No. 1 (1970).

Tsypkin, Ya. Z., Kelmans, G. K., and Epstein, L. E.
[1] Learning control systems. *Congr. IFAC, 4th, Warsaw, July, 16–21, 1969.*

Turbovich, I. T., ed.
[1] "Pattern Recognition." Nauka, Moscow, 1968 (in Russian).

Vapnik, V. N., Lerner, A. Ya., and Chervonenkis, A. Ya.
[1] Training of machines to recognize patterns based on the method of generalized patterns. *Proc. All-Union Conf. Automat. Control and Eng. Cybernetics, 3rd*, **3**. Nauka, Moscow, 1967 (in Russian).

Vasilyev, V. I.
[1] "Pattern Recognition Systems." Naukova Dumka, Kiev, 1969.

Wolverton, C. T., and Wagner, T. J.
[1] Asymptotically optimal discriminant functions for pattern classification. *IEEE Trans. Information Theory* **IT-15**, No. 2 (1969).

Yakubovich, V. A.
[1] Three theoretical schemes of pattern recognition learning systems. *Proc. All-Union Conf. Automat. Control and Eng. Cybernetics 3rd*, **3**. Nauka, Moscow, 1967.

Yau, S. S., and Schumpert, J. M.
[1] Design of pattern classifiers with the undating property using stochastic approximation. *IEEE Trans. Comput.* **C-17**, No. 9 (1968).

Zagoruyko, N. G.
[1] Present state of the problems of pattern recognition. *In* "Computing Systems," Vol. 28. Siberian Section, Akademia Nauk, Novosibirsk, 1967 (in Russian).

Chapter VI

Self-Learning Systems of Classification

For everything today, yesterday seems like delirium.

E. VERHARN

6.1 Introduction

In learning with supervision (or with reinforcement), which was considered in the preceding chapter, the teacher always provides the correct classification of each situation observed by the system. However, in a number of systems such information does not exist. A system may have to be trained to make decisions without reinforcement. In learning without supervision (or without reinforcement), we can talk about regions or clusters that can be separated with the help of a decision rule and not about actual classes. Therefore, we prefer to discuss learning without supervision in terms of classification or clustering, and not of recognition.

As before, the goal of learning consists of finding the decision rule that minimizes a certain functional of the average risk type, but this goal can be reached only on the basis of observed situations without any additional information from the outside.

This chapter is devoted to the discussion of various possible approaches to the design of self-learning systems.

6.2 Goal of Self-Learning

Self-learning, or learning without supervision, corresponds to minimal *a priori* information. Here, both the probabilistic characteristics of the situations, P_k, $p_k(\mathbf{x})$, and the additional information regarding the classification of the observed situations are unknown. Therefore, in self-learning we cannot use the concepts of errors of the first and the second type which play an important role in learning with reinforcement. Let us introduce for yet unknown regions X_k $(k = 1, 2, \ldots, M)$ the penalty functions $F_k(\mathbf{x}, \vec{\mathbf{c}})$, where $\vec{\mathbf{c}} = (\mathbf{c}_1, \ldots, \mathbf{c}_M)$ is also an unknown parameter vector. The average risk, which evaluates the quality of classification, can be written in the following form:

$$R = \sum_{k=1}^{M} P_k \int_{X_k} F_k(\mathbf{x}, \vec{\mathbf{c}}) p_k(\mathbf{x})\, d\mathbf{x} \tag{6.1}$$

or, by assuming that the sought regions are not intersecting,

$$R = \sum_{k=1}^{M} \int_{X_k} F_k(\mathbf{x}, \vec{\mathbf{c}}) p(\mathbf{x})\, d\mathbf{x}. \tag{6.2}$$

Here, $p(\mathbf{x})$ is the mixture probability density function:

$$p(\mathbf{x}) = \sum_{k=1}^{M} P_k p_k(\mathbf{x}). \tag{6.3}$$

The goal of learning consists of finding such boundaries of the regions, and such a vector $\vec{\mathbf{c}} = \vec{\mathbf{c}}^*$ for which the average risk R is minimized using the observed situations. The conditions of the minimum R can be found from the general conditions (5.2) and (5.3), if we consider the regions X_k instead of the classes $X_k{}^0$. Thus, by setting

$$F_{km}(\mathbf{x}, \vec{\mathbf{c}}) = F_k(\mathbf{x}, \vec{\mathbf{c}}), \qquad k = 1, 2, \ldots, M, \tag{6.4}$$

into (5.3) and (5.2), we obtain from the condition of the average risk (5.2)

$$\nabla_{\vec{\mathbf{c}}} R = \sum_{k=1}^{M} \int_{X_k} \nabla_{\vec{\mathbf{c}}} F_k(\mathbf{x}, \vec{\mathbf{c}}) p(\mathbf{x})\, d\mathbf{x} = 0, \tag{6.5}$$

and the equation of the decision rule (5.3)

$$f_{km}(\mathbf{x}, \vec{\mathbf{c}}) = F_k(\mathbf{x}, \vec{\mathbf{c}}) - F_m(\mathbf{x}, \vec{\mathbf{c}}) = 0, \qquad \mathbf{x} \in \Lambda_{km}, \tag{6.6}$$

because $p(\mathbf{x}) > 0$.

Condition (6.5) can be written in the abbreviated form

$$\mathsf{M}\left\{\sum_{k=1}^{M} \theta_k(\mathbf{x}, \vec{\mathbf{c}}) \, \nabla_{\vec{\mathbf{c}}} F_k(\mathbf{x}, \vec{\mathbf{c}})\right\} = 0, \tag{6.7}$$

where

$$\theta_k(\mathbf{x}, \vec{\mathbf{c}}) = \begin{cases} 1 & \text{when} \quad \mathbf{x} \in X_k \\ 0 & \text{when} \quad \mathbf{x} \,\overline{\in}\, X_k \end{cases} \tag{6.8}$$

is a characteristic function.

A situation $\mathbf{x}$ is placed into the region X_k according to the following decision rule:

$$\mathbf{x} \in X_k \qquad \text{if for all} \quad m \neq k \quad f_{km}(\mathbf{x}, \vec{\mathbf{c}}) < 0. \tag{6.9}$$

It is important that the loss function $F_k(\mathbf{x}, \vec{\mathbf{c}})$ uniquely defines the equation of the decision rule (6.6).

Therefore, the goal of learning is reduced to finding the vector $\vec{\mathbf{c}} = \vec{\mathbf{c}}^*$ that satisfies the condition (6.5) using the observed situations $\mathbf{x}$.

6.3 Binary Case

For two classes, $M = 2$, we obtain the expression of the average risk from (6.1) and (6.7):

$$R = \int_{X_1} F_1(\mathbf{x}, \vec{\mathbf{c}}) p(\mathbf{x}) \, d\mathbf{x} + \int_{X_2} F_2(\mathbf{x}, \vec{\mathbf{c}}) p(\mathbf{x}) \, d\mathbf{x}. \tag{6.10}$$

The condition of its minimum is

$$\mathsf{M}\{\theta_1(\mathbf{x}, \vec{\mathbf{c}}) \, \nabla_{\vec{\mathbf{c}}} F_1(\mathbf{x}, \vec{\mathbf{c}}) + \theta_2(\mathbf{x}, \vec{\mathbf{c}}) \, \nabla_{\vec{\mathbf{c}}} F_2(\mathbf{x}, \vec{\mathbf{c}})\} = 0, \tag{6.11}$$

where

$$\theta_1(\mathbf{x}, \vec{\mathbf{c}}) = \begin{cases} 1 & \text{when} \quad \mathbf{x} \in X_1 \\ 0 & \text{when} \quad \mathbf{x} \in X_2, \end{cases}$$
$$\theta_2(\mathbf{x}, \vec{\mathbf{c}}) = \begin{cases} 0 & \text{when} \quad \mathbf{x} \in X_1 \\ 1 & \text{when} \quad \mathbf{x} \in X_2, \end{cases} \tag{6.12}$$

and

$$f_{12}(\mathbf{x}, \vec{\mathbf{c}}) = F_1(\mathbf{x}, \vec{\mathbf{c}}) - F_2(\mathbf{x}, \vec{\mathbf{c}}) = 0, \qquad \mathbf{x} \in \Lambda. \tag{6.13}$$

From now on we shall consider this binary case. A general case can easily be obtained if one has a little patience.

6.4 Algorithms of Self-Learning

In order to design self-learning systems, we use discrete (2.6) or hybrid (2.8) algorithms. From (6.11), using (6.12) and (6.13), we find:

Discrete algorithms:

$$\vec{\mathbf{c}}[n] = \vec{\mathbf{c}}[n-1] - \Gamma_1[n]\,\nabla_{\vec{\mathbf{c}}} F_1(\mathbf{x}[n], \vec{\mathbf{c}}[n-1]) \tag{6.14}$$

if

$$f_{12}(\mathbf{x}[n], \vec{\mathbf{c}}[n-1]) = F_1(\mathbf{x}[n], \vec{\mathbf{c}}[n-1]) - F_2(\mathbf{x}[n], \vec{\mathbf{c}}[n-1]) < 0, \tag{6.15}$$

and

$$\vec{\mathbf{c}}[n] = \vec{\mathbf{c}}[n-1] - \Gamma_2[n]\,\nabla_{\vec{\mathbf{c}}} F_2(\mathbf{x}[n], \vec{\mathbf{c}}[n-1]) \tag{6.16}$$

if

$$f_{12}(\mathbf{x}[n], \vec{\mathbf{c}}[n-1]) > 0; \tag{6.17}$$

Hybrid algorithms:

$$d\vec{\mathbf{c}}(t)/dt = -\Gamma_1(t)\,\nabla_{\vec{\mathbf{c}}} F_1(\mathbf{x}[t], \vec{\mathbf{c}}(t)) \tag{6.18}$$

if

$$f_{12}(\mathbf{x}[t], \vec{\mathbf{c}}(t)) = F_1(\mathbf{x}[t], \vec{\mathbf{c}}(t)) - F_2(\mathbf{x}[t], \vec{\mathbf{c}}(t)) < 0, \tag{6.19}$$

and

$$d\vec{\mathbf{c}}(t)/dt = -\Gamma_2(t)\,\nabla_{\vec{\mathbf{c}}} F_2(\mathbf{x}[t], \vec{\mathbf{c}}(t)) \tag{6.20}$$

if

$$f_{12}(\mathbf{x}[t], \vec{\mathbf{c}}(t)) > 0, \tag{6.21}$$

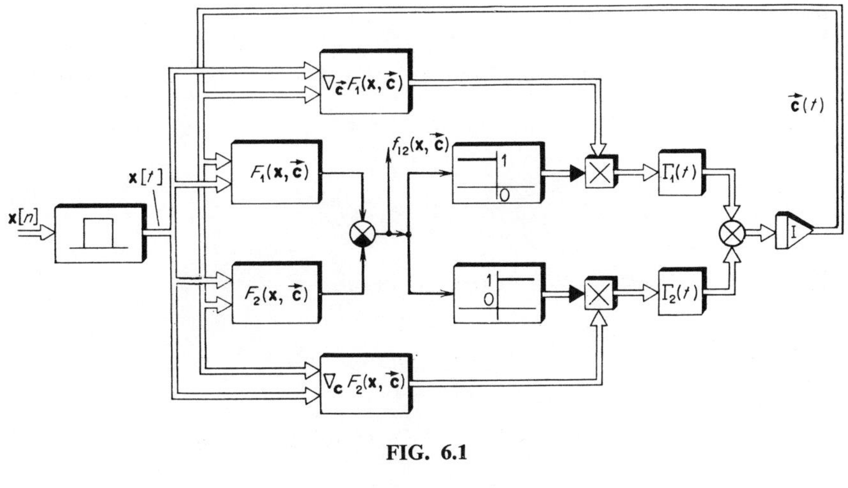

FIG. 6.1

where, we should recall,

$$\mathbf{x}[t] = \mathbf{x}(nT) = \mathbf{x}[n] \qquad \text{when} \quad (n-1)T < t \leq nT. \tag{6.22}$$

The block diagram of the self-learning system realizing these algorithms is shown in Fig. 6.1. It consists of two mutually coupled learning systems.

Discrete algorithms (6.14)–(6.17) have as their special case various algorithms known earlier, and they are listed in Table 6.1.

6.5 Algorithms of Optimal Self-Learning

In the general case of arbitrary penalty functions $F_k(\mathbf{x}, \vec{\mathbf{c}})$ $(k = 1, 2)$, there are no rigorously optimal discrete algorithms of the form (6.14) and (6.15). At the same time, hybrid algorithms can in principle be made rigorously optimal with a suitable choice of $\Gamma_1(t)$ and $\Gamma_2(t)$. Using the results of Section 3.10, we obtain the conditions of optimality

$$(d/dt)\int_0^t \theta_1(\mathbf{x}[\tau], \vec{\mathbf{c}}(t))\, \nabla_{\vec{\mathbf{c}}} F_1(\mathbf{x}[\tau], \vec{\mathbf{c}}(t))\, d\tau = 0 \tag{6.23}$$

and

$$(d/dt)\int_0^t \theta_2(\mathbf{x}[\tau], \vec{\mathbf{c}}(t))\, \nabla_{\vec{\mathbf{c}}} F_2(\mathbf{x}[\tau], \vec{\mathbf{c}}(t))\, d\tau = 0. \tag{6.24}$$

By differentiating with respect to t and using Algorithms (6.18) and (6.20), we find by following the approach described in Section 3.10 for the simplest case

$$\Gamma_1(t) = \left[\int_0^t \theta_1(\mathbf{x}[\tau], \vec{\mathbf{c}}(t))\, \nabla_{\vec{\mathbf{c}}}^2 F_1(\mathbf{x}[\tau], \vec{\mathbf{c}}(t))\, d\tau\right]^{-1} \tag{6.25}$$

and

$$\Gamma_2(t) = \left[\int_0^t \theta_2(\mathbf{x}[\tau], \vec{\mathbf{c}}(t))\, \nabla_{\vec{\mathbf{c}}}^2 F_2(\mathbf{x}[\tau], \mathbf{c}(t))\, d\tau\right]^{-1}. \tag{6.26}$$

These optimal matrices satisfy the equations

$$\begin{aligned} d\Gamma_1(t)/dt = -\Gamma_1(t)\Big[&\theta_1(\mathbf{x}[t], \mathbf{c}(t))\, \nabla_{\vec{\mathbf{c}}}^2 F_1(\mathbf{x}[t], \vec{\mathbf{c}}(t)) \\ &+ \int_0^t \theta_1(\mathbf{x}[\tau], \vec{\mathbf{c}}(t))\, \nabla_{\vec{\mathbf{c}}}^3 F_1(\mathbf{x}[\tau], \vec{\mathbf{c}}(t))\, d\tau\, d\vec{\mathbf{c}}(t)/dt\Big]\Gamma_1(t) \end{aligned} \tag{6.27}$$

TABLE 6.1

	Loss function	Algorithms
1	$F_1(\mathbf{x}, \vec{\mathbf{c}})$, $F_2(\mathbf{x}, \vec{\mathbf{c}})$, $\vec{\mathbf{c}} = (\mathbf{c}_1, \mathbf{c}_2)$	$\vec{\mathbf{c}}[n] = \vec{\mathbf{c}}[n-1] - \Gamma_1[n]\nabla_{\vec{\mathbf{c}}}F_1(\mathbf{x}[n], \vec{\mathbf{c}}[n-1])$ if $f_{12}(\mathbf{x}[n], \vec{\mathbf{c}}[n-1]) < 0$; $\vec{\mathbf{c}}[n] = \vec{\mathbf{c}}[n-1] - \Gamma_2[n]\nabla_{\vec{\mathbf{c}}}F_2(\mathbf{x}[n], \vec{\mathbf{c}}[n-1])$ if $f_{12}(\mathbf{x}[n], \vec{\mathbf{c}}[n-1]) > 0$
2	$F_1(\mathbf{x}, \vec{\mathbf{c}}) = \Vert \boldsymbol{\varphi}(\mathbf{x}) - \mathbf{c}_1 \Vert^2$ $F_2(\mathbf{x}, \vec{\mathbf{c}}) = \Vert \boldsymbol{\varphi}(\mathbf{x}) - \mathbf{c}_2 \Vert^2$	$\mathbf{c}_1[n] = \mathbf{c}_1[n-1] + \gamma_1[n](\boldsymbol{\varphi}(\mathbf{x}[n]) - \mathbf{c}_1[n-1])$; $\mathbf{c}_2[n] = \mathbf{c}_2[n-1]$ if $2(\mathbf{c}_1^{\mathrm{T}}[n-1] - \mathbf{c}_2^{\mathrm{T}}[n-1])\boldsymbol{\varphi}(\mathbf{x}[n]) - (\Vert \mathbf{c}_1[n-1] \Vert^2 - \Vert \mathbf{c}_2[n-1] \Vert^2) < 0$; $\mathbf{c}_1[n] = \mathbf{c}_1[n-1]$; $\mathbf{c}_2[n] = \mathbf{c}_2[n-1] + \gamma_2[n](\boldsymbol{\varphi}(\mathbf{x}[n]) - \mathbf{c}_2[n-1])$ if $2(\mathbf{c}_1^{\mathrm{T}}[n-1] - \mathbf{c}_2^{\mathrm{T}}[n-1])\boldsymbol{\varphi}(\mathbf{x}[n]) - (\Vert \mathbf{c}_1[n-1] \Vert^2 - \Vert \mathbf{c}_2[n-1] \Vert^2) > 0$
3	$F_1(\mathbf{x}, \vec{\mathbf{c}}) = \Vert \boldsymbol{\varphi}(\mathbf{x}) - \mathbf{c}_1 \Vert^2 + \Vert \mathbf{c}_2 \Vert^2$, $F_2(\mathbf{x}, \vec{\mathbf{c}}) = \Vert \boldsymbol{\varphi}(\mathbf{x}) - \mathbf{c}_2 \Vert^2 + \Vert \mathbf{c}_1 \Vert^2$	$\mathbf{c}_1[n] = \mathbf{c}_1[n-1] + \gamma_1[n](\boldsymbol{\varphi}(\mathbf{x}[n]) - \mathbf{c}_1[n-1])$; $\mathbf{c}_2[n] = \mathbf{c}_2[n-1]$ if $(\mathbf{c}_1^{\mathrm{T}}[n-1] - \mathbf{c}_2^{\mathrm{T}}[n-1])\boldsymbol{\varphi}(\mathbf{x}[n]) < 0$; $\mathbf{c}_1[n] = \mathbf{c}_1[n-1]$; $\mathbf{c}_2[n] = \mathbf{c}_2[n-1] + \gamma_2[n](\boldsymbol{\varphi}(\mathbf{x}[n]) - \mathbf{c}_2[n-1])$ if $(\mathbf{c}_1^{\mathrm{T}}[n-1] - \mathbf{c}_2^{\mathrm{T}}[n-1])\boldsymbol{\varphi}(\mathbf{x}[n]) > 0$; $\gamma_1[n] = (N[n])^{-1}$, $\gamma_2[n] = (n - N[n])^{-1}$; $N[n]$—number of patterns $\mathbf{x}$ placed into the region X

and

$$d\Gamma_2(t)/dt = -\Gamma_2(t)\Big[\theta_2(\mathbf{x}[t], \mathbf{c}(t))\, \nabla_{\vec{c}}^2 F_2(\mathbf{x}[t], \vec{c}(t)) + \int_0^t \theta_2(\mathbf{x}[\tau], \mathbf{c}(t))\, \nabla_{\vec{c}}^3 F_2(\mathbf{x}[\tau], \vec{c}(t))\, d\tau\, d\vec{c}(t)/dt\Big]\Gamma_2(t). \quad (6.28)$$

Since the initial conditions $\vec{c}(t_0)$ and matrices $\Gamma_1(t_0)$ and $\Gamma_2(t_0)$ are unknown, we can only talk about suboptimal self-learning systems.

The block diagram of such suboptimal self-learning systems is symbolically shown in Fig. 6.2. An explanation of the term "symbolic," relative to the block diagrams of optimal learning systems, was given in Section 3.10.

In the special case of quadratic loss functions in $\vec{c}$, the algorithms for obtaining optimal matrices are considerably simplified:

$$d\Gamma_1(t)/dt = -\Gamma_1(t)\theta_1(\mathbf{x}[t], \vec{c}(t))\, \nabla_{\vec{c}}^2 F_1(\mathbf{x}[t], \vec{c}(t))\Gamma_1(t) \quad (6.29)$$

and

$$d\Gamma_2(t)/dt = -\Gamma_2(t)\theta_2(\mathbf{x}[t], \mathbf{c}(t))\, \nabla_{\vec{c}}^2 F_2(\mathbf{x}[t], \vec{c}(t))\Gamma_2(t). \quad (6.30)$$

In this case $\nabla_{\vec{c}}^2 F_k(\mathbf{x}[t], \vec{c}(t))$ does not depend on $\vec{c}(t)$.

For quadratic loss functions in $\vec{c}$, when

$$\Gamma_1[n] = \left[\sum_{m=1}^{n} \theta_1(\mathbf{x}[m], \mathbf{c}[n])\, \nabla_{\vec{c}}^2 F_1(\mathbf{x}[m], \vec{c}[n])\right]^{-1} \quad (6.31)$$

and

$$\Gamma_2[n] = \left[\sum_{m=1}^{n} \theta_2(\mathbf{x}[m], \mathbf{c}[n])\, \nabla_{\vec{c}}^2 F_2(\mathbf{x}[m], \vec{c}[n])\right]^{-1}, \quad (6.32)$$

discrete algorithms have the form

$$\vec{c}[n] = \vec{c}[n-1] - \Gamma_1[n]\, \nabla_{\vec{c}} F_1(\mathbf{x}[n], \vec{c}[n-1]) \quad (6.33)$$

if

$$f_{12}(\mathbf{x}[n], \vec{c}[n-1]) < 0, \quad (6.34)$$

and

$$\vec{c}[n] = \vec{c}[n-1] - \Gamma_2[n]\, \nabla_{\vec{c}} F_2(\mathbf{x}[n], \vec{c}[n-1]) \quad (6.35)$$

if

$$f_{12}(\mathbf{x}[n], \vec{c}[n-1]) > 0. \quad (6.36)$$

The block diagram of the suboptimal discrete self-learning system that corresponds to Algorithms (6.33)–(6.36), has a considerably simpler form

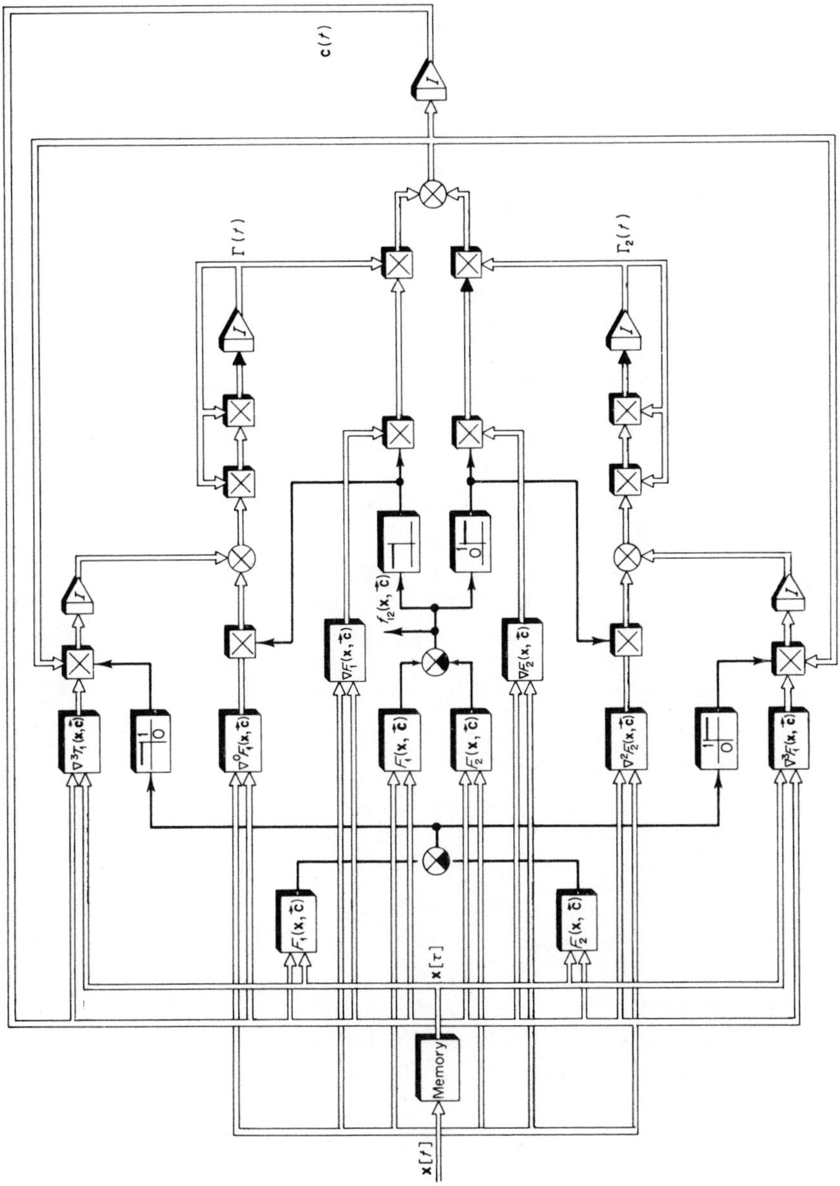

FIG. 6.2

than one shown in Fig. 6.2, since in this case $\nabla^3 F_1(\mathbf{x}, \vec{\mathbf{c}}) = \nabla^3 F_2(\mathbf{x}, \vec{\mathbf{c}}) \equiv 0$. We shall not present it here. Readers can produce it without difficulties when needed.

6.6 Adaptive Bayes Approach

We shall attempt to use the adaptive Bayes approach in the design of self-learning systems. For the Siegert–Kotelnikov maximum *a posteriori* probability decision rule, the discriminant function is

$$f(x) = P_2 p_2(\mathbf{x}) - P_1 p_1(\mathbf{x}). \tag{6.37}$$

Let us assume now that the products of a priori probabilities and density functions $P_1 p_1(\mathbf{x})$ and $P_2 p_2(\mathbf{x})$ can be approximated by a finite series

$$P_2 p_2(\mathbf{x}) \approx \mathbf{a}^{\mathrm{T}} \boldsymbol{\varphi}(\mathbf{x}), \qquad P_1 p_1(\mathbf{x}) \approx \mathbf{b}^{\mathrm{T}} \boldsymbol{\psi}(\mathbf{x}). \tag{6.38}$$

Here, $\mathbf{a} = (a_1, \ldots, a_{N_1})$, $\mathbf{b} = (b_1, \ldots, b_{N_2})$ are unknown vectors, and $\boldsymbol{\varphi}(\mathbf{x}) = (\varphi_1(\mathbf{x}), \ldots, \varphi_{N_1}(\mathbf{x}))$, $\boldsymbol{\psi}(\mathbf{x}) = (\psi_1(\mathbf{x}), \ldots, \psi_{N_2}(\mathbf{x}))$ are known vector functions. For simplicity, their component functions are assumed to form an orthonormal system.

The decision rule (6.37) can then be written in the form

$$\hat{f}(\mathbf{x}, \mathbf{a}, \mathbf{b}) = \mathbf{a}^{\mathrm{T}} \boldsymbol{\varphi}(\mathbf{x}) - \mathbf{b}^{\mathrm{T}} \boldsymbol{\psi}(\mathbf{x}), \tag{6.39}$$

and the decision rule is determined by finding the vectors **a** and **b**. But these vectors can be found in the following manner. Noticing that due to (6.38) the probability density function

$$p(\mathbf{x}) = P_1 p_1(\mathbf{x}) + P_2 p_2(\mathbf{x}) \tag{6.40}$$

is approximately equal to

$$p(\mathbf{x}) \approx \hat{p}(\mathbf{x}) = \mathbf{a}^{\mathrm{T}} \boldsymbol{\varphi}(\mathbf{x}) + \mathbf{b}^{\mathrm{T}} \boldsymbol{\psi}(\mathbf{x}), \tag{6.41}$$

it is simple to understand that the problem of determining the vectors **a** and **b** is reduced to the restoration (estimation) of the mixture probability density function. Let us introduce the functional

$$J(\mathbf{a}, \mathbf{b}) = \int_X [p(\mathbf{x}) - \mathbf{a}^{\mathrm{T}} \boldsymbol{\varphi}(\mathbf{x}) - \mathbf{b}^{\mathrm{T}} \boldsymbol{\psi}(\mathbf{x})]^2 \, d\mathbf{x}. \tag{6.42}$$

By differentiating this functional with respect to **a** and **b**, and considering the orthonormality of the component functions $\boldsymbol{\varphi}(\mathbf{x})$ and $\boldsymbol{\psi}(\mathbf{x})$, we find the conditions of the minimum in the form

$$\begin{aligned} \nabla_{\mathbf{a}} J(\mathbf{a}, \mathbf{b}) &= \mathsf{M}\{\boldsymbol{\varphi}(\mathbf{x})\} - \mathbf{a} - G\mathbf{b} = 0, \\ \nabla_{\mathbf{b}} J(\mathbf{a}, \mathbf{b}) &= \mathsf{M}\{\boldsymbol{\psi}(\mathbf{x})\} - G^{\mathrm{T}}\mathbf{a} - \mathbf{b} = 0, \end{aligned} \tag{6.43}$$

where the matrix

$$G = \int_X \boldsymbol{\varphi}(x)\boldsymbol{\psi}^{\mathrm{T}}(\mathbf{x})\, d\mathbf{x}. \tag{6.44}$$

By solving Eqs. (6.43) with respect to **a** and **b**, we obtain

$$\mathbf{a} = \mathsf{M}_{\mathbf{x}}\{U(\boldsymbol{\varphi}(\mathbf{x}) - G\boldsymbol{\psi}(\mathbf{x}))\}, \tag{6.45}$$

$$\mathbf{b} = \mathsf{M}_{\mathbf{x}}\{U^{\mathrm{T}}(\boldsymbol{\psi}(\mathbf{x}) - G^{\mathrm{T}}\boldsymbol{\varphi}(\mathbf{x}))\}, \tag{6.46}$$

where $U_1 = (I - GG^{\mathrm{T}})^{-1}$.

Now using the simplest optimal algorithms we obtain

$$\begin{aligned} \mathbf{a}[n] &= \mathbf{a}[n-1] - n^{-1}(\mathbf{a}[n-1] - U[\boldsymbol{\varphi}(\mathbf{x}[n]) - G\boldsymbol{\psi}(\mathbf{x}[n])]), \\ \mathbf{b}[n] &= \mathbf{b}[n-1] - n^{-1}(\mathbf{b}[n-1] - U^{\mathrm{T}}[\boldsymbol{\psi}(\mathbf{x}[n]) - G^{\mathrm{T}}\boldsymbol{\varphi}(\mathbf{x}[n])]). \end{aligned} \tag{6.47}$$

The learning decision rule will have the form

$$\hat{f}(\mathbf{x}[n], \mathbf{a}[n-1], \mathbf{b}[n-1]) = \mathbf{a}^{\mathrm{T}}[n-1]\boldsymbol{\varphi}(\mathbf{x}[n]) - \mathbf{b}^{\mathrm{T}}[n-1]\boldsymbol{\psi}(\mathbf{x}[n]). \tag{6.48}$$

The block diagram of the self-learning system that uses these algorithms is shown in Fig. 6.3.

Therefore, in the adaptive Bayes approach, the problem of constructing decision rule is reduced to the problem of restoring (estimating) the mixture probability density function.

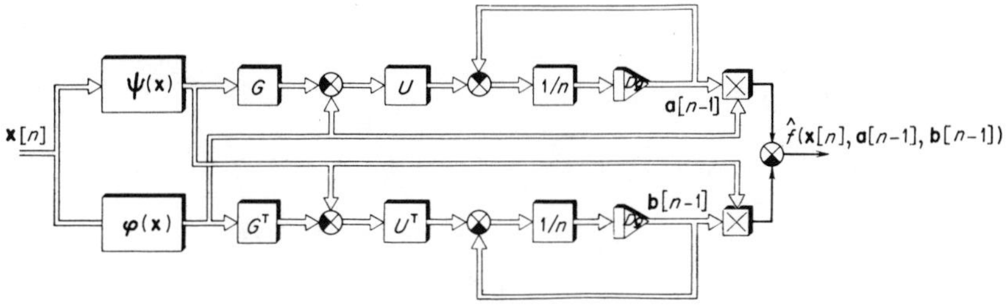

FIG. 6.3

6.7 Self-Learning When the Number of Regions Is Known

Let us assume that the number of regions is $M > 2$ and that the penalty functions are

$$F_k(\mathbf{x}, \vec{\mathbf{c}}) = F(\mathbf{x} - \mathbf{c}_k), \qquad k = 1, 2, \ldots, M. \tag{6.49}$$

In this case the average risk (6.2) becomes

$$R = \sum_{k=1}^{M} \int_{X_k} F(\mathbf{x} - \mathbf{c}_k) p(\mathbf{x})\, d\mathbf{x}, \tag{6.50}$$

and from (6.6)–(6.8) we obtain the conditions of the minimum

$$\mathsf{M}\left\{\sum_{k=1}^{M} \theta_k(\mathbf{x}, \vec{\mathbf{c}})\, \nabla_{\mathbf{c}_k} F_k(\mathbf{x} - \mathbf{c}_k)\right\} = 0, \tag{6.51}$$

where

$$\theta_k(\mathbf{x}, \vec{\mathbf{c}}) = \begin{cases} 1 & \text{if } \mathbf{x} \in X_k \\ 0 & \text{if } \mathbf{x} \mathrel{\overline{\in}} X_k \end{cases} \tag{6.52}$$

and

$$f_{km}(\mathbf{x}, \vec{\mathbf{c}}) = F(\mathbf{x} - \mathbf{c}_k) - F(\mathbf{x} - \mathbf{c}_m) = 0, \qquad \mathbf{x} \in \Lambda_{km}. \tag{6.53}$$

Using discrete algorithms, we obtain from (6.51)–(6.53)

$$\begin{aligned} \mathbf{c}_k[n] &= \mathbf{c}_k[n-1] + \gamma_k[n]\, \nabla_{\mathbf{c}_k} F(\mathbf{x}[n] - \mathbf{c}_k[n-1]), \quad k = 1, 2, \ldots, M, \\ \mathbf{c}_m[n] &= \mathbf{c}_m[n-1], \qquad m \neq k, \end{aligned} \tag{6.54}$$

if for all $m \neq k$

$$f_{km}(\mathbf{x}[n], \vec{\mathbf{c}}[n-1]) = F(\mathbf{x}[n] - \mathbf{c}_k[n-1]) - F(\mathbf{x}[n] - \mathbf{c}_m[n-1]) < 0. \tag{6.55}$$

The block diagram of the self-learning system representing these algorithms is presented in Fig. 6.4.

In the special case for

$$F(\mathbf{x} - \mathbf{c}_k) = \| \mathbf{x} - \mathbf{c}_k \|^2, \tag{6.56}$$

we obtain optimal algorithms

$$\mathbf{c}_k[n] = \mathbf{c}_k[n-1] + (N_k[n])^{-1} (\mathbf{x}[n] - \mathbf{c}_k[n-1]), \quad k = 1, 2, \ldots, M, \tag{6.57}$$

$$\begin{aligned} f(\mathbf{x}[n], \vec{\mathbf{c}}[n-1]) &= -2(\mathbf{c}_k^{\mathrm{T}}[n-1] - \mathbf{c}_m^{\mathrm{T}}[n-1])x[n] \\ &\quad + \| \mathbf{c}_k[n-1] \|^2 - \| \mathbf{c}_m[n-1] \|^2, \end{aligned} \tag{6.58}$$

where $N_k[n]$ is the number of situations $\mathbf{x}$ that were related to the region X_k.

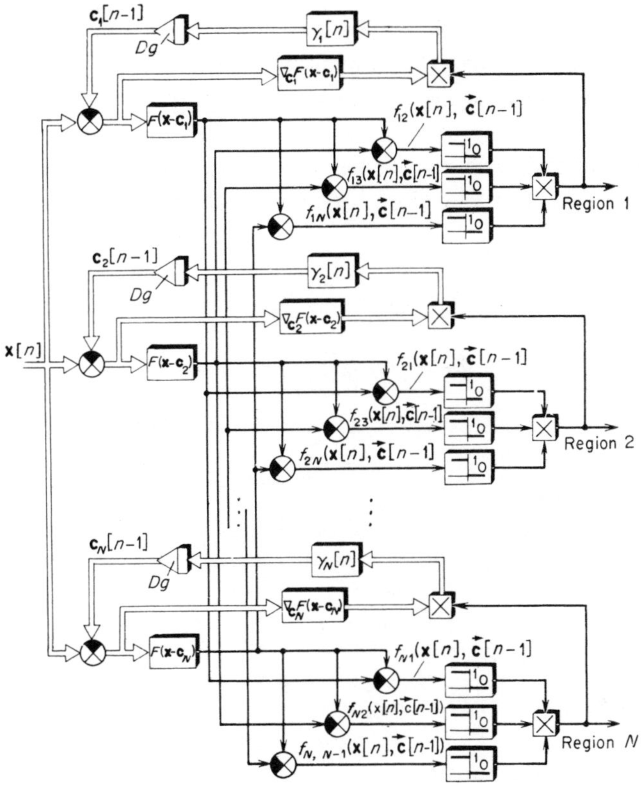

FIG. 6.4

The block diagram of the optimal learning system that realizes these algorithms differs from the one shown in Fig. 6.4; the functional transformer $\nabla_{\mathbf{c}_k} F(\mathbf{x} - \mathbf{c}_k)$ is not present.

6.8 Self-Learning When the Number of Regions Is Unknown: I

In the algorithms of self-learning given above, it was assumed that the number of regions M into which the observed situations have to be clustered is given in advance (for simplicity and clarity, it was assumed to equal 2). Although this does not look like a significant limitation, since for $M > 2$ we can repeatedly use the binary case (frequently called "dichotomy"), it is still needed to remove the necessity of specifying a fixed number of regions. In other words, it is desired not only to relate observed situations to proper regions but also to determine the correct number of these regions.

Sufficiently complete information about the regions of the situations **x** is contained in the mixture probability density function (6.3). We can assume that the peaks of the estimated mixture probability density function (Fig. 6.5) correspond to the "centers" of the regions, and the lines passing along the valleys of this relief are the boundaries of the regions; the number of existing peaks in $p(\mathbf{x})$ defines the number of regions.

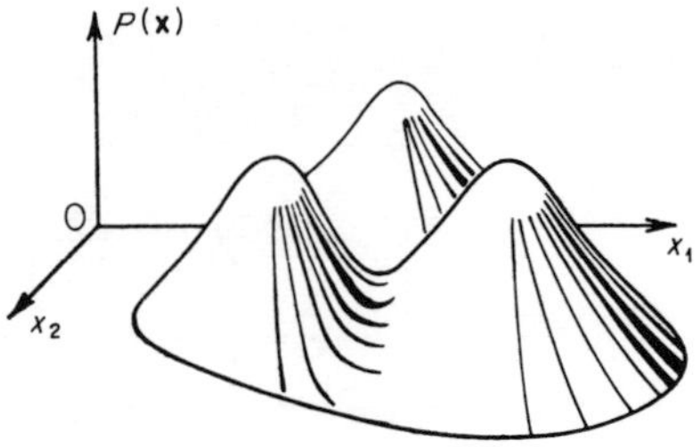

FIG. 6.5

In order to restore (estimate) the mixture probability density function $p(\mathbf{x})$, we shall approximate it by

$$\hat{p}(\mathbf{x}) = \mathbf{a}^{\mathrm{T}}\boldsymbol{\varphi}(\mathbf{x}), \tag{6.59}$$

where $\boldsymbol{\varphi}(\mathbf{x})$ is a vector function with orthonormal components.

We now form the functionals

$$J(\mathbf{c}) = \int_X [p(\mathbf{x}) - \mathbf{a}^{\mathrm{T}}\boldsymbol{\varphi}(\mathbf{x})]^2 \, d\mathbf{x}. \tag{6.60}$$

It is obtained from the functional (6.42) for $\mathbf{b} \equiv 0$. Thus, by setting in (6.45) and (6.46) and the obtained algorithms (6.47),

$$\mathbf{b} \equiv 0, \qquad U = 1, \qquad \boldsymbol{\psi}(\mathbf{x}) \equiv 0, \qquad G \equiv 0,$$

we obtain

$$\mathbf{a} = M\{\boldsymbol{\varphi}(\mathbf{x})\}, \tag{6.61}$$

and therefore

$$\mathbf{a}[n] = \mathbf{a}[n-1] - n^{-1}(\mathbf{a}[n-1] - \boldsymbol{\varphi}(\mathbf{x}[n])). \tag{6.62}$$

According to (6.59),

$$\hat{p}_{n-1}(\mathbf{x}[n]) = \mathbf{a}^{\mathrm{T}}[n-1]\boldsymbol{\varphi}(\mathbf{x}[n]). \tag{6.63}$$

The system realizing Algorithms (6.62) and (6.63) is presented in Fig. 6.6.

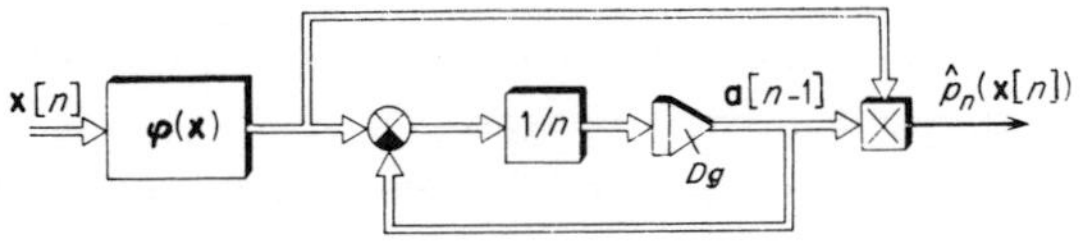

FIG. 6.6

Therefore, we can form an estimate of the mixture probability density function. A slightly different approach to restoration (estimation) of $p(\mathbf{x})$ is also possible. As mentioned in Section 3.2, the empirical mixture probability density function is defined in the following way:

$$\hat{p}_n(\mathbf{x}) = n^{-1} \sum_{m=1}^{n} \delta(\mathbf{x} - \mathbf{x}[m]), \tag{6.64}$$

where $\delta(\mathbf{x})$ is a δ-function. But no continuous line corresponds to this estimate. In the expression (6.64), excessively large weight is given to the observed situations $\mathbf{x}[m]$, and the weights of all other situations are equal to zero.

In order to obtain a smoother estimate of the empirical probability density function, we replace δ-function by a certain bell-shaped function $k(\mathbf{x}, \mathbf{x}[m])$ (Fig. 6.7) that gives the largest weight to the observed situation $\mathbf{x}[m]$, and for the other situation, the weights are different from zero. Then instead of (6.64) we obtain

$$\tilde{p}_n(\mathbf{x}) = n^{-1} \sum_{m=1}^{n} k(\mathbf{x}, \mathbf{x}[m]), \tag{6.65}$$

or, in the recursive form,

$$\tilde{p}_n(\mathbf{x}) = \tilde{p}_{n-1}(\mathbf{x}) - n^{-1}(\tilde{p}_{n-1}(\mathbf{x}) - k(\mathbf{x}, \mathbf{x}[n])). \tag{6.66}$$

This algorithm of learning, like the algorithm of learning (6.62) and (6.63), can be used in the estimation of the mixture probability density function,

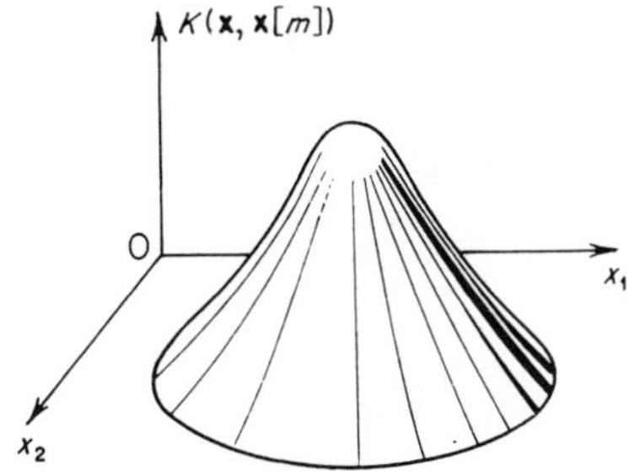

FIG. 6.7

and thus also in finding the number of regions or groups and their corresponding situations.

The algorithm of self-learning (6.66) can be generalized if we replace a fixed function $k(\mathbf{x}, \mathbf{x}[n])$ by a function $k_n(\mathbf{x}, \mathbf{x}[n])$ that varies at each step, for instance,

$$k_n(\mathbf{x}, \mathbf{x}[n]) = (h[n])^{-1} k\left(\frac{\mathbf{x} - \mathbf{x}[n]}{h[n]}\right), \tag{6.67}$$

where $h[n]$ is a certain decreasing sequence of positive numbers.

It should be noticed that the algorithms of learning (6.62) and (6.63) are the special cases of the algorithm of learning (6.66). Actually, by setting

$$k(\mathbf{x}, \mathbf{x}[n]) = \boldsymbol{\varphi}^{\mathrm{T}}(\mathbf{x})\boldsymbol{\varphi}(\mathbf{x}[n]) \tag{6.68}$$

in (6.66), and by introducing $\hat{p}_k(x)$ from (6.63), we obtain the algorithm of learning (6.62) after a division by $\boldsymbol{\varphi}(\mathbf{x})$.

We have described above the ways toward the restoration (estimation) of the mixture probability density functions. For multidimensional vectors of the situations $\mathbf{x}$, this restoration is very difficult when smoothness has to be maintained. It is even more difficult to extract the desired regions.

6.9 Self-Learning When the Number of Regions Is Unknown: II

In order to avoid the difficulties related to clear presentation of the mixture probability density function, we shall rank the situations simultaneously with the restoration of $\tilde{p}_n(\mathbf{x})$. Naturally, this requires that a complete set of all observations $\mathbf{x}$ be at our disposal.

Let us observe an arbitrary situation $\tilde{\mathbf{x}}[1]$ from the collection $\{\mathbf{x}[1], \ldots, \mathbf{x}[s]\}$. Then, according to (6.66) for $n = 1$,

$$\tilde{p}_1(\mathbf{x}) = k(\mathbf{x}, \tilde{\mathbf{x}}[1]). \tag{6.69}$$

Among the remaining situations we search for the second situation $\tilde{\mathbf{x}}[2]$ such that

$$\tilde{p}_1(\tilde{\mathbf{x}}[2]) = \max_{\mathbf{x}} k(\mathbf{x}, \tilde{\mathbf{x}}[1]). \tag{6.70}$$

Among the remaining situations we search for the third situation $\tilde{\mathbf{x}}[3]$ such that

$$\begin{aligned} p_2(\tilde{\mathbf{x}}[3]) &= \max_{\mathbf{x}}[\tilde{p}_1(\mathbf{x}) - \tfrac{1}{2}(p_1(\mathbf{x}) - k(\mathbf{x}, \tilde{\mathbf{x}}[2]))] \\ &= \max_{\mathbf{x}} \tfrac{1}{2} \sum_{m=1}^{2} k(\mathbf{x}, \tilde{\mathbf{x}}[m]), \end{aligned} \tag{6.71}$$

and so forth, until we obtain

$$p_s(\tilde{\mathbf{x}}[s+1]) = \max_{\mathbf{x}}[p_{s-1}(\mathbf{x}) - s^{-1}(p_{s-1}(x) - k(\mathbf{x}, \tilde{\mathbf{x}}[s]))]$$
$$= \max_{\mathbf{x}} s^{-1} \sum_{m=1}^{s} k(\mathbf{x}, \tilde{\mathbf{x}}[m]). \tag{6.72}$$

The obtain values $\tilde{p}_n(\tilde{\mathbf{x}}[n+1])$ are displayed in the coordinate system $(p_n(\tilde{\mathbf{x}}[n+1]), n)$ (Fig. 6.8). From this display, we can see that the situations of the first region are first selected or enumerated, then those of the second region, and so forth. The transitions from one region to the next are characterized by a sharp decrease in $\tilde{p}_n(\mathbf{x}[n+1])$ (Fig. 6.8).

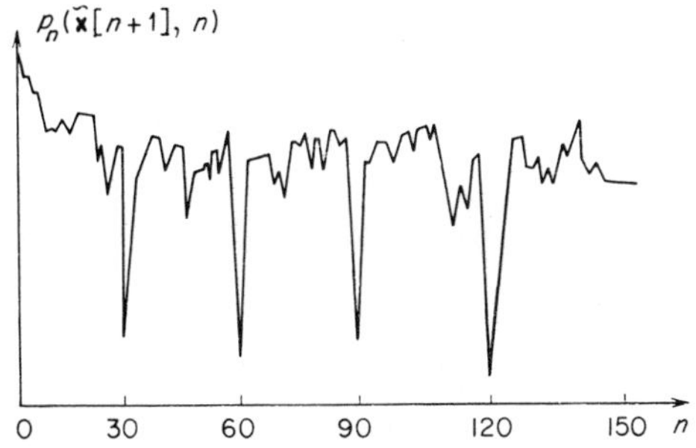

FIG. 6.8

The algorithms of self-learning presented, although of a specific nature, lead us again to the various estimates of the mixture probability density. For the time being, obviously, there are no other ways of constructing algorithms of self-learning.

6.10 Discussion

The problem of constructing self-learning systems, until recently still a mystical one, actually consists of estimating the mixture probability density function or certain boundaries that are directly or indirectly related to this density function. In the latter case, as in the problem of learning with supervision, the goal of learning is again the minimum of the average risk, but with incompletely defined loss functions. Therefore, the problems of learning with and without supervision, which correspond to the problem of recognition and to the problem of classification, are considered from the standpoint of a single goal of learning, but this goal of learning is achieved by different means.

We have not considered here all possible approaches to the design of self-learning systems based on learning with supervision. Only supervision (reinforcement) defined by the answers of the self-learning system and not by classifications provided by a teacher was discussed. The actions of such self-learning systems are similar to the actions of a trusting optimist or of a doubting pessimist, who always accept as correct those decisions that they consider respectively as desirable or undesirable. Although similar systems can find the boundaries between the regions, they cannot uniquely recognize these regions. It should be clear now that the symmetric construction of self-learning systems, which represents a combination of two perceptrons, compensates for the lack of classifications provided by a teacher and classifies the situations uniquely into the regions.

6.11 Conclusion

Learning without supervision plays a very important role in the cases when observed situations or patterns have to be classified into a number of known or *a priori* unknown regions without any training samples that correspond to the correct classifications provided by a teacher. It could be expected that learning without supervision would take a longer time than learning with supervision under the same conditions. We have again encountered a simple fact that ignorance must be paid for. In the problem of learning, the cost is an increase in learning time.

Comments

6.1 A survey of various principles of learning without supervision in the case of sufficient a priori information can be found in the paper by Spragins [1]. This approach was studied by Cooper and Cooper [1] and Fralick [1].

6.3 A variational formulation of the problem of learning with supervision was given by Shlezinger [1]. He has considered the average risk for quadratic loss function. This same problem, but in slightly different terms, was later considered by Braverman [1]. General formulation of this problem for arbitrary loss functions was given by the author and Kelmans [1].

6.4 General algorithms of learning without supervision were obtained by the author and Kelmans [1], and also by the author [3]. Table 6.1

contains algorithms by Braverman [1] (Algorithm 2) and Dorofeyuk [1] (Algorithm 3) which were obtained in another way.

6.5 See also the article by the author [1].

6.6 An idea of a similar adaptive approach to learning without supervision was described by Schwartz [1] on the basis of the results by the author [1, 2]. He has obtained incomplete forms of the algorithms.

6.8 Estimation of the probability density function with the algorithms (6.62), (6.63) was described by the author [1, 2], Blaydon [1], Kashyap and Blaydon [1], and Laski [1], and with Algorithms (6.65)–(6.67) by Parzen [1], and especially by Tarasenko [1] and Chavchanidze and Kumsishvili [1].

6.9 A statistical interpretation of the algorithm of self-learning "Spectar" proposed by Dorofeyuk [1] was given here. Very interesting results using algorithms of self-learning in the prediction of reliability can be found in the papers by Gorenkov *et al.* [1] and by Bugaets *et al.* [1] on the systematization of minerals.

REFERENCES

Blaydon, C. C.

[1] Approximation of distribution and density functions. *Proc. IEEE* **55**, No. 2 (1967).

Braverman, E. M.

[1] Potential function method in the problem of machine learning without a teacher. *Avtomat. i Telemeh.* No. 11 (1966).

Bugaets, A. N., Dorofeyuk, A. A., Matsak, A. P., and Serova, L. I.

[1] Application of algorithms of automatic classification to the systematization of minerals. *Avtomat. i Telemeh.* No. 6 (1966).

Chavchanidze, V. V., and Kumsishvili, V. V.

[1] On estimation of probability distributions based on a small number of observations. *In* "Application of Computers in Automatization." Mashgiz, 1961 (in Russian).

Cooper, D., and Cooper, P.

[1] Non-superwised adaptive signal detection. *IEEE Trans. Information Theory* **IT-11,** No. 2 (1965).

Dorofeyuk, A. A.

[1] Algorithms of learning without a teacher which are based on the potential function method. *Avtomat. i Telemeh.* No. 11 (1966).

Fralick, S. C.

[1] Learning to recognize patterns without a teacher. *IEEE Trans. Information Theory* **IT-13,** No. 1 (1967).

Gorenkov, E. V., Dorofeyuk, A. A., and Zhitkikh, I. I.

[1] Application of the method of automatic classification to the individual prediction of the life time of powerful klystron tubes. *Avtomat. i Telemeh.* No. 1 (1969).

Kashyap, R. L., and Blaydon, C. C.
[1] Estimation of probability density and distribution functions. *IEEE Trans. Information Theory* **IT-14**, No. 4 (1968).

Laski, J.
[1] On the probability density estimation. *Proc. IEEE* **56**, No. 5 (1968).

Parzen, E.
[1] On estimation of a probability density and mode. *Ann. Math. Statist.* **33**, No. 3 (1962).

Schwartz, S. C.
[1] An example of nonsupervised adaptive pattern classification. *IEEE Trans. Automatic Control* **AC-13**, No. 1 (1968).

Shlezinger, M. I.
[1] On arbitrary pattern classification. *In* "Reading Automata." Kiev, 1965 (in Russian).
[2] Relationship between learning and self-learning in pattern recognition. *Kibernetika (Kiev)* No. 2 (1968).

Spragins, J. J.
[1] Learning without a teacher. *IEEE Trans. Information Theory* **IT-12** (1966).

Tarasenko, F. P.
[1] On evaluation of an unknown probability density function, the direct estimation, of the entropy from independent observations of a continuous random variable and the distribution-free entropy test of goodness. *Proc. IEEE* **56**, No. 1 (1968).

Tsypkin, Ya. Z.
[1] Application of the method of stochastic approximation to estimation of unknown probability density functions using observations. *Avtomat. i Telemeh.* No. 3 (1966).
[2] On algorithms for estimation of probability density functions and moments using observations. *Avtomat. i Telemeh.* No. 7 (1967).
[3] Self-learning, what is it? *IEEE Trans. Automatic Control* **AC-13**, No. 1 (1968).

Tsypkin, Ya. Z., and Kelmans, G. K.
[1] Recursive algorithms of self-learning. *Izv. Akad. Nauk SSSR Tehn. Kibernet.* No. 5 (1967).

Volohov, Yu. P., and Zaichenko, Yu. P.
[1] Dispersion method of spontaneous partition of the space into compact sets (Patterns). *Avtomatika* **11**, No. 5 (1966).

Watson, G. S., and Leadbetter, M.
[1] On the estimation of the probability density. *Ann. Math. Statist.* **34**, No. 2 (1963).

Zhuravliev, O. G., and Torgovitskii, I. Sh.
[1] Optimal method of objective classification in the problems of pattern recognition. *Avtomat. i Telemeh.* **26**, No. 11 (1965).

Chapter VII

Learning Models

Physical models are as different from the world as a geographical map is from the surface of the earth.

L. BRILLOUIN

7.1 Introduction

Learning models, which change their structure and parameters in order to approach the behavior of the systems under study, can be used for system identification. The problem of system identification is very similar to the problem of pattern recognition considered in Chapter V. In the problem of pattern recognition, the learning system estimates the discriminant function, and the sign of this function defines the class to which the observed situation belongs. In the problem of identification, this same discriminant function represents the sought characteristic of the system. The problem of system identification is a very broad one, since the systems can be described by differential or integral equations of various types.

We do not wish to examine this problem in depth, and thus we limit our discussion in this chapter to a sufficiently general way of describing systems by operator equations.

7.2 Description of the System

We shall describe dynamic systems by operator equations of two types:

$$y(t) = \mathcal{Q}(y(t), x(t)) \tag{7.1}$$

or

$$y = \mathcal{Q}^0(x(t)), \tag{7.2}$$

where $\mathcal{Q}(y, x)$ and $\mathcal{Q}^0(x)$ are certain operators, $x(t)$ is input, and $y(t)$ is output of the system (Fig. 7.1).

Operator equation (7.2) represents an explicit equation in y. Therefore, it can be viewed as a solution of Eq. (7.1). Furthermore, it is assumed that the system is in the regime of normal operation, that is, $\mathbf{x}(t)$ and $y(t)$ are stationary random processes. For linear systems

$$\begin{aligned} y(t) &= \mathcal{Q}(y(t), x(t)) \\ &= \int_0^\infty k_y(\tau) y(t-\tau)\, d\tau + \int_0^\infty k_x(\tau) x(t-\tau)\, d\tau \end{aligned} \tag{7.3}$$

and

$$y(t) = \mathcal{Q}^0(x(t)) = \int_0^\infty k(\tau) x(t-\tau)\, d\tau, \tag{7.4}$$

where $k_y(\tau)$, $k_x(\tau)$, and $k(\tau)$ are impulse responses, and $k(\tau)$ depends, generally speaking, in a very complicated fashion on $k_y(\tau)$ and $k_x(\tau)$. Equations (7.3) and (7.4) are actually of convolution type, where (7.4) describes the relationship between the input and the output of the system, that is, Eq. (7.4) is the solution of Eq. (7.3).

For a nonlinear system

$$\begin{aligned} y(t) &= \mathcal{Q}(y(t), x(t)) \\ &= \sum_{m=1}^{\infty} \underbrace{\int_0^\infty \cdots \int_0^\infty}_{m \text{ times}} k_y(\tau_1, \ldots, \tau_m) y(t-\tau_1) \cdots y(t-\tau_m)\, d\tau_1 \cdots d\tau_m \\ &\quad + \sum_{m=1}^{\infty} \underbrace{\int_0^\infty \cdots \int_0^\infty}_{m \text{ times}} k_x(\tau_1, \ldots, \tau_m) x(t-\tau_1) \cdots x(t-\tau_m)\, d\tau_1 \cdots d\tau_m \end{aligned} \tag{7.5}$$

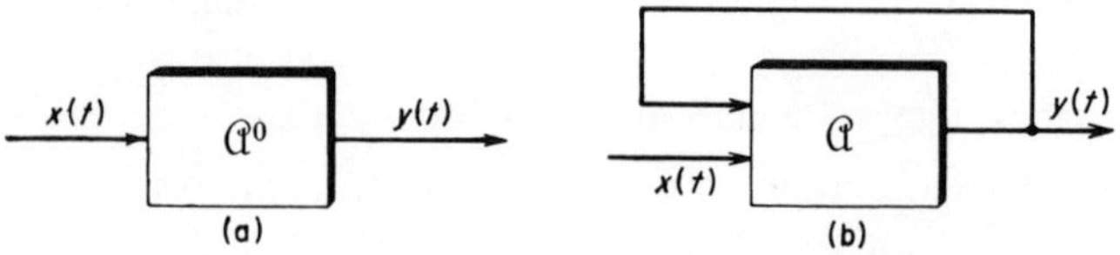

FIG. 7.1

and

$$y(t) = \mathfrak{A}^0(x(t))$$

$$= \sum_{m=1}^{\infty} \underbrace{\int_0^{\infty} \cdots \int_0^{\infty}}_{m \text{ times}} k(\tau_1, \ldots, \tau_m) x(t - \tau_1) \ldots x(t - \tau_m) \, d\tau_1 \cdots d\tau_m. \tag{7.6}$$

Series (7.6) is usually called the Volterra series. It defines the solution of nonlinear equations of the type (7.5). In practice, the number of terms in (7.5) and (7.6) is finite.

7.3 Structure of the Model

The equation of the learning model is assumed to be

$$\hat{y}(t) = \mathfrak{B}(y(t), x(t), \mathbf{c}) \tag{7.7}$$

or

$$\hat{y}(t) = \mathfrak{B}^0(x(t), \mathbf{c}), \tag{7.8}$$

where $\mathfrak{B}(y, x, \mathbf{c})$ and $\mathfrak{B}^0(x, \mathbf{c})$ are known operators that depend on unknown parameter vector

$$\mathbf{c} = (c_1, \ldots, c_N). \tag{7.9}$$

In Eqs. (7.7) and (7.8), $\hat{y}(t)$ is the output of the model, and $y(t)$ and $x(t)$ are the inputs. Let us also assume that the operator can be represented in the form of a linear combination of the simplest operators, that is,

$$\mathfrak{B}(y, x, \mathbf{c}) = \mathbf{c}^T \mathfrak{B}(y, x) \tag{7.10}$$

or

$$\mathfrak{B}^0(x, \mathbf{c}) = \mathbf{c}^T \mathfrak{B}(x), \tag{7.11}$$

where

$$\mathfrak{B}(y, x) = (\mathfrak{B}_1(y, x), \ldots, \mathfrak{B}_N(y, x)), \tag{7.12}$$

$$\mathfrak{B}(x) = (\mathfrak{B}_1(x), \ldots, \mathfrak{B}_N(x)), \tag{7.13}$$

are vector operators with the simplest linearly independent operators. Equations of the learning model (7.7) and (7.8) can then be written as

$$\hat{y}(t) = \mathbf{c}^T \mathfrak{B}(y(t), x(t)) \tag{7.14}$$

or

$$\hat{y}(t) = \mathbf{c}^T (\mathfrak{B}^0 x(t)). \tag{7.15}$$

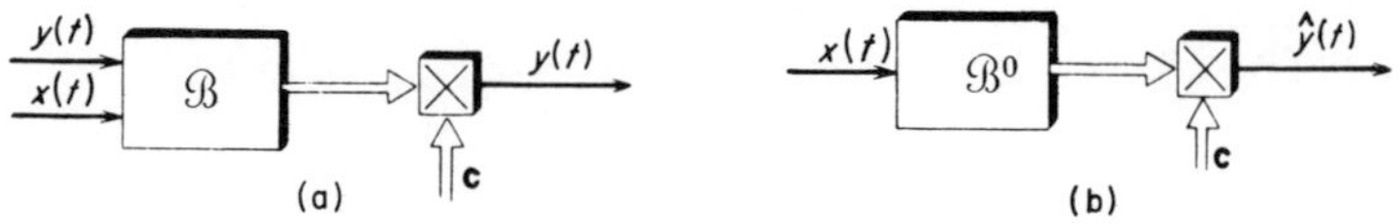

FIG. 7.2

In accordance with this equation, the structure of the learning system can be represented by the diagrams shown in Fig. 7.2. In the first case, we have two inputs, and in the second case, one.

7.4 Goal of Learning

Let us apply to the input of the learning model signal $x(t)$ [and when it is necessary, output $y(t)$], and compare the output of the system $y(t)$ and the model $\hat{y}(t)$. Their difference characterizes the instantaneous error

$$\varepsilon(t) = y(t) - \hat{y}(t). \tag{7.16}$$

We form the functional

$$J(\mathbf{c}) = \mathsf{M}\{F(y(t) - \mathbf{c}^{\mathrm{T}}\mathfrak{B}(y(t), x(t)))\} \tag{7.17}$$

or

$$J(\mathbf{c}) = \mathsf{M}\{F(y(t) - \mathbf{c}^{\mathrm{T}}\mathfrak{B}^0(x(t)))\}, \tag{7.18}$$

where $F(\,\cdot\,)$ is a convex, usually quadratic, function. The goal of learning is the minimum of functional (7.17), or (7.18), and the problem of learning in a model consists of selecting $\mathbf{c} = \mathbf{c}^*$ for which the goal of learning is reached.

7.5 Algorithms of Learning

The condition of the minimum of the functional (7.17) has the form

$$\nabla J(\mathbf{c}) = -\mathsf{M}_{\mathbf{x}}\{F'(y(t) - \mathbf{c}^{\mathrm{T}}\mathfrak{B}(y(t), x(t)))\mathfrak{B}(y(t), x(t))\} = 0. \tag{7.19}$$

Using continuous algorithms of learning, we obtain from (7.19)

$$d\mathbf{c}(t)/dt = \gamma(t)F'(y(t) - \mathbf{c}^{\mathrm{T}}(t)\mathfrak{B}(y(t), x(t)))\mathfrak{B}(y(t), x(t)), \tag{7.20}$$

or, more briefly,

$$d\mathbf{c}(t)/dt = \gamma(t)F'(y(t) - \hat{y}(t, t))\mathfrak{B}(y(t), x(t)), \tag{7.21}$$

where

$$\hat{y}(t, t) = \mathbf{c}^{\mathrm{T}}(t)\mathfrak{B}(y(t), x(t)). \tag{7.22}$$

The block diagram of the learning model representing these algorithms is shown in Fig. 7.3. This is a learning model with two inputs. Similarly, for the functional (7.18) we have

$$\nabla J(\mathbf{c}) = -\mathsf{M}_{\mathbf{x}}\{F'(y(t) - \mathbf{c}^{\mathrm{T}}\mathfrak{B}^{0}(x(t)))\mathfrak{B}^{0}(x(t))\} = 0. \tag{7.23}$$

In this case, the algorithms of learning have the form

$$d\mathbf{c}(t)/dt = \gamma(t)F'(y(t) - \mathbf{c}^{\mathrm{T}}(t)\mathfrak{B}^{0}(x(t)))\mathfrak{B}^{0}(x(t)), \tag{7.24}$$

or, more briefly,

$$d\mathbf{c}(t)/dt = \gamma(t)F'(y(t) - \hat{y}(t, t))\mathfrak{B}^{0}(x(t)), \tag{7.25}$$

where

$$\hat{y}(t, t) = \mathbf{c}^{\mathrm{T}}(t)\mathfrak{B}^{0}(x(t)). \tag{7.26}$$

The block diagram of the learning model that corresponds to these algorithms is shown in Fig. 7.4. This is a learning model with one input. In a number of cases it may be more convenient to use the estimate $\hat{y}(t, t)$ instead of $y(t)$ in (7.20), that is, to replace Algorithm (7.20) by

$$d\mathbf{c}(t)/dt = \gamma(t)F'(y(t) - \mathbf{c}^{\mathrm{T}}(t)\mathfrak{B}(\hat{y}(t, t), x(t)))\mathfrak{B}(\hat{y}(t, t), x(t)), \tag{7.27}$$

where

$$\hat{y}(t, t) = \mathbf{c}^{\mathrm{T}}(t)\mathfrak{B}(\hat{y}(t, t), x(t)).$$

Obviously, this substitution is legitimate only when $\hat{y}(t, t)$ is in a certain sense close to $y(t)$. The block diagram of such a learning system differs from one shown in Fig. 7.3: the input $y(t)$ is replaced by $\hat{y}(t, t)$. This is accomplished by a simple switch in the block diagram shown in Fig. 7.5. When the switch is in position 1, Algorithm (7.20) is realized; position 2 is for Algorithm (7.27). This learning model receives the data about input and output signals and it makes an estimate $\hat{y}(t, t)$ that approaches $y(t)$ due to the changes in the parameter vector. In other words, the learning model approaches the dynamic system under study in the best way. This justifies the usuage of learning models in modeling various systems.

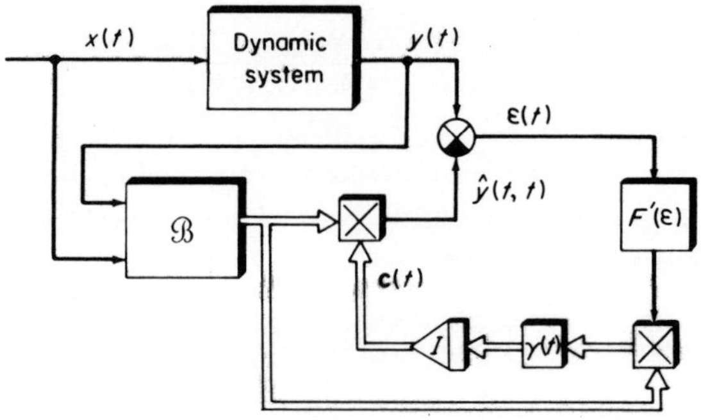

FIG. 7.3

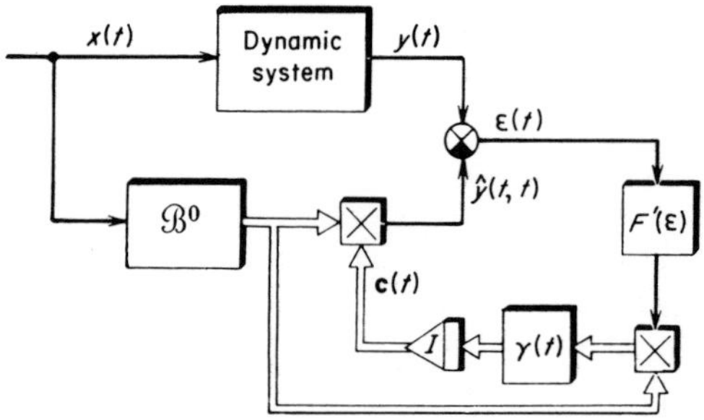

FIG. 7.4

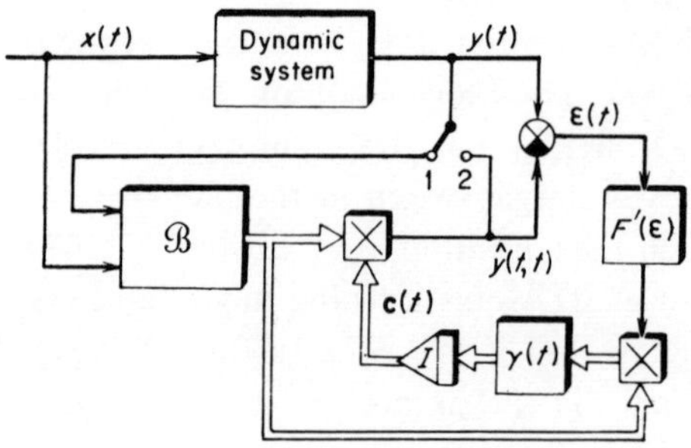

FIG. 7.5

7.6 Linear Learning Model

Let us consider the linear learning model. The equation of this model (7.7) is given in the form

$$\hat{y}(t) = \mathcal{B}(y(t), x(t), \mathbf{c}) = \mathbf{c}_y^{\mathrm{T}}\boldsymbol{\varphi}_y(t) + \mathbf{c}_x^{\mathrm{T}}\boldsymbol{\varphi}_x(t), \tag{7.28}$$

where the vector function is defined by

$$\begin{aligned} \boldsymbol{\varphi}_y(t) &= \int_0^\infty \mathbf{k}_y(\tau)y(t-\tau)\,d\tau, \\ \boldsymbol{\varphi}_x(t) &= \int_0^\infty \mathbf{k}_x(\tau)x(t-\tau)\,d\tau. \end{aligned} \tag{7.29}$$

In these expressions

$$\begin{aligned} \mathbf{k}_y(\tau) &= (k_{y_1}(\tau), \ldots, k_{y_{N_k}}(\tau)), \\ \mathbf{k}_x(\tau) &= (k_{x_1}(\tau), \ldots, k_{x_{N_k}}(\tau)), \end{aligned} \tag{7.30}$$

are vector impulse characteristics.

If the goal of learning is the minimum of the functional

$$J(\mathbf{c}_y, \mathbf{c}_x) = \mathsf{M}\{F(y(t) - \mathbf{c}_y^{\mathrm{T}}\boldsymbol{\varphi}_y(t) - \mathbf{c}_x^{\mathrm{T}}\boldsymbol{\varphi}_x(t))\}, \tag{7.31}$$

then, according to (7.21), we obtain the algorithms of learning

$$\begin{aligned} d\mathbf{c}_y(t)/dt &= \gamma_y(t)F'(y(t) - \hat{y}(t, t))\boldsymbol{\varphi}_y(t), \\ d\mathbf{c}_x(t)/dt &= \gamma_x(t)F'(y(t) - \hat{y}(t, t))\boldsymbol{\varphi}_x(t), \end{aligned} \tag{7.32}$$

where

$$\hat{y}(t, t) = \mathbf{c}_y^{\mathrm{T}}(t)\boldsymbol{\varphi}_y(t) + \mathbf{c}_x^{\mathrm{T}}(t)\boldsymbol{\varphi}_x(t). \tag{7.33}$$

The block diagram of a linear learning model with two inputs is shown in Fig. 7.6.

If instead of (7.28) we use

$$\hat{y}(t) = \mathcal{B}^0(x(t), \mathbf{c}) = \mathbf{c}^{\mathrm{T}}\boldsymbol{\varphi}(t), \tag{7.34}$$

where

$$\boldsymbol{\varphi}(t) = \int_0^\infty \mathbf{k}(\tau)x(t-\tau)\,d\tau \tag{7.35}$$

and

$$\mathbf{k}(\tau) = (k_1(\tau), \ldots, k_N(\tau)), \tag{7.36}$$

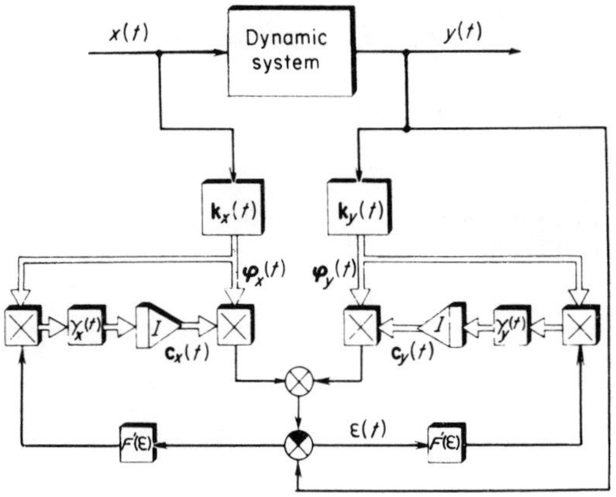

FIG. 7.6

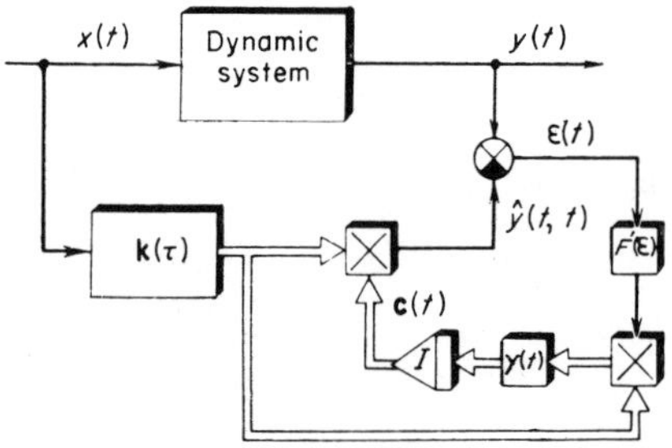

FIG. 7.7

then, by setting

$$\boldsymbol{\varphi}_y(t) \equiv 0, \qquad \boldsymbol{\varphi}_x(t) = \boldsymbol{\varphi}(t), \qquad \mathbf{c}_x = \mathbf{c}, \tag{7.37}$$

we obtain

$$d\mathbf{c}(t)/dt = \gamma(t)F'(y(t) - \hat{y}(t, t))\boldsymbol{\varphi}(t), \tag{7.38}$$

where

$$\hat{y}(t, t) = \mathbf{c}^{\mathrm{T}}(t)\boldsymbol{\varphi}(t). \tag{7.39}$$

The block diagram of a linear learning system with one input is presented in Fig. 7.7. If the system under study is linear, then a linear learning model after a period of learning defines the characteristic of the system. If the studied system is nonlinear, the linear learning system defines then a linear statistical equivalent of a nonlinear dynamic system, that is, statistical linearization of a nonlinear dynamic system is accomplished.

7.7 Optimal Learning Linear Model

For optimal, or more accurately, suboptimal learning of a linear model with one input (see Fig. 7.7), according to the results of Section 3.10, the algorithms of optimal learning have the form

$$d\mathbf{c}(t)/dt = \Gamma(t)F'(y(t) - \hat{y}(t, t))\boldsymbol{\varphi}(t), \tag{7.40}$$

where $\Gamma(t)$ is a matrix defined by

$$d\Gamma(t)/dt = -\Gamma(t)\Big[\nabla_{\mathbf{c}}^2 F(y(t) - \hat{y}(t, t)) + \int_0^t \nabla_{\mathbf{c}}^3 F(y(\tau) - \hat{y}(t, \tau))\, d\tau \,\frac{d\mathbf{c}(t)}{dt}\Big]\Gamma(t). \tag{7.41}$$

In the special case of quadratic performance index

$$\begin{aligned} F(y(t) - \hat{y}(t, t)) &= \tfrac{1}{2}(y(t) - \hat{y}(t, t))^2, \\ \nabla_{\mathbf{c}} F(y(t) - \hat{y}(t, t)) &= -(y(t) - \hat{y}(t, t))\boldsymbol{\varphi}(t), \\ \nabla_{\mathbf{c}}^2 F(y(t) - \hat{y}(t, t)) &= \boldsymbol{\varphi}(t)\boldsymbol{\varphi}^{\mathrm{T}}(t), \\ \nabla_{\mathbf{c}}^3 F(y(\tau) - \hat{y}(t, \tau)) &= 0. \end{aligned} \tag{7.42}$$

Therefore,

$$d\mathbf{c}(t)/dt = \Gamma(t)(y(t) - \hat{y}(t, t))\boldsymbol{\varphi}(t) \tag{7.43}$$

and

$$d\Gamma(t)/dt = -\Gamma(t)[\boldsymbol{\varphi}(t)\boldsymbol{\varphi}^{\mathrm{T}}(t)]\Gamma(t). \tag{7.44}$$

The block diagram of optimal learning linear system is presented in Fig. 7.8. In a similar fashion, we can obtain algorithms of optimal learning systems with two inputs.

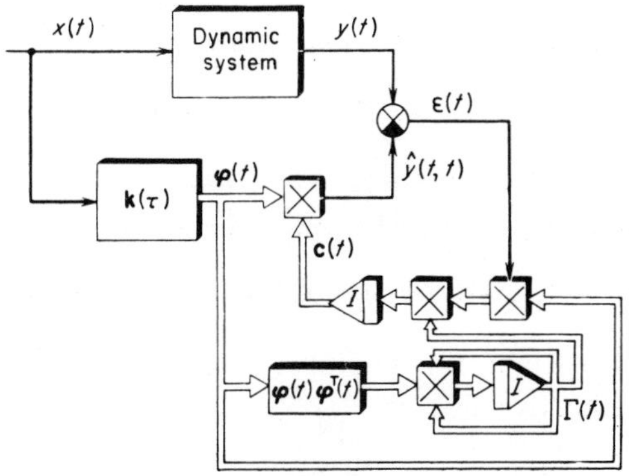

FIG. 7.8

7.8 Nonlinear Learning Model: I

The nonlinear learning models with two inputs are described in general by

$$\hat{y}(t) = \mathcal{B}(y(t), x(t), \mathbf{c}) = \sum_{m=1}^{N_y} \mathbf{c}_{my}^{\mathrm{T}} \boldsymbol{\varphi}_{my}(t) + \sum_{m=1}^{N_x} \mathbf{c}_{mx}^{\mathrm{T}} \boldsymbol{\varphi}_{mx}(t), \tag{7.45}$$

where

$$\begin{aligned} \boldsymbol{\varphi}_{my}(t) &= \underbrace{\int_0^\infty \cdots \int_0^\infty}_{m \text{ times}} \mathbf{k}_y(\tau_1, \ldots, \tau_m) y(t-\tau_1) \cdots y(t-\tau_m)\, d\tau_1 \cdots d\tau_m, \\ \boldsymbol{\varphi}_{mx}(t) &= \underbrace{\int_0^\infty \cdots \int_0^\infty}_{m \text{ times}} \mathbf{k}_x(\tau_1, \ldots, \tau_m) x(t-\tau_1) \cdots x(t-\tau_m)\, d\tau_1 \cdots d\tau_m, \end{aligned} \tag{7.46}$$

and

$$\begin{aligned} \mathbf{k}_y(\tau_1, \ldots, \tau_m) &= (k_{1y}(\tau_1, \ldots, \tau_m), \ldots, k_{N_y y}(\tau_1, \ldots, \tau_m)), \\ \mathbf{k}_x(\tau_1, \ldots, \tau_m) &= (k_{1x}(\tau_1, \ldots, \tau_m), \ldots, k_{N_x x}(\tau_1, \ldots, \tau_m)) \end{aligned} \tag{7.47}$$

are vectors of Volterra kernels.

By introducing components of the parameter vectors

$$\begin{aligned} \vec{\mathbf{c}}_y &= (\mathbf{c}_{1y}, \ldots, \mathbf{c}_{N_y y}), \\ \vec{\mathbf{c}}_x &= (\mathbf{c}_{1x}, \ldots, \mathbf{c}_{N_x x}) \end{aligned} \tag{7.48}$$

and component vector functions

$$\begin{aligned} \vec{\boldsymbol{\varphi}}_y(t) &= (\boldsymbol{\varphi}_{1y}(t), \ldots, \boldsymbol{\varphi}_{N_y y}(t)), \\ \vec{\boldsymbol{\varphi}}_x(t) &= (\boldsymbol{\varphi}_{1x}(t), \ldots, \boldsymbol{\varphi}_{N_x x}(t)), \end{aligned} \tag{7.49}$$

we can write Eq. (7.45) in the compact form

$$\hat{y}(t) = \vec{\mathbf{c}}_y^{\mathrm{T}} \vec{\boldsymbol{\varphi}}_y(t) + \vec{\mathbf{c}}_x^{\mathrm{T}} \vec{\boldsymbol{\varphi}}_x(t), \tag{7.50}$$

that differs from (7.28) by the presence of the component vectors instead of resultant vectors. By selecting the minimum of the functional

$$J(\vec{\mathbf{c}}_y, \vec{\mathbf{c}}_x) = \mathsf{M}\{F(y(t) - \vec{\mathbf{c}}_y^{\mathrm{T}} \vec{\boldsymbol{\varphi}}_y(t) - \vec{\mathbf{c}}_x^{\mathrm{T}} \vec{\boldsymbol{\varphi}}_x(t))\}, \tag{7.51}$$

to be the goal of learning we obtain in accordance with (7.21) the corresponding algorithms of learning

$$\begin{aligned} d\vec{\mathbf{c}}_y(t)/dt &= \Gamma_y(t) F'(y(t) - \hat{y}(t, t)) \vec{\boldsymbol{\varphi}}_y(t), \\ d\vec{\mathbf{c}}_x(t)/dt &= \Gamma_x(t) F'(y(t) - \hat{y}(t, t)) \vec{\boldsymbol{\varphi}}_x(t), \end{aligned} \tag{7.52}$$

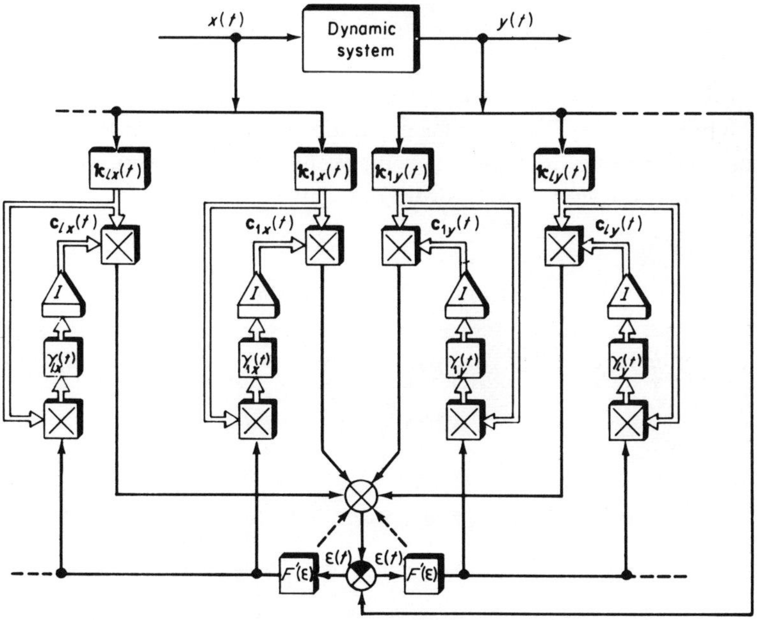

FIG. 7.9

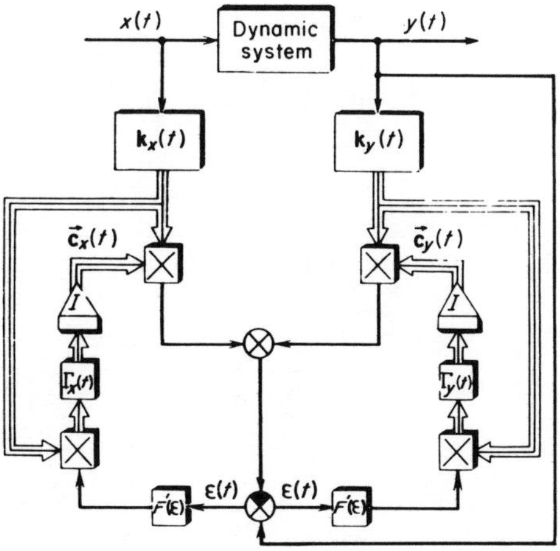

FIG. 7.10

where

$$\hat{y}(t, t) = \vec{\mathbf{c}}_y^{\mathrm{T}}(t)\vec{\boldsymbol{\varphi}}_y(t) + \vec{\mathbf{c}}_x^{\mathrm{T}}(t)\vec{\boldsymbol{\varphi}}_x(t), \tag{7.53}$$

and $\Gamma_x(t)$, and $\Gamma_y(t)$ are diagonal matrices of type (3.14).

The block diagram of a nonlinear learning system is presented in Fig. 7.9. By using triple lines to represent component vector connections, the block diagram takes a very simple form (Fig. 7.10).

7.9 Nonlinear Learning Model: II

For nonlinear learning systems with one input, Eq. (7.50) is replaced by

$$\hat{y}(t) = \mathcal{B}^0(x(t), \mathbf{c}) = \vec{\mathbf{c}}^{\mathrm{T}}\vec{\boldsymbol{\varphi}}(t), \tag{7.54}$$

where

$$\vec{\boldsymbol{\varphi}}(t) = (\boldsymbol{\varphi}_1(t), \ldots, \boldsymbol{\varphi}_N(t)), \tag{7.55}$$

$$\boldsymbol{\varphi}_m(t) = \underbrace{\int_0^\infty \cdots \int_0^\infty}_{m \text{ times}} \mathbf{k}(\tau_1, \ldots, \tau_m) x(t-\tau_1) \cdots x(t-\tau_m)\, d\tau_1 \cdots d\tau_m, \tag{7.56}$$

and

$$\mathbf{k}(\tau_1, \ldots, \tau_m) = (k_1(\tau_1, \ldots, \tau_m), \ldots, k_{N_0}(\tau_1, \ldots, \tau_m)). \tag{7.57}$$

In order to obtain algorithms of learning, we set

$$\vec{\boldsymbol{\varphi}}_y(t) \equiv 0, \qquad \vec{\boldsymbol{\varphi}}_x(t) = \vec{\boldsymbol{\varphi}}(t) \tag{7.58}$$

into the results of Section 7.8.

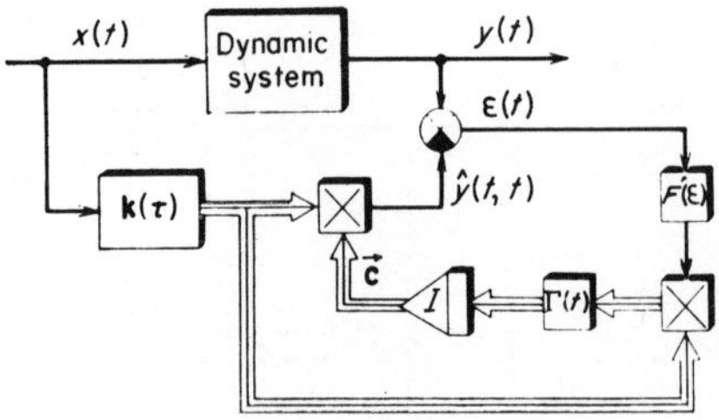

FIG. 7.11

Then from (7.52) and (7.53) we obtain

$$d\mathbf{c}(t)/dt = \Gamma(t)F'(y(t) - \hat{y}(t, t))\vec{\boldsymbol{\varphi}}(t), \tag{7.59}$$

where

$$\hat{y}(t, t) = \vec{\mathbf{c}}^{\mathrm{T}}(t)\vec{\boldsymbol{\varphi}}(t). \tag{7.60}$$

The block diagram of such a nonlinear learning model with one input is shown in Fig. 7.11.

7.10 Discussion

The simplicity of the block diagrams of nonlinear learning models (see Figs. 7.10 and 7.11) and their external similarity with the block diagrams of linear learning models (see Figs. 7.7 and 7.8) can lead to an incorrect impression that linear and nonlinear models do not differ very much from each other. This impression is quickly dispersed after the number of component vectors that define the algorithms of learning are counted. For linear learning models with one input, vector $\mathbf{c}$ has N components. For nonlinear models with one input, the number of components in the vector $\vec{\mathbf{c}}$ is equal to $N_0 \sum_{m=1}^{N} N_m$. For learning systems with two inputs, the number of components is even larger, and there exists a real danger that the "curse of dimensionality" may not permit us to find all these coefficients. It is therefore extremely important to find the methods for overcoming this difficulty. The most complicated methods are most probably related to the decomposition, that is, to substitution of a complex problem of large dimensionality by several simpler problems of smaller dimensionality that have independent solutions. Until such methods are found, we must be satisfied with simple nonlinear learning models.

7.11 Influence of Noise

We thus have assumed that noise is not present. In many cases, this assumption is not justified and we have to consider noise. Let us first examine a simple case when noise exists at the output of the dynamic system (Fig. 7.12).

In this case the functional (7.18) is replaced by

$$J(\mathbf{c}) = \mathsf{M}\{F(y(t) - \mathbf{c}^{\mathrm{T}}\mathfrak{B}^0(x(t)) + \xi(t))\}, \tag{7.61}$$

and the condition of the minimum of (7.23) becomes

$$\nabla J(\mathbf{c}) = -\mathsf{M}\{F'(y(t) - \mathbf{c}^{\mathrm{T}}\mathfrak{B}^0(x(t)) + \xi(t))\mathfrak{B}^0(x(t))\} = 0. \tag{7.62}$$

For a quadratic functional, we obtain from (7.62)

$$\mathsf{M}\{(y(t) - \mathbf{c}^{\mathrm{T}}\mathcal{B}^0(x(t)) + \xi(t))\mathcal{B}^0(x(t))\} = 0. \tag{7.63}$$

If noise $\xi(t)$ and input signal $x(t)$ are uncorrelated,

$$\mathsf{M}\{\xi(t)\mathcal{B}^0(x(t))\} = 0, \tag{7.64}$$

and the condition (7.63) becomes

$$-\mathsf{M}\{(y(t) - \mathbf{c}^{\mathrm{T}}\mathcal{B}^0(x(t)))\mathcal{B}^0(x(t))\} = 0, \tag{7.65}$$

which is identical to (7.23). Therefore, in this case the estimate $\mathbf{c}^*$, obtained through the algorithm of learning, does not depend on noise, that is, it is an unbiased estimate. This is a very important property of quadratic loss functions.

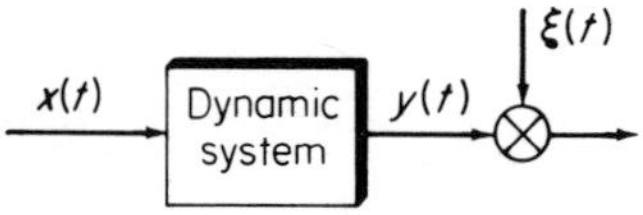

FIG. 7.12

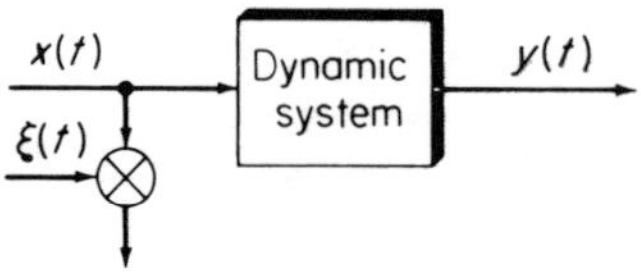

FIG. 7.13

Let us assume that the input of the dynamic system is measured with certain error (Fig. 7.13). Then instead of (7.61) and (7.62) we obtain, respectively,

$$J(\mathbf{c}) = \mathsf{M}\{F(y(t) - \mathbf{c}^{\mathrm{T}}\mathcal{B}^0(x(t) + \xi(t)))\} \tag{7.66}$$

and

$$\nabla J(\mathbf{c}) = -\mathsf{M}\{F'(y(t) - \mathbf{c}^{\mathrm{T}}\mathcal{B}^0(x(t)+\xi(t)))(\mathcal{B}^0(x(t)+\xi(t))\} = 0. \tag{7.67}$$

For quadratic functionals and linear systems we obtain

$$\begin{aligned}\nabla J(\mathbf{c}) = -\mathsf{M}\{[&y(t) - \mathbf{c}^{\mathrm{T}}\mathcal{B}^0(x(t)) \\ &-\mathbf{c}^{\mathrm{T}}\mathcal{B}^0(\xi(t))][\mathcal{B}^0(x(t)) + \mathcal{B}^0(\xi(t))]\} = 0.\end{aligned} \tag{7.68}$$

If noise $\xi(t)$ and signal $x(t)$ are uncorrelated, then

$$\mathsf{M}\{\mathcal{B}^0(x(t))\mathcal{B}^{0\mathrm{T}}(\xi(t))\} = 0. \tag{7.69}$$

By introducing notation

$$\mathsf{M}\{\mathcal{B}^{0}(\xi(t))\mathcal{B}^{0\mathrm{T}}(\xi(t))\} = D_B, \tag{7.70}$$

we simplify the condition (7.68):

$$\nabla J(\mathbf{c}) = -\mathsf{M}\{[y(t) - \mathbf{c}^{\mathrm{T}}\mathcal{B}^{0}(x(t))]\mathcal{B}^{0}(x(t)) - D_B\mathbf{c}\} = 0. \tag{7.71}$$

In this case (7.71) differs from (7.63), and thus the estimate is biased; it depends on D_B.

Nonlinear systems can be similarly examined if

$$\mathcal{B}^{0}(x(t) + \xi(t)) \tag{7.72}$$

is represented by a power series of the simplest operators $\mathcal{B}_1^{0\nu}(x(t))$, $\mathcal{B}_2^{0\mu}(\xi(t))$. Using a similar approach, we can also consider the case when the loss function is not quadratic.

7.12 Removing the Influence of Noise

In order to remove noise that causes the bias in the estimate, *a priori* information about noise is necessary. Let us assume that we know matrix D_B. It follows from (7.71) that for the unbiased estimate

$$\nabla J(\mathbf{c}^*) = D_B\mathbf{c}^* \neq 0. \tag{7.73}$$

But if we correct (7.71), that is, if we consider

$$\nabla J(\mathbf{c}) - D_B\mathbf{c} = -\mathsf{M}\{[y(t) - \mathbf{c}^{\mathrm{T}}\mathcal{B}^{0}(x(t)+\xi(t))]\mathcal{B}^{0}(x(t)+\xi(t))+D_B\mathbf{c}\} = 0, \tag{7.74}$$

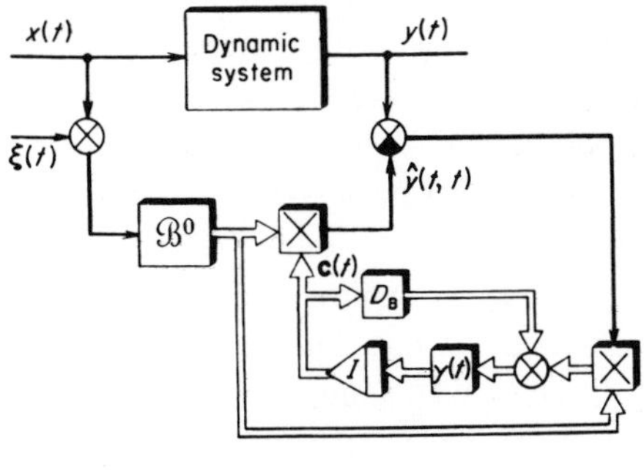

FIG. 7.14

it becomes equal to zero for $\mathbf{c} = \mathbf{c}^*$. From (7.38) we obtain the algorithm of learning

$$d\mathbf{c}(t)/dt = \gamma(t)\{[y(t) - \hat{y}(t, t)]\mathfrak{B}^0(x(t) + \xi(t)) + D_B\mathbf{c}(t)\}, \qquad (7.75)$$

that provides unbiased estimates.

The block diagram of such a general linear model is shown in Fig. 7.14. The case described can be generalized to the case of a nonlinear model.

7.13 Conclusion

Learning models can converge to the system under study in the best way according to the chosen criterion. Therefore, after reaching their goal of learning, learning models give us the characteristics of the studied systems. It is not difficult to establish a close relationship between learning models that perform identification of the systems under study and the learning systems of pattern recognition that recognize and classify situations.

Learning models permit identification of linear and nonlinear systems under normal operating conditions. Moreover, they can be used to obtain linear approximations of essentially nonlinear systems. Such linear approximations can be very useful in the analysis of nonlinear systems.

Comments

7.2 Similar functional series were introduced by Volterra [1]. They were applied in the analysis of nonlinear systems by Wiener [1] and Bode. Barret [1], Smets [1], Van Trees [1] and Roy and Sherman [1] have used functional Volterra series in the solution of concrete problems. The functional Volterra series are convenient for analysis and synthesis of nonlinear systems with analytic nonlinear dependence. In the cases when such dependence is not analytic (for instance, when the system has saturation, dead zones, hysteresis), we can apply the so-called orthonormal expansions of nonlinear functionals instead of Volterra expansions. These extensions have their roots in the works by Cameron and Martin [1]. They were systematically studied by Fan Dik Tin and Shilov [1]; also see the paper by Ahmed [1]. The case of an arbitrary measure was generalized by Popkov [1]. In this last paper, the reader can find many interesting applications of the orthogonal expansions of nonlinear functionals.

7.3 The models of similar structures were considered by Norkin [1] [the model corresponding to equation (7.7)] and by Popkov [1] [the model corresponding to Eq. (7.8)].

7.6 The problems of identification with similar models were discussed by Nemura and Arbachauskene [1, 2], Nemura and Sorkin [1], and Sakrison [1]. A scheme similar to the one shown in Fig. 7.6 was proposed and studied by Norkin [1].

7.8–7.9 Similar models in identification problems were considered in the works by Beisner [1], Roy and Sherman [1], and Shen and Rosenberg [1]. The obtained linear statistical equivalents of nonlinear systems under sufficient *a priori* information were described in the paper by Popkov [1].

7.12 An idea of a similar approach for removal of external disturbances was mentioned by V. P. Zhivoglaidov and V. H. Kaipov.

REFERENCES

Ahmed, N.
[1] Fourier analysis on Wiener measure space. *J. Franklin Inst.* **286**, No. 2 (1968).

Balakrishnan, A. V.
[1] Identification of control systems from input output data. *IFAC Symp. Identification Automat. Control Systems, Prague, 1967.*

Barret, J. F.
[1] The use of functionals in the analysis of nonlinear physical systems. Statist. Advisory Unit Rep. No. 1/57. Ministry of Supply, Great Britain, 1957.

Beisner, H. M.
[1] Recursive Bayesian method for estimation states of nonlinear system from sequential indirect observations. *IEEE Trans. System Sci. Cybernetics* **SSC-3**, No. 2 (1967).

Cameron, R. H., and Martin, W. T.
[1] The orthogonal development of nonlinear functionals in series of Fourier—Hermite functionals. *Ann. of Math.* **48**, No. 2 (1947).

Eykhoff, P.
[1] Process parameter and state estimation. *IFAC Symp. Identification Automat. Control Systems, Prague, 1967.*

Fan Dik Tin, and Shilov, G. E.
[1] Quadratic functionals in the space with gaussian metric. *Uspehi Mat. Nauk* **21**, No. 2 (1966).

Kneppo, I.
[1] Iteracna metoda identifikacie nelinearnych sustav. *Kibernetika (Kiev)* **5**, No. 3 (1969).

Nemura, A. A., and Arbachauskene, N. A.
[1] Rate of convergence of certain iterative algorithms for operation of adaptive models. *Liet. TSR Mokslu. Akad. Darb. Ser. B* **2** (53) (1968).

[2] An improvement in the rate of convergence of certain algorithms for operation of adaptive models. *Liet. TSR Mokslu. Akad. Darb. Ser. B* **2** (53) (1968).

Nemura, A. A., and Sorkin, E. D.

[1] Stability of self-organizing models. *Trudi Akad. Nauk Litovskoi SSR Ser. B.* **2**, No. 53 (1968).

Norkin, K. B.

[1] Search methods in the adjustment of model parameters for plant identification. *Avtomat. i Telemeh.* No. 11 (1968).

Popkov, Yu. S.

[1] Statistical models of nonlinear systems. *Avtomat. i Telemeh.* No. 10 (1967).

Roy, R. I., and Sherman, J.

[1] A learning technique for Volterra series representation. *IEEE Trans. Automatic Control* **AC-12**, No. 6 (1967).

Sakrison, D. J.

[1] The use of stochastic approximation to solve the system identification problem. *IEEE Trans. Automatic Control* **AC-12**, No. 5 (1967).

Shen, D. W. C., and Rosenberg, A.

[1] A nonlinear stochastic learning model. *Trans. Conf. Information Theory, Statist. Decision Functions, Random Processes, 3rd, Prague, 1964.* Czechoslovak Acad. of Sci., Prague, 1964.

Smets, H. B.

[1] Analysis and synthesis of nonlinear systems. *IRE Trans. Circuit Theory* **CT-7**, No. 4 (1960).

Taylor, L. W.

[1] Identification of human response models in manual control systems. *IFAC Symp. Identification Automat. Control Systems, Prague, 1967.*

Van Trees, G.

[1] "Synthesis of Nonlinear Control Systems." MIT Press, Cambridge, Massachusetts, 1962.

Volterra, V.

[1] "Theory of Functionals and of Integral and Integro-Differential Equations." Dover, New York, 1959.

Wiener, N.

[1] "Non-Linear Problems in Random Theory." MIT Press, Cambridge, Massachusetts, 1958.

Chapter VIII

Learning Filters

There is nothing more dangerous for new truth than old delusion.

W. GOETHE

8.1 Introduction

In this chapter, filters are considered as the systems that extract desired signals from the background noise. Very frequently the filters have to transform the signals, that is, to provide specified values of the signals and their corresponding derivatives or integrals. The synthesis of optimal filters is only possible under sufficiently complete *a priori* information, that is, when statistical characteristics of the signal and noise are known in advance. When *a priori* information is incomplete, the classical method of synthesizing optimal filters become inconvenient, and they have to be replaced by the adaptive approach. In this chapter, we present the principles of designing learning filters that can extract or transform desired signals in a best way after a period of learning in the conditions of insufficient *a priori* information.

8.2 Statement of the Problem

Let us assume that the input to the filter (Fig. 8.1) is

$$x(t) = s(t) + \xi(t), \tag{8.1}$$

where $s(t)$ is the desired signal and $\xi(t)$ is noise. From now on we shall always assume that $s(t)$ and $\xi(t)$ are uncorrelated. Both the signal and noise are stationary random processes with unknown probability density

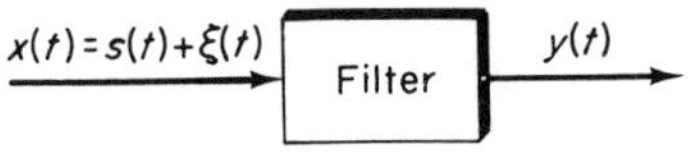

FIG. 8.1

functions. It is often required that output $y(t)$, which represents the response of the system on the input signal, converges in a certain sense to the desired function

$$y_0(t) = Ls(t), \tag{8.2}$$

where L is a certain linear operator (of prediction, integration, differentiation, and so forth). The distance measure between $y(t)$ and $y_0(t)$ is in general

$$J = \mathsf{M}\{F(y_0(t) - y(t))\}, \tag{8.3}$$

where $F(\cdot)$ is a certain convex function, or in the special case,

$$J = \mathsf{M}\{(y_0(t) - y(t))^2\}. \tag{8.4}$$

The mean-square-error criterion (8.4) was the foundation of the classical theory of optimal filtering. Thus, we have to determine the structure or the parameters of a given structure of the filter so that the functionals (8.3) and (8.4) reach their minimum. We shall clarify this problem by using the block diagram shown in Fig. 8.2. The input of the system is excited by a mixture of the signal and noise (8.1), and the input of the ideal filter is excited only by the desired signal. Outputs of these filters are then compared. The computed difference or error

$$\varepsilon(t) = y_0(t) - y(t) \tag{8.5}$$

is applied to the input of the quadratic transformer $F(\varepsilon) = \varepsilon^2$, and then averaged over the ensemble. This result is used in the classical theory of

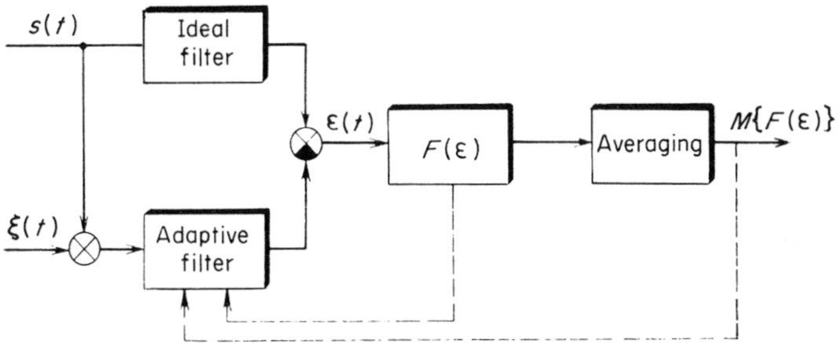

FIG. 8.2

optimal filtering. At the same time, the adaptive approach must use only a single realization of error. This difference is emphasized by the dotted line in Fig. 8.2.

The problem of designing adaptive filters would be solved if we could succeed in defining algorithms of learning that employ only the measurements of the available realization.

8.3 Structure of the Filter

Instead of the classical Kolmogorov–Wiener method, which defines the optimal characteristics of the synthetized filter, we shall here determine optimal parameters of a filter that has a sufficiently general but *a priori* given structure.

This latter approach appears to be more realistic since it avoids very complex questions of realizability. The structure of the filter is shown in Fig. 8.3. The input signal is applied to N linear filters with linearly independent impulse responses $k_\nu(t)$ $(\nu = 1, 2, \ldots, N)$. Each output signal is multiplied by a constant c_ν $(\nu = 1, 2, \ldots, N)$, and such signals are then summed to produce the output of the filter.

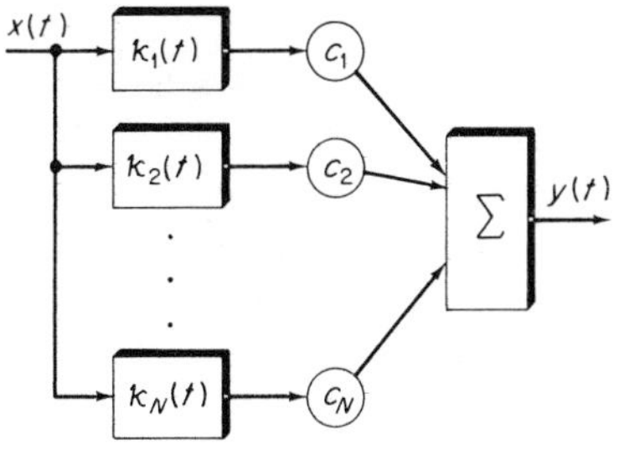

FIG. 8.3

The outputs of the corresponding linear filters are

$$\varphi_\nu(t) = \int_0^\infty k_\nu(\tau)x(t-\tau)\,d\tau = \mathcal{B}_\nu{}^0(x(t)), \tag{8.6}$$

where $\mathcal{B}_\nu$ is the convolution operator with kernel $k_\nu(t)$.

Therefore, the output of the filter is

$$\begin{aligned} y(t) &= \sum_{\nu=1}^{N} c_\nu \varphi_\nu(t) \\ &= \sum_{\nu=1}^{N} c_\nu \int_0^\infty k_\nu(\tau)x(t-\tau)\,d\tau = \sum_{\nu=1}^{N} c_\nu \mathcal{B}_\nu{}^0(x(t)). \end{aligned} \tag{8.7}$$

By introducing vector notation for the parameters

$$\mathbf{c} = (c_1, \ldots, c_N), \tag{8.8}$$

impulse characteristics

$$\mathbf{k}(t) = (k_1(t), \ldots, k_N(t)), \tag{8.9}$$

and outputs of the filters

$$\boldsymbol{\varphi}(t) = (\varphi_1(t), \ldots, \varphi_N(t)), \tag{8.10}$$

we can write (8.7) and (8.6) in the vector form

$$y(t) = \mathbf{c}^{\mathrm{T}}\boldsymbol{\varphi}(t), \tag{8.11}$$

where

$$\boldsymbol{\varphi}(t) = \int_0^\infty \mathbf{k}(\tau)x(t-\tau)\,d\tau = \mathcal{B}^0(x(t)). \tag{8.12}$$

The block diagram of the filter corresponding to (8.11) and (8.12) is shown in Fig. 8.4. The problem of designing an optimal filter is then reduced to

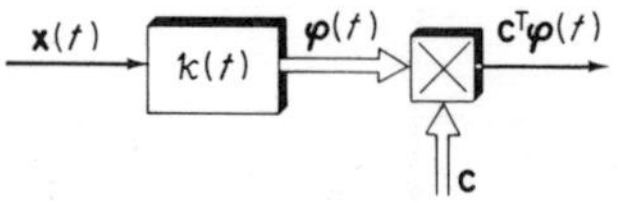

FIG. 8.4

one of finding optimal vector $\mathbf{c} = \mathbf{c}^*$ that minimizes functional (8.4). This functional, due to (8.11), has the form

$$J(\mathbf{c}) = \mathsf{M}\{(y_0(t) - \mathbf{c}^{\mathrm{T}}\boldsymbol{\varphi}(t))^2\}. \tag{8.13}$$

Depending on the degree of completeness in *a priori* information, the solution is obtained on the basis of either the classical or the adaptive approach.

8.4 Optimal Wiener Filter

Let us consider the simplest case when the desired output is the useful signal, that is,

$$y_0(t) = s(t). \tag{8.14}$$

Then from (7.13) we obtain

$$J(\mathbf{c}) = \mathsf{M}\{(s(t) - \mathbf{c}^{\mathrm{T}}\boldsymbol{\varphi}(t))^2\}. \tag{8.15}$$

The condition of the minimum of $J(\mathbf{c})$ is written in the usual form:

$$\nabla J(\mathbf{c}) = -2\mathsf{M}\{(s(t) - \mathbf{c}^{\mathrm{T}}\boldsymbol{\varphi}(t))\boldsymbol{\varphi}(t)\} = 0, \tag{8.16}$$

or

$$\mathsf{M}\{s(t)\boldsymbol{\varphi}(t)\} = \mathsf{M}\{\boldsymbol{\varphi}(t)\boldsymbol{\varphi}^{\mathrm{T}}(t)\}\mathbf{c}, \tag{8.17}$$

and from this we obtain the optimal parameter vector

$$\mathbf{c}^* = [\mathsf{M}\{\boldsymbol{\varphi}(t)\boldsymbol{\varphi}^{\mathrm{T}}(t)\}]^{-1}\mathsf{M}\{s(t)\boldsymbol{\varphi}(t)\}. \tag{8.18}$$

Taking into consideration (8.12) and (8.1), and since $s(t)$ and $\xi(t)$ are uncorrelated, we obtain

$$\begin{aligned}\mathsf{M}\{s(t)\boldsymbol{\varphi}(t)\} &= \int_0^\infty \mathbf{k}(\tau)\mathsf{M}\{s(t)x(t-\tau)\}\,d\tau \\ &= \int_0^\infty \mathbf{k}(\tau)R_{ss}(\tau)\,d\tau,\end{aligned} \tag{8.19}$$

where

$$R_{ss}(\tau) = \mathsf{M}\{s(t)s(t-\tau)\} \tag{8.20}$$

is the autocorrelation function of the useful signal. Similarly,

$$\begin{aligned}\mathsf{M}\{\boldsymbol{\varphi}(t)\boldsymbol{\varphi}^{\mathrm{T}}(t))\} &= \int_0^\infty\int_0^\infty \mathbf{k}(\tau)\mathbf{k}^{\mathrm{T}}(\lambda)\mathsf{M}\{x(t-\tau)x(t-\lambda)\}\,d\tau\,d\lambda \\ &= \int_0^\infty\int_0^\infty \mathbf{k}(\tau)\mathbf{k}^{\mathrm{T}}(\lambda)R_{xx}(\tau-\lambda)\,d\tau\,d\lambda,\end{aligned} \tag{8.21}$$

where

$$R_{xx}(\tau - \lambda) = \mathsf{M}\{x(t - \tau)x(t - \lambda)\} \tag{8.22}$$

is the autocorrelation function of the input signal. Therefore, the optimal vector of parameters (8.18) is

$$\mathbf{c}^* = \left[\int_0^\infty \int_0^\infty \mathbf{k}(\tau)\mathbf{k}^{\mathrm{T}}(\lambda)R_{xx}(\tau - \lambda)\, d\tau\, d\lambda\right]^{-1} \int_0^\infty \mathbf{k}(\tau)R_{ss}(\tau)\, d\tau. \tag{8.23}$$

The minimum of the functional (8.15) is reached for $\mathbf{c} = \mathbf{c}^*$:

$$\begin{aligned} J(\mathbf{c}^*) &= \min_{\mathbf{c}} J(\mathbf{c}) \\ &= R_{ss}(0) - \int_0^\infty \mathbf{k}^{\mathrm{T}}(\tau)R_{ss}(\tau)\, d\tau \\ &\quad \times \left[\int_0^\infty \int_0^\infty \mathbf{k}(\tau)\mathbf{k}^{\mathrm{T}}(\lambda)R_{xx}(\tau - \lambda)\, d\tau\, d\lambda\right]^{-1} \int_0^\infty \mathbf{k}(\tau)R_{ss}(\tau)\, d\tau. \end{aligned} \tag{8.24}$$

This minimal value of the functional, which characterizes the mean-square error defines the quality of the optimal filter.

It can be seen from (8.23) that in order to determine the optimal vector of parameters, we must know the autocorrelation functions $R_{ss}(\tau)$ and $R_{xx}(\tau)$. We shall now examine the cases when *a priori* information is incomplete.

8.5 Learning Wiener Filter

Let us assume that *a priori* information about statistical characteristics of the noise and the useful signal does not exist. We shall write the functional (8.15) in the following form:

$$J(\mathbf{c}) = \mathsf{M}\{\varepsilon^2(t, \mathbf{c})\}, \tag{8.25}$$

where

$$\varepsilon(t, \mathbf{c}) = s(t) - \mathbf{c}^{\mathrm{T}}\boldsymbol{\varphi}(t) \tag{8.26}$$

is the error. The condition of the minimum (8.16) then takes the form

$$\nabla J(\mathbf{c}) = -2\mathsf{M}\{\varepsilon(t, \mathbf{c})\boldsymbol{\varphi}(t)\} = 0. \tag{8.27}$$

Using continuous algorithms of learning, we obtain from (8.27)

$$d\mathbf{c}(t)/dt = \gamma(t)\varepsilon(t, t, \mathbf{c})\boldsymbol{\varphi}(t), \tag{8.28}$$

where

$$\varepsilon(t, t, \mathbf{c}) = s(t) - \hat{y}(t, t) = s(t) - \mathbf{c}^{\mathrm{T}}(t)\boldsymbol{\varphi}(t). \tag{8.29}$$

The block diagram of the learning filter designed according to this algorithm is shown in Fig. 8.5. However, in its realization, we are confronted with the following difficulty: in order to determine error, we must know the desired function, that is, in this case, the useful signal. But if the useful signal is known *a priori*, this question arises: is the filter really needed for extracting such a signal? The method presented for construction

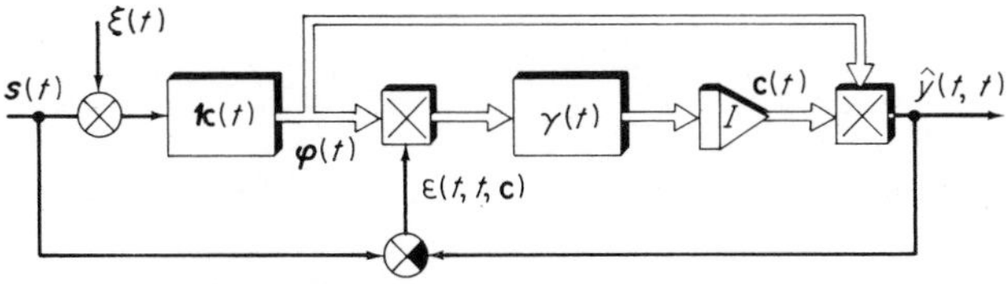

FIG. 8.5

of learning filters thus has a very narrow area of application. This is due to our desire to obtain a learning filter without any *a priori* information about the useful signal and noise. We shall now attempt to relax this condition, and use *a priori* information about statistical properties of the noise or the signal.

8.6 Learning Wiener Filter with Known *A Priori* Information about Noise

Let us now assume that we know the autocorrelation function of the noise

$$R_{\xi\xi}(\tau) = \mathsf{M}\{\xi(t)\xi(t-\tau)\}. \tag{8.30}$$

Using $s(t)$ from (8.1),

$$s(t) = x(t) - \xi(t), \tag{8.31}$$

we write the functional (8.15) in this form:

$$J(\mathbf{c}) = \mathsf{M}\{(x(t) - \mathbf{c}^{\mathrm{T}}\boldsymbol{\varphi}(t))^2\} + \mathsf{M}\{\xi^2(t)\} - 2\mathsf{M}\{(x(t) - \mathbf{c}^{\mathrm{T}}\boldsymbol{\varphi}(t))\xi(t)\}. \tag{8.32}$$

By taking into consideration the independence between $s(t)$ and $\xi(t)$, and using the expression (8.12), we find that

$$\mathsf{M}\{(x(t) - \mathbf{c}^{\mathrm{T}}\boldsymbol{\varphi}(t))\xi(t)\} = \mathsf{M}\{\xi^2(t)\} - \mathbf{c}^{\mathrm{T}} \int_0^\infty \mathbf{k}(\tau) R_{\xi\xi}(\tau)\, d\tau, \tag{8.33}$$

where $R_{\xi\xi}(\tau)$ is the autocorrelation function of the noise (8.30). We can now write the functional (8.32) as

$$J(\mathbf{c}) = \mathsf{M}\{(x(t) - \mathbf{c}^{\mathrm{T}}\boldsymbol{\varphi}(t))^2\} - R_{\xi\xi}(0) + 2\mathbf{c}^{\mathrm{T}} \int_0^\infty \mathbf{k}(\tau) R_{\xi\xi}(\tau)\, d\tau. \tag{8.34}$$

The condition of the minimum of this functional is

$$\nabla J(\mathbf{c}) = -2\mathsf{M}\left\{(x(t) - \mathbf{c}^{\mathrm{T}}\boldsymbol{\varphi}(t))\boldsymbol{\varphi}(t) - \int_0^\infty \mathbf{k}(\tau) R_{\xi\xi}(\tau)\, d\tau\right\} = 0. \tag{8.35}$$

Using continuous algorithms of learning (2.7), we obtain from (8.35)

$$d\mathbf{c}(t)/dt = \gamma(t)[(x(t) - \hat{y}(t, t))\boldsymbol{\varphi}(t) - \mathbf{r}^{\xi}], \tag{8.36}$$

where

$$\hat{y}(t, t) = \mathbf{c}^{\mathrm{T}}(t)\boldsymbol{\varphi}(t), \tag{8.37}$$

and vector

$$\mathbf{r}^{\xi} = \int_0^\infty \mathbf{k}(\tau) R_{\xi\xi}(\tau)\, d\tau \tag{8.38}$$

is computed in advance according to the vector impulse characteristic of the noise autocorrelation function. The algorithm of learning (8.36), in contrast to the algorithm of learning (8.28), employs only those quantities that can be measured directly: input signal $x(t)$ and output of the filter, $\hat{y}(t, t) = \mathbf{c}^{\mathrm{T}}(t)\boldsymbol{\varphi}(t)$.

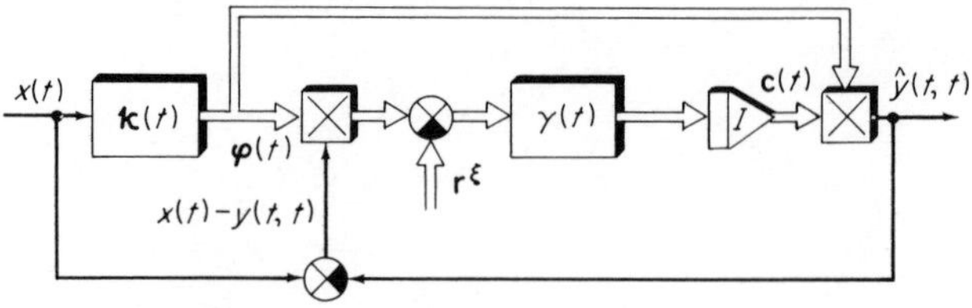

FIG. 8.6

The block diagram of the learning Wiener filter is shown in Fig. 8.6. The available *a priori* information—vector $\mathbf{r}^{\xi}$ (Eq. (8.38))—generates the correction in the random gradient.

8.7 Learning Wiener Filter with Known *A Priori* Information about the Signal

We shall now assume that the autocorrelation function of the signal

$$R_{ss}(\tau) = \mathsf{M}\{s(t)s(t-\tau)\} \tag{8.39}$$

is known. In this case, it is convenient to represent the functional (8.15) in the form

$$J(\mathbf{c}) = \mathsf{M}\{(\mathbf{c}^{\mathrm{T}}\boldsymbol{\varphi}(t))^2\} + \mathsf{M}\{s^2(t)\} - 2\mathsf{M}\{(\mathbf{c}^{\mathrm{T}}\boldsymbol{\varphi}(t))s(t)\}. \tag{8.40}$$

Due to the independence of $s(t)$ and $\xi(t)$, and using (8.12),

$$\mathsf{M}\{(\mathbf{c}^{\mathrm{T}}\boldsymbol{\varphi}(t))s(t)\} = \mathbf{c}^{\mathrm{T}} \int_0^\infty \mathbf{k}(\tau)R_{ss}(\tau)\, d\tau, \tag{8.41}$$

since

$$\mathsf{M}\{s^2(t)\} = R_{ss}(0), \tag{8.42}$$

Eq. (8.40) can be written in the form

$$J(\mathbf{c}) = \mathsf{M}\{(\mathbf{c}^{\mathrm{T}}\boldsymbol{\varphi}(t))^2\} + R_{ss}(0) - 2\mathbf{c}^{\mathrm{T}} \int_0^\infty \mathbf{k}(\tau)R_{ss}(\tau)\, d\tau. \tag{8.43}$$

The condition of the minimum of $J(\mathbf{c})$ is

$$\nabla J(\mathbf{c}) = 2\mathsf{M}\left\{(\mathbf{c}^{\mathrm{T}}\boldsymbol{\varphi}(t))\boldsymbol{\varphi}(t) - \int_0^\infty \mathbf{k}(\tau)R_{ss}(\tau)\, d\tau\right\} = 0. \tag{8.44}$$

Using continuous algorithms of learning (2.7), we obtain from (8.43)

$$d\mathbf{c}(t)/dt = -\gamma(t)[\hat{y}(t, t)\boldsymbol{\varphi}(t) - \mathbf{r}^s], \tag{8.45}$$

where $\hat{y}(t, t)$ is obtained according to (8.37), and the vector

$$\mathbf{r}^s = \int_0^\infty \mathbf{k}(\tau)R_{ss}(\tau)\, d\tau \tag{8.46}$$

is computed in advance using vector impulse characteristic and the autocorrelation function of the signal. In this case, the algorithm of learning (8.45) employs only those quantities that can be directly measured.

The block diagram of the learning filter is shown in Fig. 8.7. The available *a priori* information—vector $\mathbf{r}^s$—provides the correction to the random gradient.

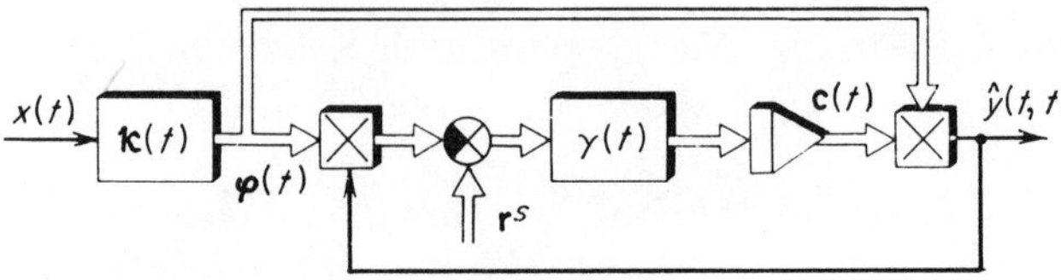

FIG. 8.7

Learning Wiener filters described above are asymptotically optimal. Their realization is simple since they use a single "scalar" amplifier with the time-varying gain $\gamma(t)$. But this simplicity is obtained at the cost of suboptimal learning.

8.8 A Generalization

Until now these learning Wiener filters have been solving a relatively simple problem of extracting a signal $s(t)$ from the background noise $\xi(t)$. But when *a priori* information about the signal is available, the learning Wiener filter can perform the more complex operations mentioned in Section 8.2. Let the desired function have the form (8.12). The examples of such desired functions are presented in Table 8.1.

TABLE 8.1

Operation	Desired function	Operator
Reproduction	$y_0(t) = s(t)$	1
Prediction	$y_0(t) = s(t)$	e^{pt_0}
Differentiation	$y_0(t) = ds(t)/dt$	p
Integration	$y_0(t) = \int_0^t s(\tau)\, d\tau$	$1/p$

By substituting $s(t)$ with $y_0(t)$ in (8.40), we obtain

$$J(\mathbf{c}) = \mathsf{M}\{(\mathbf{c}^{\mathrm{T}}\boldsymbol{\varphi}(t))^2\} + \mathsf{M}\{y_0^2(t)\} - 2\mathsf{M}\{(\mathbf{c}^{\mathrm{T}}\boldsymbol{\varphi}(t))y_0(t)\}. \tag{8.47}$$

Since $s(t)$ and $\xi(t)$, and thus $y_0(t)$ and $\xi(t)$ are uncorrelated, instead of (8.41), we obtain

$$\mathsf{M}\{(\mathbf{c}^{\mathrm{T}}\boldsymbol{\varphi}(t))y_0(t)\} = \mathbf{c}^{\mathrm{T}} \int_0^\infty \mathbf{k}(\tau)R_{y_0 s}(\tau)\, d\tau, \tag{8.48}$$

where

$$R_{y_0s}(\tau) = \mathsf{M}\{y_0(t)s(t-\tau)\}. \tag{8.49}$$

Instead of the autocorrelation function of the useful signal, $R_{ss}(\tau)$, we now obtain the cross-correlation function of the desired function and the useful signal $R_{y_0s}(\tau)$. The form of the algorithm (8.45) stays unchanged:

$$d\mathbf{c}(t)/dt = -\gamma(t)[\hat{y}(t, t)\boldsymbol{\varphi}(t) - \mathbf{r}^{y_0s}], \tag{8.50}$$

$$\hat{y}(t, t) = \mathbf{c}^{\mathrm{T}}(t)\boldsymbol{\varphi}(t), \tag{8.51}$$

but now

$$\mathbf{r}^{y_0s} = \int_0^\infty \mathbf{k}(\tau)R_{y_0s}(\tau)\,d\tau. \tag{8.52}$$

Therefore, in order to design the learning Wiener filter that extracts not only a signal $s(t)$ but also a signal that is defined by a linear transformation of the useful signal, it is sufficient to replace vector $\mathbf{r}^s$ in Fig. 8.7 by a vector $\mathbf{r}^{y_0s}$ (Eq. (8.52)).

8.9 Optimal Learning Wiener Filters

If it is necessary to learn in a certain best sense, then, as already shown in Chapter III, the solution becomes more complex. First of all, the scalar amplifier $\gamma(t)$ is replaced by a matrix amplifier, and then instead of (8.36), we obtain

$$d\mathbf{c}(t)/dt = \Gamma(t)[(x(t) - \hat{y}(t, t))\boldsymbol{\varphi}(t) - \mathbf{r}^{\xi}]. \tag{8.53}$$

The matrix $\Gamma(t)$ must satisfy Eq. (3.82), which in this case has the form

$$d\Gamma(t)/dt = -\Gamma(t)[\boldsymbol{\varphi}(t)\boldsymbol{\varphi}^{\mathrm{T}}(t)]\Gamma(t). \tag{8.54}$$

If we could compute in advance the initial conditions $\mathbf{c}(t_0)$ and $\Gamma(t_0)$, we would be able to build an optimal learning Wiener filter. For arbitrary initial conditions, we obtain only a suboptimal learning Wiener filter.

The block diagram of such a suboptimal Wiener filter, which represents Algorithms (8.53) and (8.54), is shown in Fig. 8.8. Similarly, we obtain a suboptimal algorithm corresponding to (8.45):

$$d\mathbf{c}(t)/dt = -\Gamma(t)[(\hat{y}(t, t))\boldsymbol{\varphi}(t) - \mathbf{r}^s], \tag{8.55}$$

where $\Gamma(t)$ satisfies Eq. (8.54).

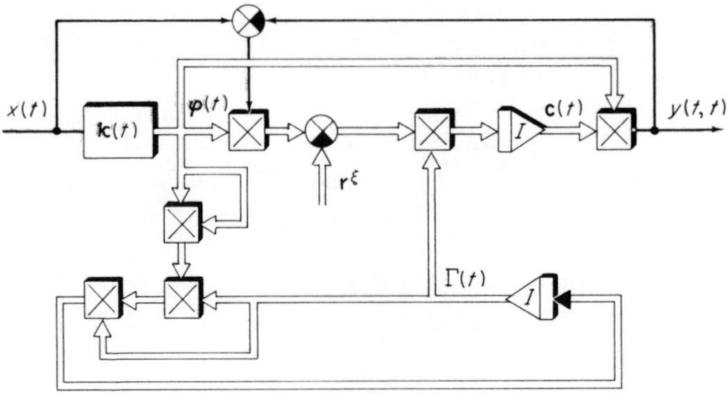

FIG. 8.8

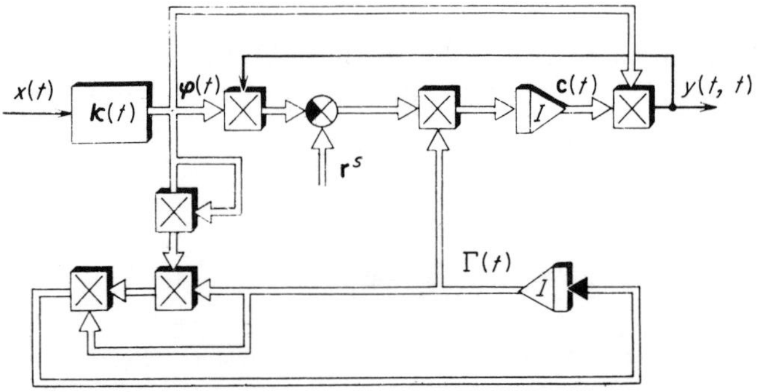

FIG. 8.9

The block diagram of the suboptimal learning Wiener filter that realizes Algorithms (8.55) and (8.54) is shown in Fig. 8.9. If $\mathbf{r}^s$ is replaced in it by $\mathbf{r}^{y_0 s}$, this filter can accomplish a more complex operation than extraction of a useful signal from a background noise. Therefore, the increased complexity of learning filters permits an improvement in learning. For an external signal $x(t)$ of duration t, the obtained estimates $\mathbf{c}(t_*)$, which form the output signal $\hat{y}(t, t)$, have minimal variance. In other words, for an optimal learning filter

$$\mathsf{M}\{\| \mathbf{c}(t_*) - \mathbf{c}^* \|^2\} \to \min. \tag{8.56}$$

8.10 Learning Filters of Another Type

In the preceding section, we considered learning filters of the Kolmogorov–Wiener type. For such filters, the goal of learning is minimization of the mean-square error. In practice, we are usually confronted by the necessity to consider other goals of learning. For instance, we may have to train the filter to extract a narrow-band signal of unknown frequency either from the background noise or from other narrow-band signals of less power. For the solution of this problem, we must use a functional different from (8.4).

Let us designate

$$y(t) = (\mathbf{c} + \mathbf{e}_N a)^{\mathrm{T}} \boldsymbol{\varphi}(t), \tag{8.57}$$

where

$$\mathbf{c} = (c_1, \ldots, c_{2N}), \qquad \mathbf{e}_N = (\underbrace{0, \ldots, 0, 1}_{N}, 0, \ldots, 0), \tag{8.58}$$

and

$$\boldsymbol{\varphi}(t) = \int_0^\infty \mathbf{k}(\tau) x(t - \tau)\, d\tau \tag{8.59}$$

is the output signal of the filter. Similarly,

$$y_\xi(t) = (\mathbf{c} + \mathbf{e}_N a)^{\mathrm{T}} \boldsymbol{\varphi}_\xi(t), \tag{8.60}$$

where

$$\boldsymbol{\varphi}_\xi(t) = \int_0^\infty k(\tau) \xi(t - \tau)\, d\tau \tag{8.61}$$

is the component of the output signal caused by noise.

As a goal of learning, we shall select now the maximum of the difference between signal and noise power, that is, the maximum of

$$J(\mathbf{c}) = \mathsf{M}\{y^2(t)\} - \mathsf{M}\{y_\xi^2(t)\}. \tag{8.62}$$

Since

$$\mathsf{M}\{y_\xi^2(t)\} = \mathsf{M}\{[(\mathbf{c} + \mathbf{e}_N a)^{\mathrm{T}} \boldsymbol{\varphi}_\xi(t)]^2\}, \tag{8.63}$$

or

$$\mathsf{M}\{y_\xi^2(t)\} = (\mathbf{c} + \mathbf{e}_N a)^{\mathrm{T}} U (\mathbf{c} + e_N a), \tag{8.64}$$

where

$$U = \int_0^\infty \int_0^\infty \mathbf{k}^{\mathrm{T}}(\tau) R_{\xi\xi}(\tau - \lambda) \mathbf{k}(\lambda)\, d\tau\, d\lambda, \tag{8.65}$$

is a matrix that depends on the statistical properties of noise, we can write (8.62) in the form

$$J(\mathbf{c}) = \mathsf{M}\{y^2(t)\} - (\mathbf{c} + \mathbf{e}_N a)^{\mathrm{T}} U (\mathbf{c} + \mathbf{e}_N a). \tag{8.66}$$

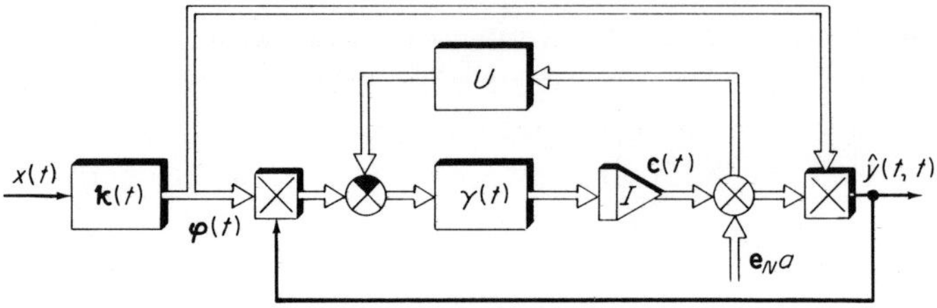

FIG. 8.10

The condition of the minimum of $J(\mathbf{c})$ is then

$$\nabla J(\mathbf{c}) = 2\mathsf{M}\{y(t)\,\nabla_{\mathbf{c}} y(t) - U(\mathbf{c} + \mathbf{e}_N a)\} = 0. \tag{8.67}$$

Considering that

$$\nabla_{\mathbf{c}} y(t) = \nabla_{\mathbf{c}}[(\mathbf{c} + \mathbf{e}_N a)^{\mathrm{T}} \boldsymbol{\varphi}(t)] = \boldsymbol{\varphi}(t), \tag{8.68}$$

we write (8.67) as

$$\mathsf{M}\{y(t)\boldsymbol{\varphi}(t) - U(\mathbf{c} + \mathbf{e}_N a)\} = 0. \tag{8.69}$$

Now using continuous algorithms of learning, we obtain

$$d\mathbf{c}(t)/dt = \gamma(t)[\hat{y}(t, t)\boldsymbol{\varphi}(t) - U(\mathbf{c}(t) + \mathbf{e}_N a)], \tag{8.70}$$

where

$$\hat{y}(t, t) = (\mathbf{c}(t) + \mathbf{e}_N a)^{\mathrm{T}} \boldsymbol{\varphi}(t). \tag{8.71}$$

The block diagram of the learning filter that realizes Algorithm (8.70) is shown in Fig. 8.10.

8.11 Optimal Learning Filter

By substituting a scalar coefficient $\gamma(t)$ in (8.70) with the matrix $\Gamma(t)$, we obtain

$$d\mathbf{c}(t)/dt = \Gamma(t)[\hat{y}(t, t)\boldsymbol{\varphi}(t) - U(\mathbf{c}(t) + \mathbf{e}_N a)]. \tag{8.72}$$

We shall constrain the behavior of $\Gamma(t)$ by Eq. (3.82), which in this case has the form

$$d\Gamma(t)/dt = -\Gamma(t)(\boldsymbol{\varphi}(t)\boldsymbol{\varphi}^{\mathrm{T}}(t) - U)\Gamma(t). \tag{8.73}$$

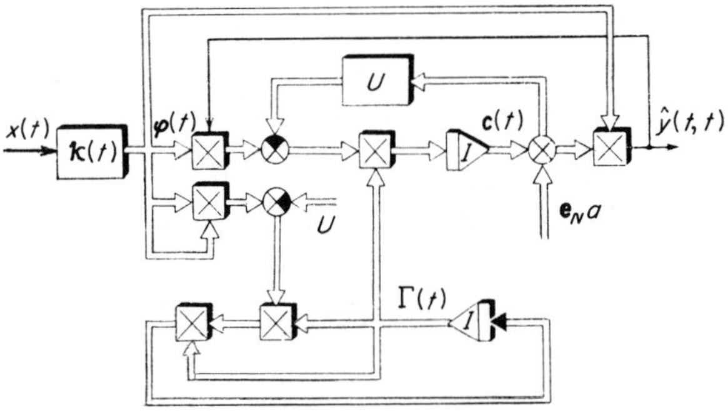

FIG. 8.11

For arbitrary $\mathbf{c}(t_0)$ and $\Gamma(t_0)$ we obtain algorithms of suboptimal learning.

The block diagram of such a suboptimal filter that realizes algorithms of learning (8.72) and (8.73) is presented in Fig. 8.11.

8.12 Conclusion

Learning filters differ from the learning pattern recognition systems and learning models. In pattern recognition systems, the correct classification of each situation is provided by a teacher, and in the case of learning models, for each value of the input signal, we know the corresponding output signal. This last quantity corresponds to the classifications provided by the teacher. It seems that such a role should be played in the problems of filtering by the desired function that represents a useful signal or its transformation. But in this lies the difficulty. As a rule, the desired function cannot be physically realized, and the whole idea of building learning filters consists of employing minimal *a priori* information (for instance, autocorrelation functions of the signal or of the noise) in order to use only observed or measured realizations. This idea permeated the chapter. In addition to the design of learning Wiener filters, we have also considered the possibility of designing filters of another type.

Comments

8.2 The problem of synthesizing optimal filters arose in the 1940s. The first work related to the filtering of random series was by Kolmogorov [1]. The theory of optimal filters for random processes was developed by Wiener [1].

8.3 Similar filter structures were described by many authors. We mention a very interesting paper by Sakrison [1] that covers a sufficiently large number of communication and also filtering problems.

8.4 At first, the specialists in the design of radar systems considered the theory of optimal Wiener filters to be very complicated. But as time passed, the mathematical level of the specialists sharply increased and the Kolmogorov–Wiener theory is considered to be self-understood and trivial. In our opinion, this evaluation of the theory is the highest possible one. The Kolmogorov–Wiener theory lead to the design of optimal transfer functions of the filter. Knowing the optimal transfer function, one may attempt to determine the structure and the parameters of the optimal filter. However, as is often the case, the optimal filter cannot be realized, and then one has to be satisfied by a quasioptimal filter.

The well-known mathematician Phillips (see James *et al.* [1]), who also had an interest in practical problems, suggested the design of optimal filters with a given structure. This meant that optimal parameters of the filter had to be found. If the optimum existed, then all the questions of physical realizability do not apply since such an optimal filter is physically realizable. This approach introduced by Phillips was used here.

8.5 We have given the name of Wiener filter to the designed optimal filter although the method of design was not suggested by Wiener. This method of solution is close to one proposed by Phillips (see James *et al.* [1]).

8.6 A similar approach to the design of realizable learning filters when there is *a priori* information about noise was described by Sakrison [1]. Another approach was described by Davisson [1–6].

REFERENCES

Davisson, L. D.

[1] A theory of adaptive compression. *Proc. Nat. Electron. Conf.* **20** (1964).

[2] The filtering of time series with unknown signal statistics. *Proc. Nat. Electron. Conf.* **21** (1965).

[3] Adaptive linear filtering when signal distributions are unknown. *IEEE Trans. Automat. Control* **11**, No. 4 (1966).

[4] A theory of adaptive filtering. *IEEE Trans. Information Theory* **IT-12**, No. 2 (1966).

[5] A theory of adaptive data compression. *Advan. Communication Systems* **2** (1966).

[6] An approximation theory of prediction for data compression. *IEEE Trans. Information Theory* **IT-13**, No. 2 (1967).

James, H. M., Nichols, N. B., and Phillips, R. S.

[1] "Theory of Servomechanisms" (MIT Radiation Lab. Ser.), Vol. 25, pp. 308–368. McGraw-Hill, New York, 1947.

Kolmogorov, A. N.

[1] Interpolation and extrapolation of stationary random series. *Izv. Akad. Nauk SSSR Ser. Mat.* **5**, No. 1 (1941).

Sakrison, D. J.

[1] Stochastic approximation. A recursive method for solving regression problem. *Advan. Communication Systems* **2** (1966).

Wiener, N.

[1] "Nonlinear Problems in Random Theory." MIT Press, Cambridge, Massachusetts, 1958.

Chapter IX

Examples of Learning Systems

It is a fact that all general theories grow from studies of particular problems and they do not have any meaning unless they can explain more specific questions and bring some order in them.

R. COURANT

9.1 Introduction

This final chapter is devoted to the application of learning algorithms in the construction of various learning systems. Specific examples of learning systems of pattern recognition, classification, identification, filtering, and control are presented. Special attention is given to the learning systems for solving the problems of standardization and fault detection.

Learning systems can be either built in the form of a special analog, discrete or hybrid devices, or realized on digital computers. In the latter case, the algorithms of learning take the form of the corresponding digital computer programs. Experimental results are presented for several specific systems.

9.2 Perceptron

Let us examine a relatively complex goal of learning represented by the minimum of the functional

$$J(\mathbf{c}) = \mathsf{M}\{(y - \operatorname{sign} \mathbf{c}^{\mathrm{T}}\boldsymbol{\varphi}(x))\mathbf{c}^{\mathrm{T}}\boldsymbol{\varphi}(\mathbf{x})\}, \tag{9.1}$$

where

$$\operatorname{sign} \mathbf{c}^{\mathrm{T}}\boldsymbol{\varphi}(\mathbf{x}) = \begin{cases} -1 & \text{if} \quad \mathbf{c}^{\mathrm{T}}\boldsymbol{\varphi}(\mathbf{x}) < 0 \\ 1 & \text{if} \quad \mathbf{c}^{\mathrm{T}}\boldsymbol{\varphi}(\mathbf{x}) > 0 \end{cases} \tag{9.2}$$

and

$$y = \begin{cases} -1 & \text{if} \quad \mathbf{x} \in X_1^{\,0} \\ 1 & \text{if} \quad \mathbf{x} \in X_2^{\,0}. \end{cases} \tag{9.3}$$

This functional is not convex, and it becomes equal to zero for $\mathbf{c} = \mathbf{c}^*$ and $\mathbf{c} = 0$. Using the generalized gradient, (see Section 1.2), we can write the condition of the minimum (9.1) in the usual form:

$$\nabla J(\mathbf{c}) = -\mathsf{M}\{(y - \operatorname{sign} \mathbf{c}^{\mathrm{T}}\boldsymbol{\varphi}(\mathbf{x}))\boldsymbol{\varphi}(\mathbf{x})\} = 0. \tag{9.4}$$

In accordance with (9.4), we obtain an algorithm of learning

$$\mathbf{c}[n] = \mathbf{c}[n-1] + \mathfrak{a}\boldsymbol{\gamma}[n](y[n] - \operatorname{sign} \mathbf{c}^{\mathrm{T}}[n-1]\boldsymbol{\varphi}(\mathbf{x}[n]))\boldsymbol{\varphi}(\mathbf{x}[n]). \tag{9.5}$$

Let us select for the component vector functions,

$$\boldsymbol{\varphi}(\mathbf{x}) = (\varphi_1(\mathbf{x}), \ldots, \varphi_N(\mathbf{x})), \tag{9.6}$$

the threshold functions

$$\boldsymbol{\varphi}_\nu(\mathbf{x}) = \operatorname{sign}\left(\sum_{\mu=1}^{M} a_{\nu\mu}x_\mu - b_\nu\right), \tag{9.7}$$

where $a_{\nu\mu}$ and b_ν are the weights and the threshold specified in advance. Then, Algorithm (9.5) can be written in the extended form

$$\begin{aligned} c_\nu[n] = c_\nu[n-1] + \gamma_\nu[n]\Bigg[y[n] - \operatorname{sign} \sum_{\eta=1}^{N} c_\eta[n-1] \\ \times \operatorname{sign}\left(\sum_{\mu=1}^{M} a_{\nu\mu}x_\mu[n] - b_\eta\right)\Bigg] \operatorname{sign}\left(\sum_{\mu=1}^{M} a_{\nu\mu}x_\mu[n] - b_\eta\right). \end{aligned} \tag{9.8}$$

These algorithms are actually realized by the classical scheme of Rosenblatt's perceptron that is shown in Fig. 9.1. The inputs of the threshold elements are simultaneously excited by the codes $\mathbf{x}[n]$ of the patterns, and

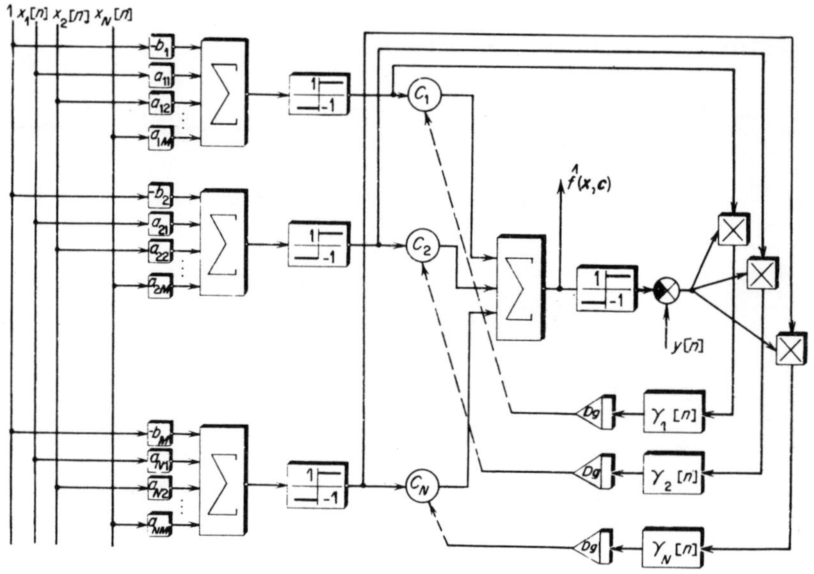

FIG. 9.1

their correct classification $y[n]$. After a period of learning, the coefficients $c_\nu[n] \to c_\nu^*$ of the discriminant function

$$\hat{f}(\mathbf{x}, \mathbf{c}^*) = \sum_{\nu=1}^{N} c_\nu^* \operatorname{sign}\left(\sum_{\mu=1}^{M} a_{\nu\mu} x_\mu[n] - b_\nu\right) \tag{9.9}$$

for two pattern classes.

9.3 Adaline

Adaline is an abbreviated name for the adaptive linear threshold elements. Adaline represents the simplest form of the perceptron that consists of a single threshold element.

Adaline's goal of learning consists of reaching the minimum of a quadratic functional

$$J(\mathbf{c}) = \mathsf{M}\{\tfrac{1}{2}(y - \mathbf{c}^T \boldsymbol{\varphi}(\mathbf{x}))^2\}, \tag{9.10}$$

in the special case when

$$\boldsymbol{\varphi}(\mathbf{x}) = \mathbf{x} = (1, x_2, \ldots, x_N), \tag{9.11}$$

and the condition of minimum has the form

$$\nabla J(\mathbf{c}) = -\mathsf{M}\{(y - \mathbf{c}^T \mathbf{x})\mathbf{x}\} = 0. \tag{9.12}$$

Therefore, the algorithm of learning is a very simple one:

$$\mathbf{c}[n] = \mathbf{c}[n-1] + \boldsymbol{\Gamma}\boldsymbol{\gamma}[n](y[n] - \mathbf{c}^{\mathrm{T}}[n-1]\mathbf{x}[n])\mathbf{x}[n] \tag{9.13}$$

or, in expanded form,

$$c_\nu[n] = c_\nu[n-1] + \gamma_\nu[n]\Big(y[n] - \sum_{\nu=1}^{N} c_\nu[n-1]x_\nu[n]\Big)x_\nu[n]. \tag{9.14}$$

Usually $\gamma_\nu[n]$ are constant and equal:

$$\gamma_\nu[n] = a_\nu/(N+1), \tag{9.15}$$

where N is the dimension of the vector $\mathbf{x}$. When noise is present, instead of (9.15)

$$\gamma_\nu[n] = a_\nu/n \tag{9.16}$$

should be used.

The block diagram of an adaline, representing the linear algorithms presented here, is shown in Fig. 9.2.

The algorithms of optimal learning according to (3.35), (3.32), and (3.38) have the form

$$\mathbf{c}[n] = \mathbf{c}[n-1] + K[n](y[n] - \mathbf{c}^{\mathrm{T}}[n-1]\mathbf{x}[n])\mathbf{x}[n], \tag{9.17}$$

where

$$K[n] = \left[\sum_{m=1}^{n} \mathbf{x}[m]\mathbf{x}^{\mathrm{T}}[m]\right]^{-1} \tag{9.18}$$

or, in recursive form,

$$K[n] = K[n-1] - \frac{(K[n-1]\mathbf{x}[n])(K[n-1]\mathbf{x}[n])^{\mathrm{T}}}{1 + \mathbf{x}^{\mathrm{T}}[n]K[n-1]\mathbf{x}[n]}. \tag{9.19}$$

The block diagram of an adaline that can learn in an optimal fashion is shown in Fig. 9.3. This scheme is very complex.

Very good results are obtained with

$$\gamma[n] = \left[\sum_{m=1}^{n} \| \mathbf{x}[m] \|^2\right]^{-1} \tag{9.20}$$

since the algorithm of learning (9.14) takes the form

$$\mathbf{c}[n] = \mathbf{c}[n-1] + \frac{\mathbf{x}[n]}{\sum_{m=1}^{n} \| \mathbf{x}[m] \|^2}(y[n] - \mathbf{c}^{\mathrm{T}}[n-1]\mathbf{x}[n]). \tag{9.21}$$

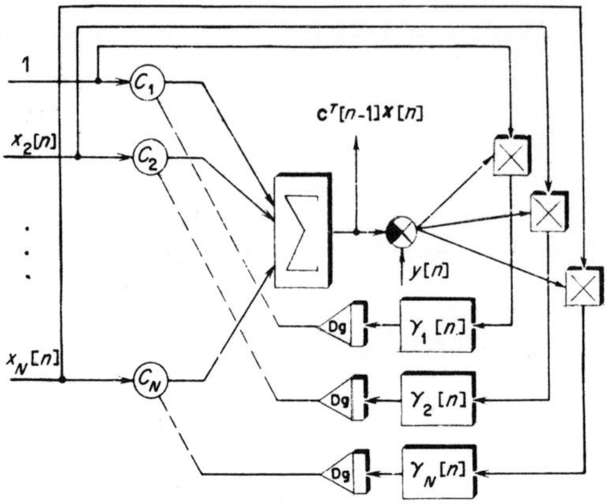

FIG. 9.2

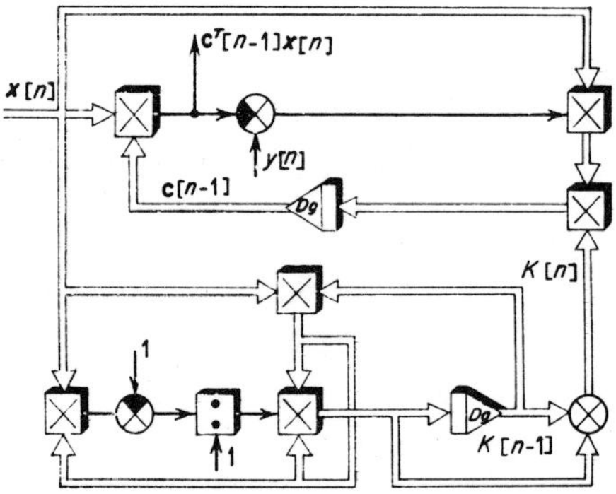

FIG. 9.3

This algorithm is sometimes called "quick and dirty." The simplicity of its realization is a good reason for being preferred over more complex algorithms of optimal learning. The block diagram of an adaline that realizes this algorithm differs only by the blocks $\gamma_\nu[n]$ from one shown in Fig. 9.2. Certain applications of adalines will be considered later.

9.4 Learning Receiver: I

Let us consider the problem of constructing a receiver of impulse signals in the background noise. When *a priori* information about the signal and noise characteristics does not exist, a learning receiver must apply the decision rule that indicates the presence or the absence of an impulse signal.

For the solution of this problem, we use adaptive Bayes approach (see Section 5.5).

Let

$$x[n] = s[n] + \xi[n], \tag{9.22}$$

where $s[n]$ is a useful impulse signal and $\xi[n]$ is noise with finite variance and mean zero.

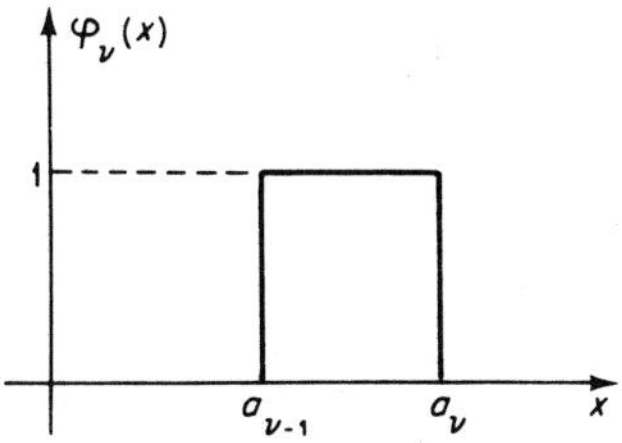

FIG. 9.4

Let us select the following system of functions $\varphi_\nu(x)$:

$$\varphi_\nu(x) = \begin{cases} 1 & \text{if } \; a_{\nu-1} < x \leq a_\nu \\ 0 & \text{if } \; a_{\nu-1} \geq x, \quad a_\nu < x. \end{cases} \tag{9.23}$$

This system of functions, as it can be seen from Fig. 9.4, has the property that

$$\varphi_\nu(x)\varphi_\mu(x) = \begin{cases} 1 & \text{when} \quad \nu = \mu \\ 0 & \text{when} \quad \nu \neq \mu. \end{cases} \tag{9.24}$$

We shall now use the results of Section 5.5. The decision rule has the form

$$\hat{f}(x[n], \mathbf{c}^*) = \sum_{\nu=1}^{N} c_\nu{}^* \varphi_\nu(x[n]), \tag{9.25}$$

where $c_\nu{}^*$ is determined by Algorithms (5.37) and (5.38).

Due to Property (9.24), the matrix H (5.33) has a very simple form

$$H = I\mathbf{a}, \tag{9.26}$$

where

$$\mathbf{a} = (a_1 - a_0, a_2 - a_1, \ldots, a_N - a_{N-1}). \tag{9.27}$$

Therefore, from (5.37), (5.38), and (5.40), we obtain

$$c_\nu[n] = c_\nu[n-1] - n^{-1}[(a_\nu - a_{\nu-1})c_\nu[n-1] - (w_{11} - w_{12})\varphi_\nu(x[n])], \tag{9.28}$$

when there is a useful signal, or

$$c_\nu[n] = c_\nu[n-1] - n^{-1}[(a_\nu - a_{\nu-1})c_\nu[n-1] - (w_{21} - w_{22})\varphi_\nu(x[n])], \quad (9.29)$$

when the useful signal is not present.

The block diagram of the learning receiver is shown in Fig. 9.5. This receiver eventually applies Bayes decision rule.

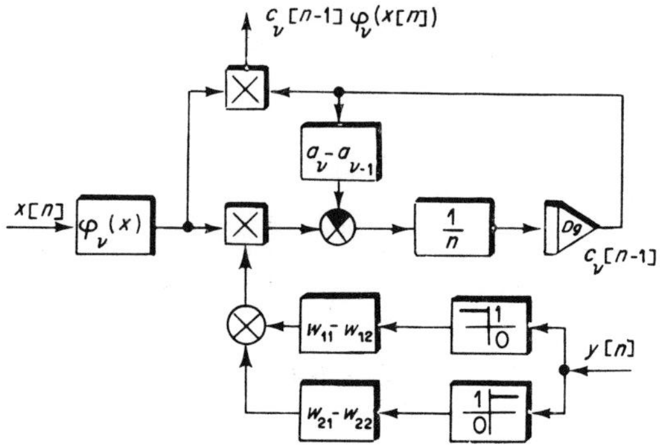

FIG. 9.5

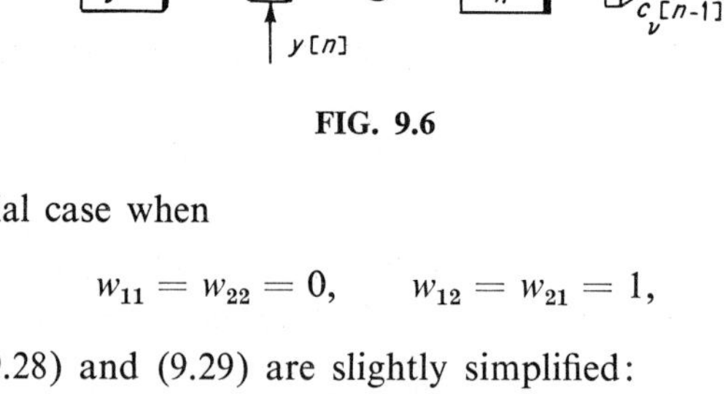

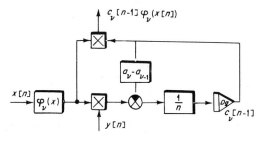

FIG. 9.6

In the special case when

$$w_{11} = w_{22} = 0, \qquad w_{12} = w_{21} = 1, \quad (9.30)$$

Algorithms (9.28) and (9.29) are slightly simplified:

$$c_\nu[n] = c_\nu[n-1] - n^{-1}[(a_\nu - a_{\nu-1})c_\nu[n-1] - y[n]\varphi_\nu(x[n])], \quad (9.31)$$

where

$$y[n] = \begin{cases} -1 & \text{when signal is present} \\ 1 & \text{when signal is not present} \end{cases} \quad (9.32)$$

represents correct classifications provided by a "teacher."

The block diagram of a learning receiver based on Algorithm (9.31) is shown in Fig. 9.6. This learning receiver applies the Siegert–Kotelnikov decision rule.

9.5 Learning Receiver: II

Let us now use a slightly different criterion of optimality: we ask that the probabilities of errors of the first and the second kind be equal, that is,

$$\mathsf{P}\{x \in X_1^0; s = 0\} = \mathsf{P}\{x \,\bar{\in}\, X_1^0; s \neq 0\}. \tag{9.33}$$

According to the formula of total probability,

$$\mathsf{P}\{x \in X_1^0\} = \mathsf{P}\{x \in X_1^0; s = 0\} + \mathsf{P}\{x \in X_1^0; s \neq 0\}. \tag{9.34}$$

Also

$$\mathsf{P}\{s \neq 0\} = \mathsf{P}\{x \,\bar{\in}\, X_1^0; s \neq 0\} + \mathsf{P}\{x \in X_1^0; s \neq 0\}. \tag{9.35}$$

By subtracting (9.35) from (9.34), and using (9.33), we obtain

$$\mathsf{P}\{x \in X_1^0\} = \mathsf{P}\{s \neq 0\}. \tag{9.36}$$

This equation, equivalent to (9.33), says: The probability that the decision rule indicates the presence of the signal is equal to the probability that the signal is actually present. By introducing the characteristic function

$$\theta(x, c) = \operatorname{sgn}(x - c) = \begin{cases} 1 & \text{if } x \geq c \\ 0 & \text{if } x < c, \end{cases} \tag{9.37}$$

where c is the threshold, and noticing that

$$\mathsf{M}\{\operatorname{sgn}(x - c)\} = \mathsf{P}\{x \in X_1^0\}, \qquad \mathsf{M}\{y_0\} = \mathsf{P}\{s \neq 0\}, \tag{9.38}$$

where $y_0 = (1 - y)/2$, and y is the correct decision (9.32) provided by the "teacher," we write (9.36) as

$$\mathsf{M}\{\operatorname{sgn}(x - c) - y_0\} = 0. \tag{9.39}$$

Finally we obtain the algorithms of learning:

Discrete:

$$c[n] = c[n-1] + \gamma[n](\operatorname{sgn}(x[n] - c[n-1]) - y_0[n]), \tag{9.40}$$

Continuous:

$$dc(t)/dt = \gamma(t)(\operatorname{sgn}(x(t) - c(t)) - y_0(t)). \tag{9.41}$$

The block diagram of the learning receiver is given in Fig. 9.7. This receiver can learn the value of the threshold $c = c^*$ for which the criterion (9.33) is satisfied. According to this criterion, the useful signal is present when x exceeds the threshold, and it is not present when x is less than the threshold. The processes of generating the threshold and the output of the receiver are depicted in Fig. 9.8.

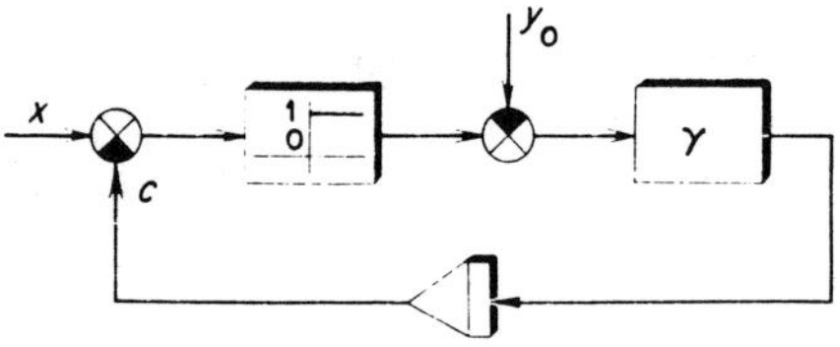

FIG. 9.7

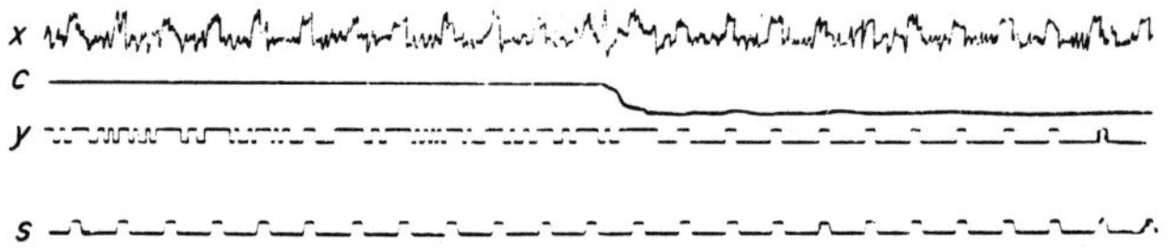

FIG. 9.8

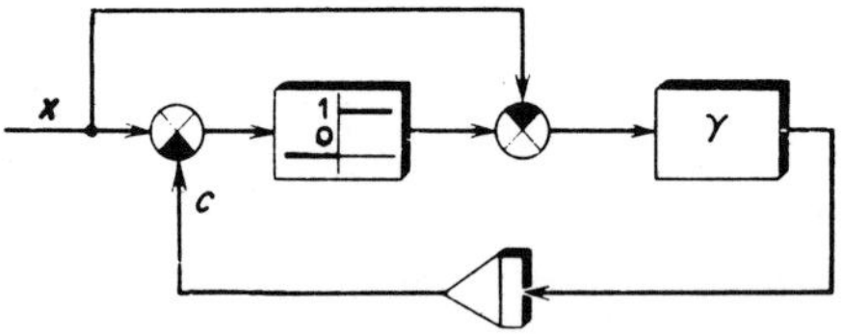

FIG. 9.9

If the correct decisions y of the "teacher" do not exist, then instead of y_0 we can use the input x directly as shown in Fig. 9.9. In this case, if in the input signal

$$x(t) = s(t) + \xi(t), \tag{9.42}$$

the useful signal $s(t)$ is normalized, and the mean value of $\xi(t)$ is zero, the criterion (9.39) is replaced by

$$\mathsf{M}\{\operatorname{sgn}(x - c) - x\} = \mathsf{M}\{\operatorname{sgn}(x - c) - s\} = 0. \tag{9.43}$$

Instead of Algorithms (9.40) and (9.41), we obtain

$$c[n] = c[n-1] + \gamma[n](\operatorname{sgn}(x[n] - c[n-1] - x[n]), \tag{9.44}$$

and

$$dc(t)/dt = \gamma(t)(\operatorname{sgn}(x(t) - c(t)) - x(t)). \tag{9.45}$$

The processes of generating the threshold and the outputs in this case are presented in Fig. 9.10. They do not differ considerably from the processes when the correct decisions of the "teacher" do not exist.

Finally, we assume that the input signal (9.42) is of finite duration but sufficiently long for establishing the threshold. In this case we must use algorithms of learning with repetition that we described in Section 3.15. In Fig. 9.11a–d, the processes of generating the threshold and output are

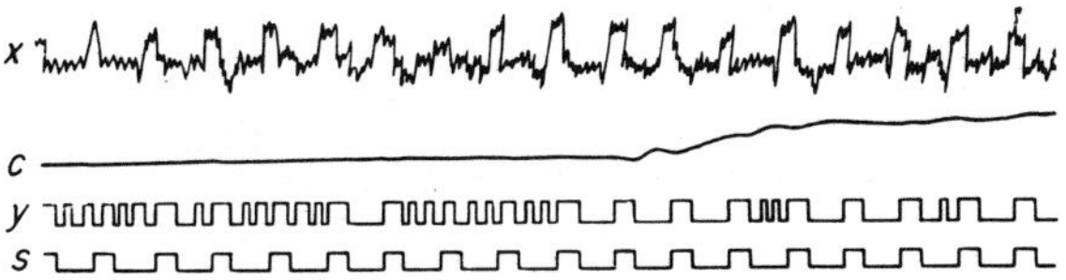

FIG. 9.10

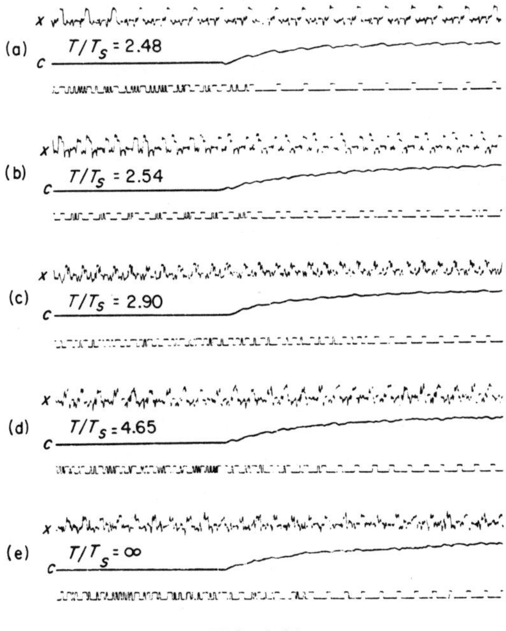

FIG. 9.11

TABLE 9.1[a]

	1	2	3	4	5
T/T_s	2.48	2.54	2.90	4.65	∞
$c_{\text{thresh}}/(c_{\text{thresh}})_{T\to\infty}$	0.98	0.98	1.01	0.99	1.0
t_l	0.54	0.56	0.55	0.56	0.56

[a] c, threshold; T, length of the sample; t_l, period of learning; T_s, repetition period of the signal.

shown. As can be seen in Table 9.1, the time for estimating the threshold and the optimal threshold depend considerably on the length of time for reception of the input signal.

9.6 Self-Learning Classifier

Let $x(t)$ be an input signal. The problem of a self-learning classifier consists of classifying the input signals into two groups: the signals of large and small amplitude; the useful signals and noise, etc. It is also assumed that additional information does not exist.

The loss functions (6.4) are the simplest quadratic functions

$$F_1(\mathbf{x}, \vec{\mathbf{c}}) = (c_1 - x)^2, \qquad F_2(\mathbf{x}, \vec{\mathbf{c}}) = (c_2 - x)^2. \tag{9.46}$$

Then the equation that defines the decision rule (6.6) is simply

$$\hat{f}(\mathbf{x}, \vec{\mathbf{c}}) = (c_1 - x)^2 - (c_2 - x)^2 \tag{9.47}$$

or

$$\hat{f}(\mathbf{x}, \vec{\mathbf{c}}) = (c_1 - c_2)(c_1 + c_2 - 2x). \tag{9.48}$$

In order to determine unknown parameters, we use continuous algorithms of self-learning which are obtained from hybrid algorithms (6.18)–(6.21) by substituting the step function $x[t]$ with a continuous function $x(t)$. Taking into consideration (9.46), we obtain

$$dc_1(t)/dt = -\gamma_1(t)[c_1(t) - x(t)] \tag{9.49}$$

if

$$(c_1(t) - c_2(t))(c_1(t) + c_2(t) - 2x(t)) < 0, \tag{9.50}$$

and

$$dc_2(t)/dt = -\gamma_2(t)[c_2(t) - x(t)] \tag{9.51}$$

if

$$(c_1(t) - c_2(t))(c_1(t) + c_2(t) - 2x(t)) > 0. \tag{9.52}$$

Using the function

$$\operatorname{sgn} z = \begin{cases} 1 & \text{if} \quad z > 0 \\ 0 & \text{if} \quad z < 0, \end{cases} \tag{9.53}$$

instead of (9.49)–(9.52), we obtain

$$\begin{aligned} dc_1(t)/dt = &-\gamma_1(t)[c_1(t) - x(t)] \\ &\times \operatorname{sgn}[(c_1(t) - c_2(t))(2x(t) - c_1(t) - c_2(t))], \end{aligned} \tag{9.54}$$

and

$$\begin{aligned} dc_2(t)/dt = &-\gamma_2(t)[c_1(t) - x(t)] \\ &\times \operatorname{sgn}[(c_1(t) - c_2(t))(c_1(t) + c_2(t) - 2x(t)]. \end{aligned} \tag{9.55}$$

The block diagram of the self-learning classifier is shown in Fig. 9.12. In the case when $c_1(t) > c_2(t)$,

$$\operatorname{sgn}[(c_1(t) - c_2(t))(2x(t) - c_1(t) - c_2(t))] = \operatorname{sgn}(x(t) - x^0(t)), \tag{9.56}$$

where

$$x^0(t) = [c_1(t) + c_2(t)]/2 \tag{9.57}$$

is the threshold value. The process of self-learning for this case is shown in Fig. 9.13. The learning classifier can classify with equal success large and small signals as well as useful signals and noise.

For obtaining algorithms of optimal learning, we must determine optimal values $\gamma_1(t)$ and $\gamma_2(t)$ according to (3.80), and use them in Algorithms (9.49)–(9.52).

These optimal values are equal:

$$\gamma_{1\,\mathrm{opt}}(t) = \left[\int_0^t \operatorname{sgn}[c_1(t) - c_2(t)][x(\tau) - x^0(t)]\, d\tau\right]^{-1}, \tag{9.58}$$

$$\gamma_{2\,\mathrm{opt}}(t) = \left[\int_0^t \operatorname{sgn}[c_1(t) - c_2(t)][x^0(t) - x(\tau)]\, d\tau\right]^{-1}. \tag{9.59}$$

Optimal values $\gamma_{1\,\mathrm{opt}}(t)$ and $\gamma_{2\,\mathrm{opt}}(t)$ can be determined from the differential

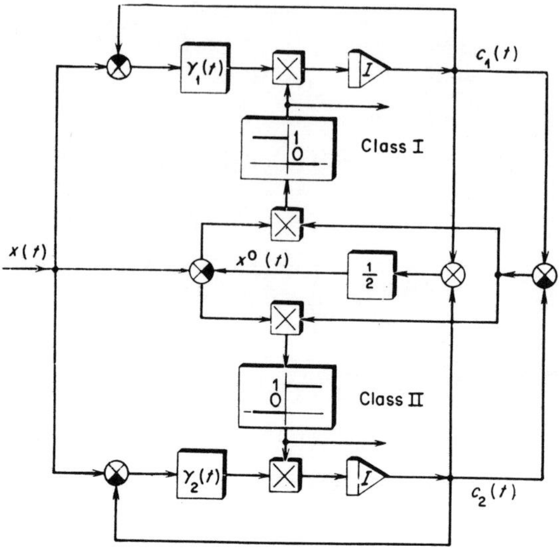

FIG. 9.12

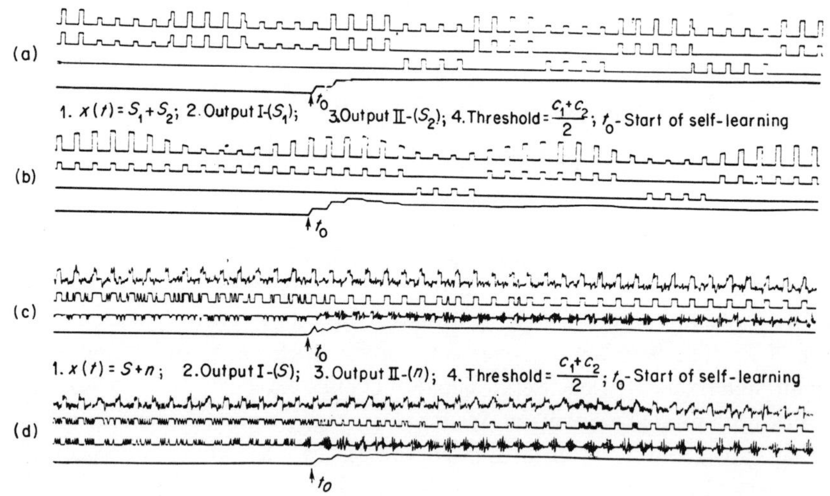

FIG. 9.13

equations (3.82). In the given case, they can be obtained more simply by direct differentiation of (9.58) and (9.59):

$$d\gamma_1(t)/dt = -\gamma_1^2(t) \operatorname{sgn}[(c_1(t) - c_2(t))(x(t) - x^0(t))] \tag{9.60}$$

and

$$d\gamma_2(t)/dt = -\gamma_2^2(t) \operatorname{sgn}[(c_1(t) - c_2(t))(x^0(t) - x(t))]. \tag{9.61}$$

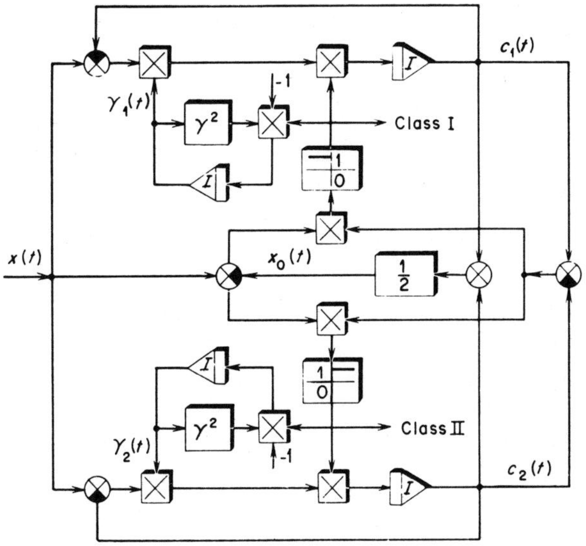

FIG. 9.14

The block diagram of the optimal self-learning classifier that represents the algorithms of self-learning (9.54) and (9.55), and (9.60) and (9.61) are shown in Fig. 9.14.

9.7 Learning Filters

It is convenient to realize the learning filters using delay lines. In this case, the impulse characteristic of the linear part of the filter is

$$k_\nu(\tau) = \delta(\tau - \nu T), \qquad \nu = 0, 1, \ldots, N, \tag{9.62}$$

where T is the delay time.

The outputs of the delay elements (8.12) have then a very simple form

$$\varphi_\nu(t) = \int_0^\infty \delta(\tau - \nu T)x(t - \tau)\, d\tau = x(t - \nu T), \tag{9.63}$$

and the output of the filter is

$$y(t) = \sum_{\nu=0}^{N} c_\nu x(t - \nu T). \tag{9.64}$$

We shall also compute the components of the vectors $\mathbf{r}^{\xi}$ (8.38) and $\mathbf{r}^{s}$ (8.46):

$$r_\nu^{\xi} = \int_0^\infty \delta(\tau - \nu T) R_{\xi\xi}(\tau)\, d\tau = R_{\xi\xi}(\nu T), \tag{9.65}$$

and

$$r_\nu^{s} = \int_0^\infty \delta(\tau - \nu T) R_{ss}(\tau)\, d\tau = R_{ss}(\nu T), \qquad \nu = 0, 1, \ldots, N. \tag{9.66}$$

The algorithms of learning and their corresponding adaptive filter can now be easily obtained.

When *a priori* information about noise exists, we can obtain from (8.36)

$$dc_\nu(t)/dt = \gamma(t)[(x(t) - \hat{y}(t, t))x(t - \nu T) - R_{\xi\xi}(\nu T)], \qquad \nu = 0, 1, \ldots, N, \tag{9.67}$$

where

$$\hat{y}(t, t) = \sum_{\nu=0}^{N} c_\nu x(t - \nu T). \tag{9.68}$$

The block diagram of the adaptive filter is given in Fig. 9.15. When *a priori* information about the signal exists, we can obtain from (8.45)

$$dc_\nu(t)/dt = -\gamma(t)[\hat{y}(t, t)x(t - \nu T) - R_{ss}(\nu T)], \tag{9.69}$$

where $\hat{y}(t, t)$ is defined by the preceding expression (9.68). The block diagram of the adaptive filter is shown in Fig. 9.16.

Let us now consider a learning filter of another type. From (8.65) and Condition (9.62), we obtain the elements of the matrix U,

$$\begin{aligned} U_{\nu\mu} &= \int_{-\infty}^{\infty}\int_{-\infty}^{\infty} \delta(\tau - \nu T)\delta(\lambda - \mu T) R_{\xi\xi}(\tau - \lambda)\, d\tau\, d\lambda \\ &= R_{\xi\xi}((\nu - \mu)T). \end{aligned} \tag{9.70}$$

Using the algorithms of learning (8.70), we obtain

$$\begin{aligned} dc_\nu(t)/dt = \gamma_\nu(t)\Big[&\hat{y}(t, t)x(t - \nu T) \\ &- \sum_{\mu=1}^{2N} R_{\xi\xi}((\nu - \mu)T)c_\mu(t) - R_{\xi\xi}((N - \nu)T)a\Big], \end{aligned} \tag{9.71}$$

where

$$\hat{y}(t, t) = \sum_{\nu=1}^{2N} c_\nu(t)x(t - \nu T) + ax(t - NT). \tag{9.72}$$

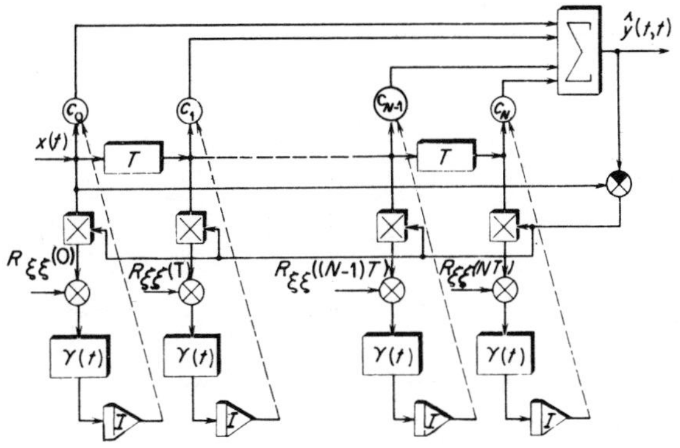

FIG. 9.15

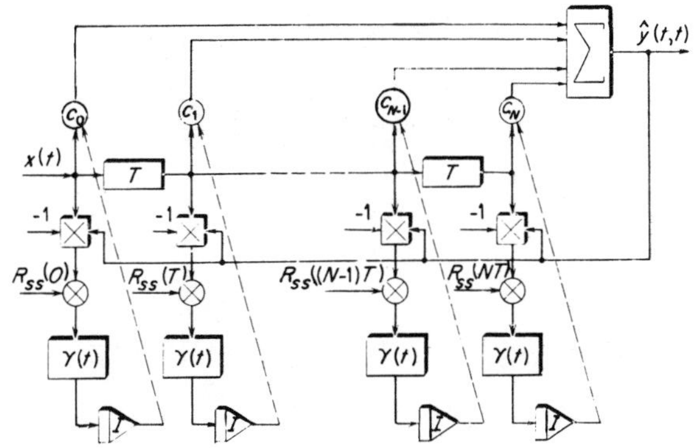

FIG. 9.16

The block diagram of the filter is given in Fig. 9.17.

In the special case when

$$R_{\xi\xi}((\nu-\mu)T) = \begin{cases} \sigma_\xi^2 & \text{when} \quad \nu = \mu \\ 0 & \text{when} \quad \nu \neq \mu, \end{cases} \tag{9.73}$$

the algorithm is simplified, and we obtain

$$dc_\nu(t)/dt = \gamma_\nu(t)[\hat{y}(t,t)x(t-\nu T) - \sigma_\xi^2 c_\nu], \qquad \nu \neq N, \tag{9.74}$$

and

$$dc_N(t)/dt = \gamma_N(t)[\hat{y}(t,t)x(t-NT) - \sigma_\xi^2(c_N + a)]. \tag{9.75}$$

These algorithms of learning can be given in the equivalent form

$$[T_\nu(t)\, dc_\nu(t)/dt] + c_\nu(t) = \sigma_\xi^{-2}\hat{y}(t,t)x(t-\nu T) \tag{9.76}$$

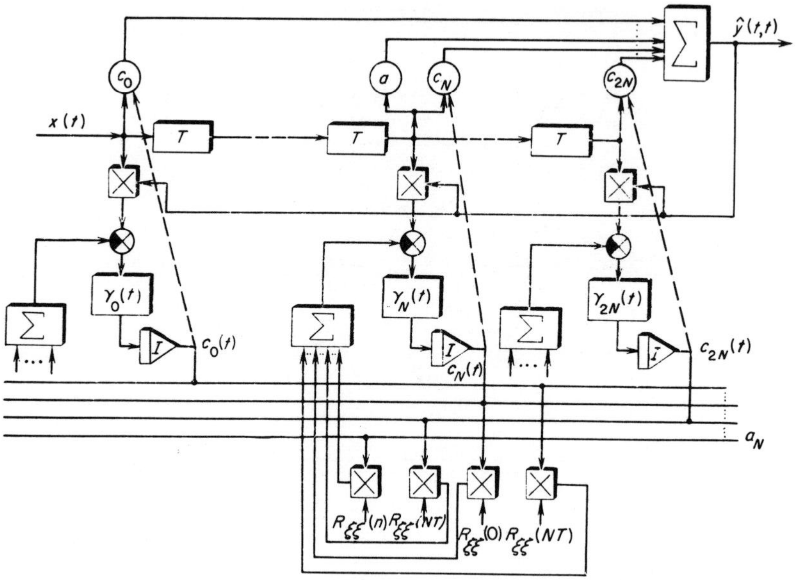

FIG. 9.17

and

$$[T_N(t)\, dc_N(t)/dt] + c_N(t) = \sigma_\xi^{-2}\hat{y}(t, t)x(t - NT) - a, \qquad (9.77)$$

where

$$T_\nu(t) = [\gamma(t)\sigma_\xi^{\ 2}]^{-1} \qquad (9.78)$$

The block diagram of such a learning filter is shown in Fig. 9.18. This block diagram contains an RC circuit with a time constant that varies according to (9.78).

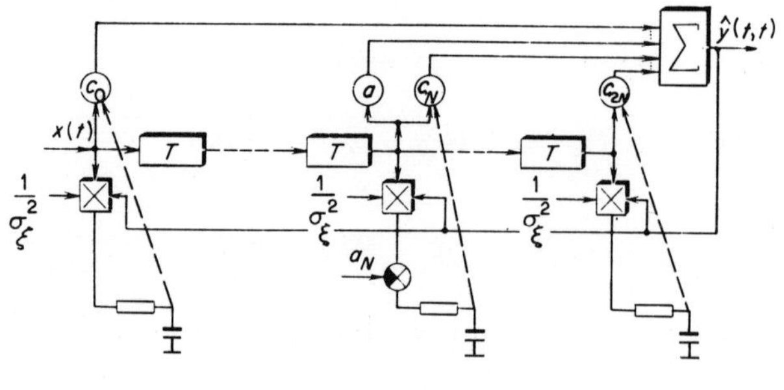

FIG. 9.18

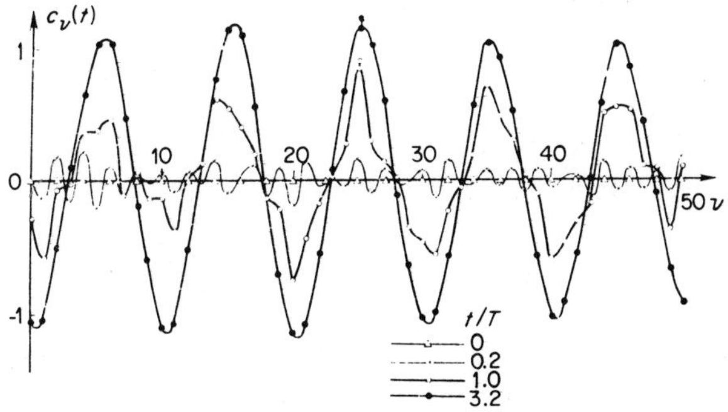

FIG. 9.19

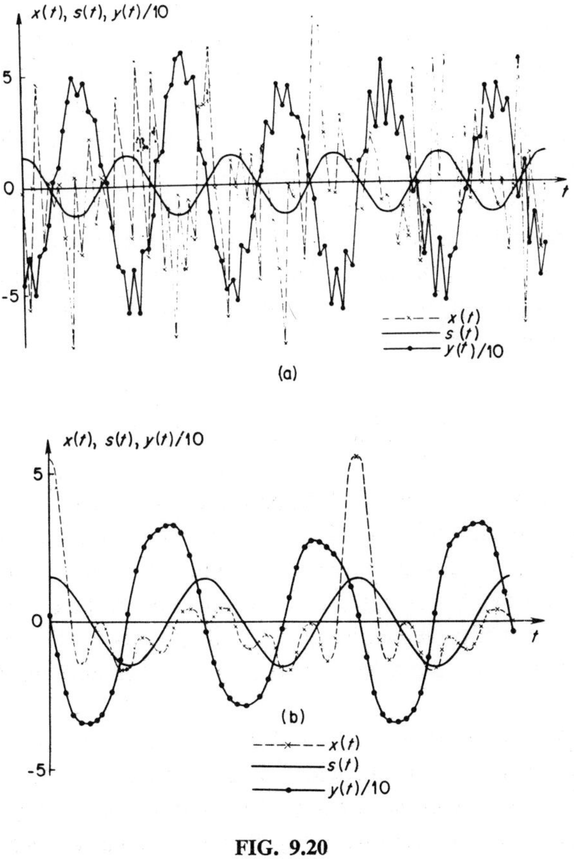

FIG. 9.20

We present the results of digital computer simulations of this learning filter. The filter specifications are

$$N = 25, \qquad T = 500\,\Delta t, \qquad a = 0.05, \tag{9.79}$$

where Δt is the sampling interval.

The useful signal is a harmonic oscillation

$$s(t) = \sqrt{2}\cos\omega t, \qquad \omega = (\pi/10)\,\Delta t. \tag{9.80}$$

Additive noise consists of (a) white noise and (b) a sum of harmonic signals of different frequencies:

$$\xi(t) = (\sqrt{2}/2)(\cos 0.5\omega t + \cos 1.5\omega t + \cos 2\omega t + \cos 2.5\omega t + \cos 3\omega t + \cos 3.5\omega t). \tag{9.81}$$

The variations of the coefficients $c_\nu(t)$ $(\nu = 1, 2, \ldots, 50)$ are shown in Fig. 9.19. The initial conditions are assumed to be $c_\nu(0) = 0$. The learning time $t = 3.2T$. Figure 9.19 clearly shows how the characteristics of the filter that is tuned to the frequency ω are being formed. Figure 9.20a shows the input signal $x(t)$ that represents a sum of the input signal $s(t)$ and noise $\xi(t)$, the useful signals alone, and the output signal $y(t)$ of the filter after learning. Figure 9.20a and Fig. 9.20b differ only by the noise component. In Fig. 9.20b, noise is the sum of harmonic signals. As it can be seen from these results, a learning filter can extract characteristic features of the useful signal after a learning period.

9.8 Learning Antenna System

An antenna system is designated for reception of a useful signal in the presence of spatially distributed noise sources. If the directions of the signal and noise sources are known, the removal of the influence of noise can be accomplished by the corresponding selection of the directivity pattern in the antenna system: the maximum of the directivity pattern must coincide with the direction of the signal source, and the minimums to the noise sources.

Let us now assume that the spatial distribution of the noise sources is unknown. In this case, the problem of extracting a useful signal in the presence of noise sources can be solved by a learning antenna system that is capable of modifying its directivity pattern. Actually, such an antenna system must perform spatial filtering. The antenna system represents a number of receiving antennas distributed along a circle. The output signals of each antenna are, directly or through $\frac{1}{4}$-wavelength delay lines, multiplied by the weights $c_{2\nu-1}$ and $c_{2\nu}$, and then summed. The modification of the directivity pattern is accomplished by varying the weighting coefficients using, for instance, a device of adaline type.

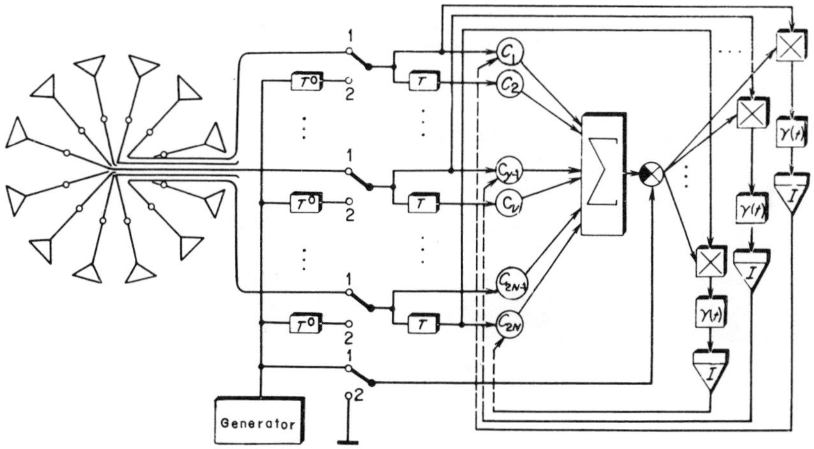

FIG. 9.21

The general block diagram of the antenna system is shown in Fig. 9.21. The goal of learning for these antenna systems consists of the minimization of the mean-square error

$$J(c) = \mathsf{M}\{\tfrac{1}{2}(y_0 - \mathbf{c}^{\mathrm{T}}\mathbf{x})^2\}, \tag{9.82}$$

where

$$\mathbf{x} = (x_1, \ldots, x_{2N}) \tag{9.83}$$

is the vector of the input signals to the antenna, and y_0 is the useful signal. The algorithms of learning are

$$dc_\nu(t)/dt = \gamma(t)\Big(y_0(t) - \sum_{\eta=1}^{2N} c_\eta(t)x_\eta(t)\Big)x_\nu(t), \qquad \nu = 1, 2, \ldots, 2N. \tag{9.84}$$

In order to train the antenna system, we must have the useful signal. But in this case, obviously, the antenna system would not be needed. Therefore, an artificially introduced signal, created by a special generator in the receiver, is used in learning. Special characteristics and the direction of arrival of this artificial signal must be analogous to the received useful

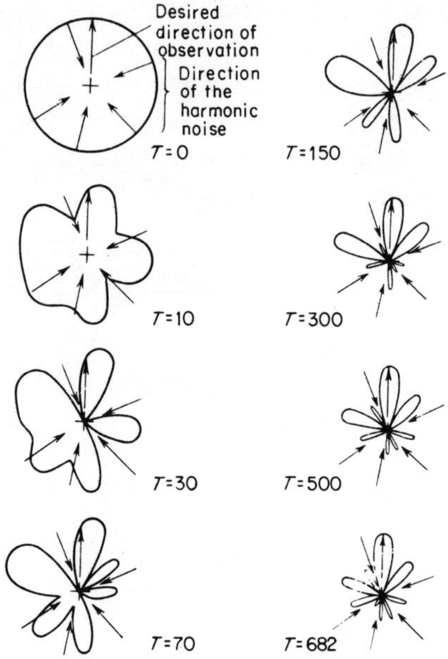

FIG. 9.22

signal. The inputs of an adaline (see Section 9.3) are connected either to the outputs of the antenna system (position 1) or to the outputs of the delay lines T_ν^0 ($\nu = 1, 2, \ldots, N$) (position 2) that are excited by the signals from the special generator (see Fig. 9.21). The delay times T_ν^0 are selected so that the obtained signals are similar to those that would exist if the antenna actually receives the signal of given direction. Positions 1 and 2 of the switches alternate sufficiently fast that the necessary direction of the directivity pattern and the minimum of noise power stay unchanged. Figure 9.22 presents experimental results of variations in the initial circular directivity pattern due to learning.

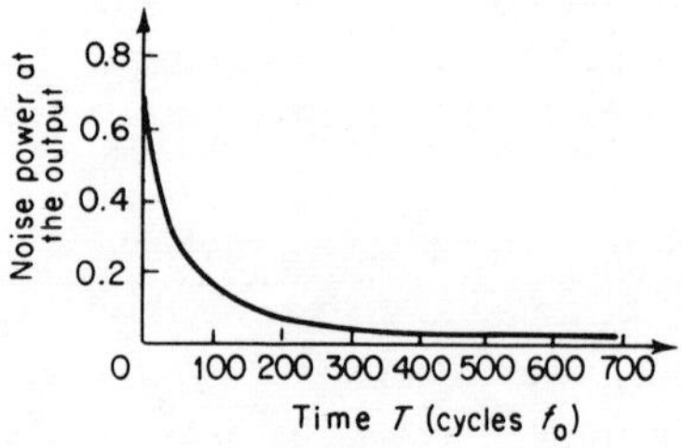

FIG. 9.23

The following notation is used: T designates the number of periods corresponding to the frequency f_0. Noise components are sinusoidal: amplitude is 0.5, and power 0.125; the frequency of the noise components were, respectively, $1.1f_0$, $0.95f_0$, f_0, $0.9f_0$, and $1.05f_0$.

The variation of the total noise power at the output of the antenna system during learning is given in Fig. 9.23. The learning period is practically equal to 400 periods of f_0; for instance, when $f = 1$ MHz, $t_{\text{learn}} = 40$ μsec.

Therefore, an adaline can form the necessary directivity pattern of an antenna system.

9.9 Learning Communication System

Two-way communication systems usually consist of two channels: a direct channel that has small power and a feedback channel that has relatively large power. Certain systems of spaceship communications are good examples of such systems. The block diagram of a two-way communication system is shown in Fig. 9.24. Let us designate an estimate of the

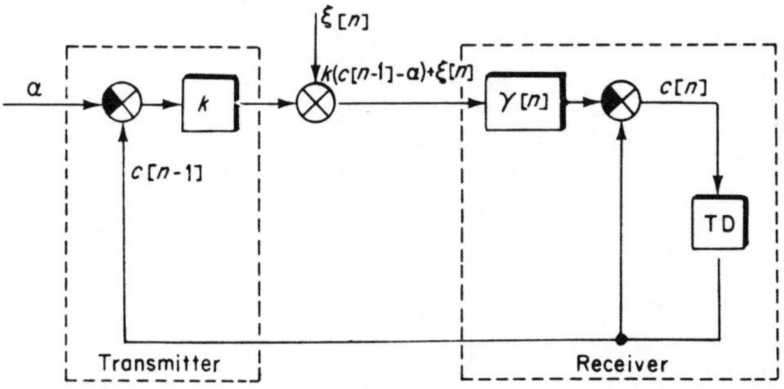

FIG. 9.24

transmitted signal α by $c[n]$, and by $k > 0$ the parameter (gain) of the transmitter. Moreover, let noise $\xi[n]$ have zero mean value. The algorithm for the operation of a two-way communication system is chosen to be

$$c[n] = c[n-1] - \gamma[n][k(c[n-1] - \alpha) + \xi[n]], \tag{9.85}$$

where $\gamma[n]$ satisfies the usual conditions. It can be easily seen that the goal of learning reached by this algorithm has the form

$$\mathsf{M}\{k(c - \alpha) + \xi\} = \mathsf{M}\{k(c - \alpha)\} = 0, \tag{9.86}$$

and that after learning $c^* = \alpha$. Therefore, the learning communication system guaranties the convergence of the estimate $c[n]$ to the transmitted signal α for any k of constant sign.

For the systems that are similar to ones already considered, it is advisable to use modified algorithms of learning discussed in Sections 2.6 and 3.8, and in particular modified algorithms of repetitive action. These algorithms allow a lower carrier frequency in the feedback channel than in the direct channel. Thus, by applying a modified algorithm of type (3.56), we obtain

$$c[N(n)] = c[N(n-1)] - \frac{\gamma[n]}{\Delta N(n-1)} \sum_{m=N(n-1)+1}^{N(n)} [k(c[N(n-1)] - \alpha) + \xi[m]], \qquad (9.87)$$

where, we should recall, $\Delta N(n-1)$ is the number of samples between the nth and the $(n-1)$th estimate, and $N(n)$ is the total number of observed sample before the nth estimate. By selecting appropriate $\gamma[n]$ (see Section 3.8), we can obtain estimates $c[N(n)]$ with the same accuracy as the estimates $c[n]$ obtained with Algorithm (9.85). The presence of noise with zero mean value in the feedback channel does not change the conclusions made above.

9.10 Learning Coding Device

The communication between earth and spaceships is usually accomplished through digital communication systems. Such systems have a direct channel, spaceship–earth, and feedback channel, earth–spaceship. Noise is practically nonexistent in the feedback channel since the power of the transmitted signals is sufficiently large.

The presence of the feedback channel, as follows from Shannon's theorem, cannot increase the channel capacity of the direct channel, but it can considerably simplify the problem of coding in order to reach the channel capacity.

Let T be the time interval used in the method of coding. This means that one coding word consists of a number of digits that are sent from a certain transmitter during time interval T. We select orthonormal functions $\varphi_\nu(t)$, with the properties

$$\int_0^T \varphi_\nu(t)\varphi_\mu(t)\,dt = \begin{cases} 1 & \text{when } \nu = \mu, \\ 0 & \text{when } \nu \neq \mu, \end{cases} \qquad \nu, \mu = 1, 2, \ldots, N. \qquad (9.88)$$

In particular, these functions can be N nonoverlapping impulses of amplitude one and duration T/N. During interval T, the signals

$$s_\nu(t) = s_\nu \varphi_\nu(t) \tag{9.89}$$

are transmitted. Let us designate by M a number of possible messages that can be sent by the transmitter. Each possible message is coded by one of the numbers

$$\vartheta_m = (2m - 1)/2M, \qquad m = 1, 2, \ldots, M, \tag{9.90}$$

uniformly spaced over a unit interval. Let the number ϑ_m be transmitted using the sequence of the signals $s_\nu(t)$ ($\nu = 1, 2, \ldots, N$). The received signal has the form

$$x(t) = \sum_{\nu=1}^{N} s_\nu \varphi_\nu(t) + \xi(t), \tag{9.91}$$

where $\xi(t)$ is noise.

In the receiver, with the help of a matched filter that has the impulse response

$$k_\nu(t) = \varphi_\nu(-t)_1 \tag{9.92}$$

the components of the signal

$$x_\nu = s_\nu + \xi_\nu. \tag{9.93}$$

are extracted.

It is assumed that ξ_ν are statistically independent random variables with zero mean and variance $\sigma^2/2$. The obtained components of the signal x_ν are used to obtain an estimate of ϑ_m. We shall designate an estimate of ϑ_m after obtaining n components of the signal x_ν by $c[n]$.

The mean-square error

$$\mathsf{M}\{(c[n] - \vartheta_m)^2\}, \qquad n = 1, 2, \ldots, N, \tag{9.94}$$

will become smaller as n increases from 1 to N.

After receiving all N quantities x_ν, the receiver must decide which ϑ_m was transmitted. It is natural to select such a value among ϑ_m ($m = 1, 2, \ldots, M$), which is closest to the estimate $c[n]$.

The probability of error is then

$$P_e = \mathsf{P}\{| c[n] - \vartheta_m |\} \geq (2M)^{-1}. \tag{9.95}$$

The method of coding must be such that P_e becomes smaller than a prespecified value for a certain transmission rate $R = \log_2 M/T$ that is smaller than the channel capacity $C = P_{av}/2\sigma^2$ with average transmission power P_{av}. In order to realize such properties of the methods of coding, it is necessary to have a sufficiently long time interval T. We shall now use the presence of the feedback channel. If the receiver sends the estimate $c[n-1]$ of the quantity ϑ_m back to the transmitter through the feedback channel, then the transmitter can only send the correction to the estimate. Since the estimate $c[n-1]$ converges to ϑ_m with increasing n, the average power P_{av} is thus reduced. Such an economy in P_{av} is sufficient for obtaining the transmission rate R that is close to the channel capacity C. Under this condition, the probability of error (9.95) can be made as small as desired by selecting suitable T. The coding scheme is shown in Fig. 9.25.

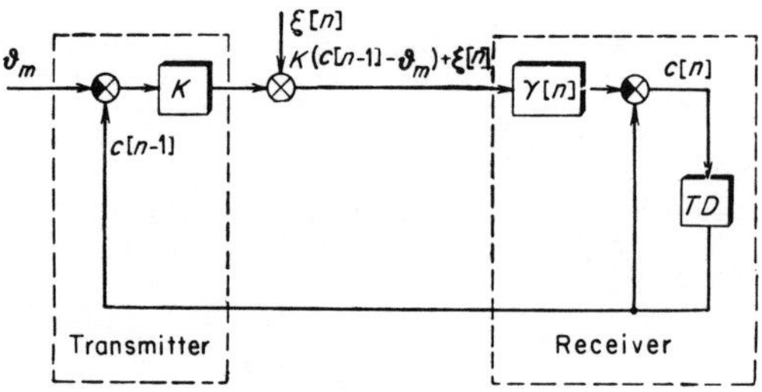

FIG. 9.25

At the instant n the transmitter sends the signal

$$s_n = k(c[n-1] - \vartheta_m), \qquad k > 0, \tag{9.96}$$

and the signal received by the receiver is

$$x_n = k(c[n-1] - \vartheta_m) + \xi_n. \tag{9.97}$$

The signal sent along the feedback channel is

$$c[n] = c[n-1] - \gamma[n][k(c[n-1] - \vartheta_m) + \xi_n], \tag{9.98}$$

where

$$\gamma[n] = (kn)^{-1}. \tag{9.99}$$

This is as we well know, the simplest optimal algorithm of learning. The only difference in this case is that n varies between 1 and N.

9.11 Self-Learning Sampler

Sampling, that is, transformation of a continuous function or its arguments into discrete sets of values, is broadly used in the sampled-data systems and digital computers. The sampling of the function values is accomplished by a sampling device (sampler) that is characterized by a stepwise function $g(x)$ (Fig. 9.26a). The sampling of a certain signal x is performed with an error that is similar to the round-off error in numerical analysis. In communication theory, this error is called quantization noise (Fig. 9.26b). Naturally, the quantization noise depends on the level of quantization c_k and the intervals $\lambda_k - \lambda_{k-1}$ $(k = 1, 2, \ldots, N)$. We should

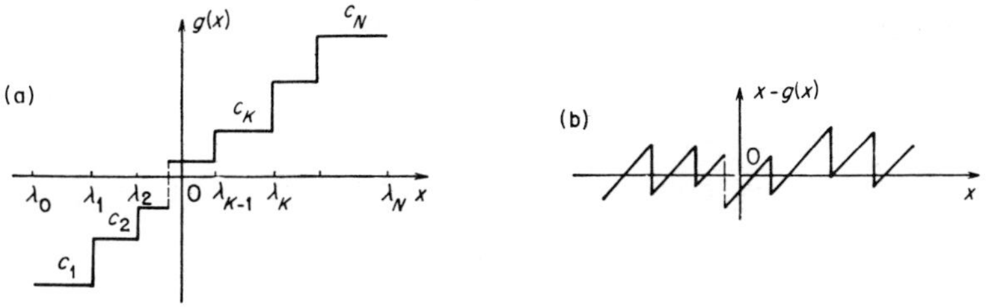

FIG. 9.26

notice the $\lambda_0 = x_{\min}$ and $\lambda_N = x_{\max}$. Therefore, the problem is to find the parameters c_k and λ_k of the sampler so that the quantization noise is minimized. We shall introduce the loss function

$$F_k(\mathbf{x}, \vec{\mathbf{c}}) = F(x - c_k), \tag{9.100}$$

where $F(\cdot)$ is an even function of its argument that is equal to zero for $x = c_k$. Then, considering that the probability density function of the quantized signal is $p(x)$, the quantization noise can be evaluated by the functional

$$J(\vec{\mathbf{c}}) = \sum_{k=1}^{N} \int_{\lambda_{k-1}}^{\lambda_k} F(x - c_k)p(x)\,dx. \tag{9.101}$$

The problem of designing an optimal sampler consists then of selecting its parameters—levels c_k and the limits of the intervals λ_k, for which the quantized signal is *a priori* known, the problems can be solved if we use a learning or, more correctly, a self-learning sampler. By comparing the functional (9.101) with the functional (6.5) that offers the algorithms of self-learning when the number of clusters (groups) is known, it is obvious that (9.101) is a special scalar case of the general functional (6.50). Therefore, we can use the conditions (6.51)–(6.53), with the simplifications that result from the fact that x, c_k, and λ_k are scalar.

Instead of (6.51), we obtain

$$\mathsf{M}\left\{\sum_{k=1}^{M} \theta_k(\mathbf{x}, \vec{\mathbf{c}}) F'(x - c_k)\right\} = 0. \tag{9.102}$$

It follows from (6.52) that

$$\theta_k(\mathbf{x}, \vec{\mathbf{c}}) = \theta(\lambda_{k-1}, \lambda_k) = \begin{cases} 1 & \text{if } \lambda_{k-1} < x \leq \lambda_k \\ 0 & \text{if } x \leq \lambda_{k-1},\, x > \lambda_k. \end{cases} \tag{9.103}$$

The boundaries are determined from the condition (6.53):

$$f_{k,k+1}(\mathbf{x}, \vec{\mathbf{c}}) = F(\lambda_k - c_k) - F(\lambda_k - c_{k+1}) = 0. \tag{9.104}$$

Using the usual procedure, we obtain the algorithms of self-learning:

$$c_k[n] = c_k[n-1] + \gamma_k[n] F'(x[n] - c_k[n-1])\theta(\lambda_{k-1}[n], \lambda_k[n]), \qquad k = 1, 2, \ldots, N, \tag{9.105}$$

where $\lambda_k[n]$ is found from the condition (9.104), that is, from the condition

$$F(\lambda_k[n] - c_k[n-1]) = F(\lambda_k[n] - c_{k+1}[n]). \tag{9.106}$$

In the special case of the quadratic loss function

$$F(x - c_k) = \tfrac{1}{2}(x - c_k)^2, \tag{9.107}$$

$$F'(x - c_k) = (x - c_k), \tag{9.108}$$

the condition (9.106) takes the form

$$(\lambda_k - c_k)^2 = (\lambda_k - c_{k+1})^2. \tag{9.109}$$

This gives

$$\lambda_k = (c_k + c_{k+1})/2, \qquad k = 1, 2, \ldots, N-1. \tag{9.110}$$

From (9.105) we obtain the algorithms of self-learning

$$c_k[n] = c_k[n-1] + \gamma_k[n](x[n] - c_k[n-1])\theta(\lambda_{k-1}[n], \lambda_k[n]), \qquad k = 1, 2, \ldots, N, \tag{9.111}$$

where

$$\lambda_k[n] = \tfrac{1}{2}(c_k[n-1] + c_{k+1}[n-1]), \qquad k = 1, 2, \ldots, N-1. \tag{9.112}$$

We should mention again that $\lambda_0 = x_{\min}$ and $\lambda_N = x_{\max}$.

The block diagram of the learning sampler that operates according to the algorithms of self-learning (9.111) and (9.112) is shown in Fig. 9.27.

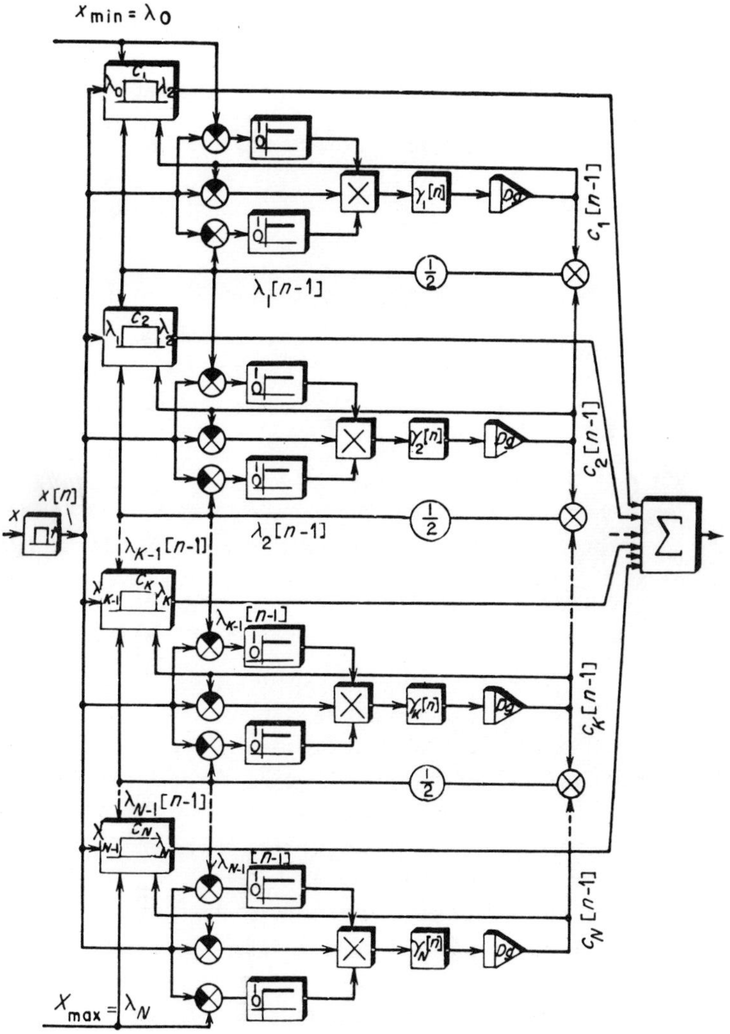

FIG. 9.27

In the general case, $\gamma_k[n]$ must satisfy the usual conditions for convergence (2.19). If we select

$$\gamma_k[n] = (r_k[n])^{-1}, \tag{9.113}$$

where r_k is the number of values that fell into the kth interval, we then obtain algorithms of optimal self-learning. In the case of absolute loss function

$$F(x - c_k) = | x - c_k |, \tag{9.114}$$

$$F'(x - c_k) = \text{sign}(x - c_k) \tag{9.115}$$

the condition (9.104) takes the form

$$| \lambda_k - c_k | = | \lambda_k - c_{k+1} |. \tag{9.116}$$

If $c_k < c_{k+1}$, then (9.110) again follows from (9.116). In this case, from (9.105), we obtain

$$c_k[n] = c_k[n-1] + \gamma_k[n] \,\text{sign}(x[n] - c_k[n-1])\theta(\lambda_{k-1}[n], \lambda_k[n]), \quad k = 1, 2, \ldots, N, \tag{9.117}$$

for which

$$\lambda_k[n] = \tfrac{1}{2}(c_k[n-1] + c_{k+1}[n-1]) \tag{9.118}$$

and again $\lambda_0 = x_{\min}$ and $\lambda_N = x_{\max}$.

The block diagram of this learning sampler, which operates according to the algorithms of self-learning (9.117) and (9.118) differs from the preceding one by the presence of a relay excited by the difference $x[n] - c_k[n-1]$.

9.12 Learning Control System

The theory of optimal control systems usually permits us to obtain the control function $u(t)$, where t is time. However, the problem of synthesizing the control law, that is, the problem of finding $u(\mathbf{x})$, where $\mathbf{x}$ is the state (or phase) variable, is still very far from an acceptable solution.

For a minimum-time control system, $u(t)$ takes one of two values ± 1, and thus the problem of synthesizing a minimum time optimal controller can be considered as a problem of classifying the state vector $\mathbf{x} = (x_1, \ldots, x_M)$ into two categories.

Let us represent the unknown switching boundary by

$$\hat{f}(\mathbf{x}, \mathbf{c}) = \mathbf{c}^T \boldsymbol{\varphi}(\mathbf{x}). \tag{9.119}$$

Then

$$u(t) = \begin{cases} -1 & \text{if } \hat{f}(\mathbf{x}, \mathbf{c}) < 0 \\ 1 & \text{if } \hat{f}(\mathbf{x}, \mathbf{c}) > 0. \end{cases} \tag{9.120}$$

Using the obtained optimal control functions $u_{\text{opt}}(t)$ and their corresponding optimal trajectories $\mathbf{x}_{\text{opt}}(t)$ for given initial conditions $\mathbf{x}(0)$, we can further employ the algorithms of learning with reinforcement since the relationship between $\mathbf{x}_{\text{opt}}(t)$ and $u_{\text{opt}}(t)$ is known.

These algorithms permit the construction of the switching boundary by the learning control system. Instead of the relationship between $\mathbf{x}_{\text{opt}}(t)$ and $u_{\text{opt}}(t)$, an actual minimum-time controller can control the plant. This optimal controller can be used to adjust the parameters of the "ordinary" controllers that are integral parts of simple learning control systems. In the course of learning, the adjustable parameters vary until the "ordinary" controller performs the role of a more expensive "optimal" controller which minimizes the number of incorrect control actions.

Let us consider another way of constructing learning control systems which does not require knowledge of the relationship between $\mathbf{x}_{\text{opt}}(t)$ and $u_{\text{opt}}(t)$. It is convenient to consider a simple example of a second-order system

$$dz(t)/dt = -ay(t), \qquad dy/dt = u(t), \tag{9.121}$$

where

$$x = -z \qquad \text{and} \qquad |u(t)| \leq 1, \tag{9.122}$$

and the transfer functions of the system are

$$K_1(p) = a/p, \qquad K_2(p) = p^{-1}. \tag{9.123}$$

For this system, the switching boundary is defined by the equation of the parabola

$$\hat{f}(x, c) = x + cy\,|y| = 0, \tag{9.124}$$

where

$$c = c^* = a/2. \tag{9.125}$$

If the parameters of the system a are unknown or time varying, there is a need to vary the coefficient c. After the first switching, the point in the phases plane that corresponds to the system under consideration travels along the trajectory that coincides with the optimal switching boundary. Therefore, it should be clear that if an approximating switching boundary lies above the true optimal boundary (that is, $c < c^*$), then after the first switching, the sign of $\hat{f}(x, c)$ is changed (Fig. 9.28). On the other hand, if the switching boundary lies below the optimal trajectory ($c > c^*$), then the point that corresponds to the system in the phase plane travels in the sliding mode toward the origin (Fig. 9.28). This fact can be used in the algorithm of learning

$$c[n] = c[n-1] + \varkappa[n]y[n] \mid y[n] \mid, \tag{9.126}$$

where

$$\varkappa[n] = \begin{cases} 1 & \text{when the sign of } \hat{f}(x, c) \text{ is changed} \\ 0 & \text{if } \hat{f}(x, c) = 0 \\ -1 & \text{for sliding mode.} \end{cases} \tag{9.127}$$

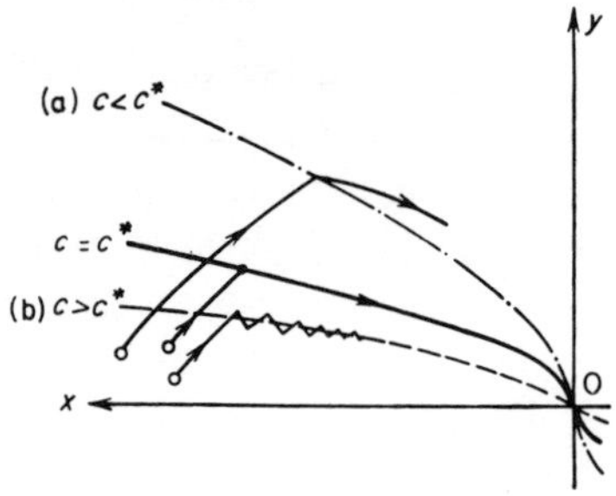

FIG. 9.28

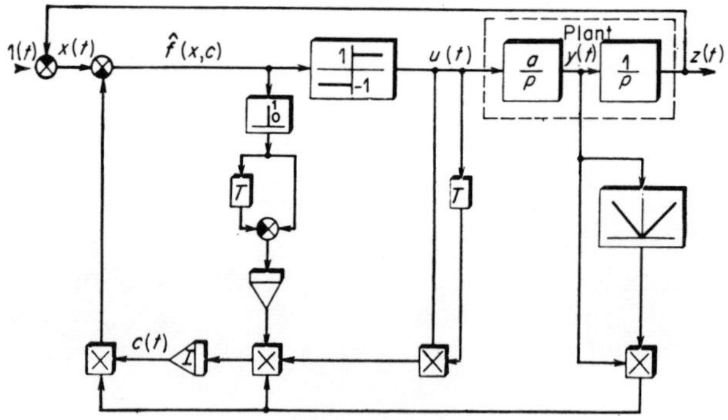

FIG. 9.29

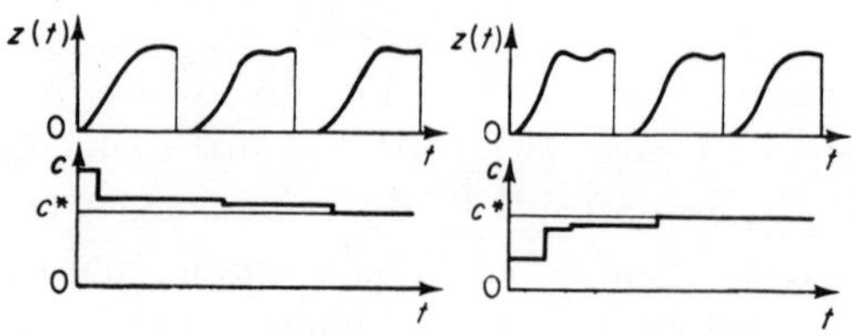

FIG. 9.30

The block diagram of such a learning system is shown in Fig. 9.29. Here, in addition to the usual elements (a functional transformer, delay lines, multipliers, integrators) we find a new element that has an output equal to one if the input signal is equal to zero, and equal to zero if the input signal is different from zero.

The oscillograms of the coefficient c, shown in Fig. 9.30, characterize the process of learning.

This simplest example illustrates the possibilities of constructing learning control systems. However, it must be emphasized that the problems of constructing closed-loop learning control systems are the most complicated and are still very far from the final solution.

9.13 Learning Diagnostic Systems

Diagnostic systems are designed to answer the questions regarding the state of the tested system: whether the system is operational or faulty, and if it is faulty, what kind of fault is present. In the following, the tested system will be a two-stage transistor amplifier (Fig. 9.31). Using the measured voltages u_1 and u_2, we must determine which one of the following situations exists: (1) the device is operational; (2) the capacitor C is in a short circuit state; (3) transistor T is in a short circuit state; (4) transistor T_2 is in a short circuit state; (5) none of the listed conditions is present. In order to solve this problem, it is necessary to partition the plane of the voltages u_1 and u_2 into 5 regions or groups that correspond to the listed situations.

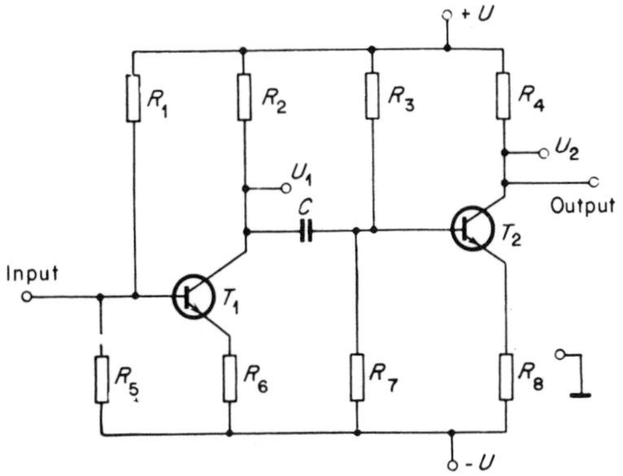

FIG. 9.31

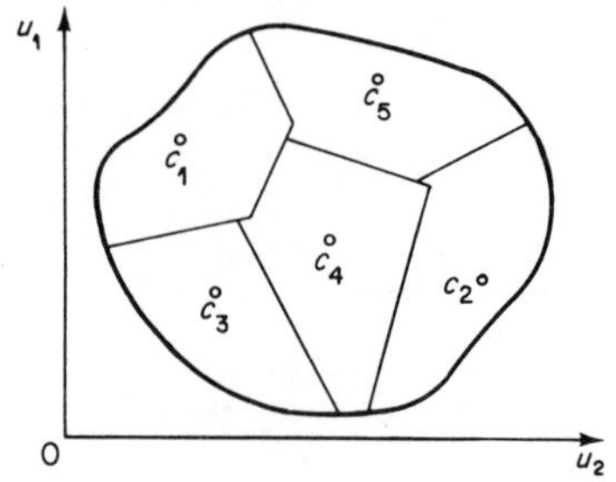

FIG. 9.32

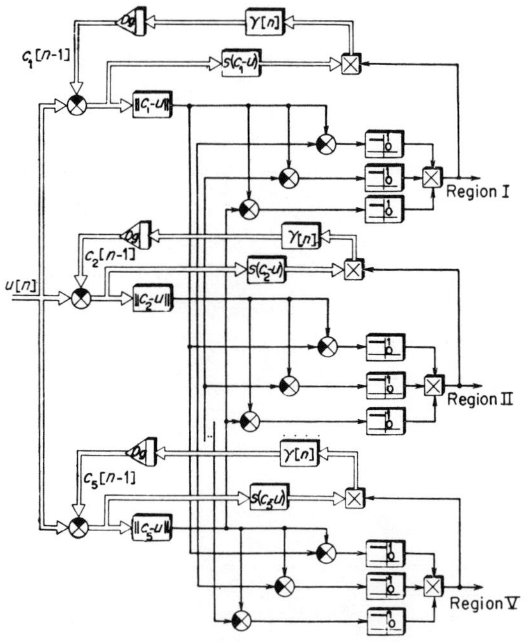

FIG. 9.33

Since the voltages u_1 and u_2 at the control points of the amplifiers are random due to the aging of the elements, temperature, humidity, and many other factors, the problem of constructing a learning diagnostic system can be formulated in the following way: find the portion of the space of voltages u_1, u_2 into the regions X_k, and such parameters c_{k1}, c_{k2} ($k = 1, 2, \ldots, 5$) for which the functional

$$R = \sum_{k=1}^{5} \int_{X_k} \| \mathbf{c}_k - \mathbf{u} \| P_k p_k(\mathbf{u}) \, d\mathbf{u}, \tag{9.128}$$

is minimal, where $\mathbf{u} = (u_1, u_2)$ is the vector of voltages, $p_k(\mathbf{u})$ is the probability density of the random vector of voltages $\mathbf{u}$ for the kth state of the amplifier, $\mathbf{c}_k = (c_{k1}, c_{k2})$ is the parameter vector, and

$$\| \mathbf{c}_k - \mathbf{u} \| = | c_{k1} - u_1 | + | c_{k2} - u_2 |. \tag{9.129}$$

Now, on the basis of results obtained in Section 6.7, we can easily obtain the algorithms of learning for the diagnostic system.

Since

$$\nabla_{\mathbf{c}_k} \| \mathbf{c}_k - \mathbf{u} \| = \mathbf{s}(\mathbf{c}_k - \mathbf{u}) = (\operatorname{sign}(c_{1k} - u_1), \operatorname{sign}(c_{2k} - u_2)),$$

we obtain

$$\mathbf{c}_k[n] = \mathbf{c}_k[n-1] - \gamma[n]\mathbf{s}(\mathbf{c}_k[n-1] - \mathbf{u}[n]), \qquad \mathbf{c}_m[n] = \mathbf{c}_m[n-1] \tag{9.130}$$

if

$$\| \mathbf{c}_k[n-1] - \mathbf{u}[n] \| < \| \mathbf{c}_m[n-1] - \mathbf{u}[n] \| \tag{9.131}$$

for all $m \neq k$, $m = 1, 2, \ldots, 5$.

The regions that correspond to the various states are defined by condition (9.131) (Fig. 9.32).

The block diagram of the learning diagnostic system is shown in Fig. 9.33. After learning, the diagnostic system will distinguish the states of the amplifiers using the position of the vector of control voltages. And now obviously, to establish the relationship between the obtained regions and the type of the amplifier states is not difficult.

The diagnostic system trained in this fashion will perform clustering of the amplifiers according to their states.

9.14 Establishment of Parametric Sequences

A parametric sequence represents a collection of standard values of the basic parameters of various parts, assemblies, devices, and machines. Establishment of parametric sequence represents the basis for unification. Thus, it is not necessary to prove the importance of developing the methods for establishment of parametric sequence. One of such methods can be based on the algorithms of self-learning. Let us assume that we have at our disposal a sufficiently large number of values for a parameter of a machine that is either in operation or requested by the user. The problem of establishing a parametric series then consists of partitioning these values into a certain number of regions, and the selection of an optimal value of the parameter in each region. The collection of these optimal values of the parameters is indeed a parametric sequence. In the one-dimensional case that will be considered here, the regions correspond to the intervals.

For certain parameters like weight, number of revolutions, dimensions, and so forth, the values of the parameters lie within the intervals. For other parameters like power, load, torque, and moment of inertia, the value corresponds to the limits of the intervals. In the first case, for the establishment of a parametric sequence, we can use the algorithms of self-learning that are similar to the algorithms of self-learning for the optimal quantization (9.111). The values c_k^* $(k = 1, 2, \ldots, N)$ found by such algorithms define the values of the parametric sequence and $\lambda_k - \lambda_{k-1}$ $(k = 1, \ldots, N)$ are the intervals of application for these values of the parameters c_k.

In the second case,

$$c_k = \lambda_k. \tag{9.132}$$

The number of terms in the parametric sequence can either be specified *a priori* or determined simultaneously with the values of its parameters. It is easy to see that the solution of the problem of establishing a parametric series can be obtained through the algorithms of self-learning when the number of regions is either known or unknown (see Sections 6.8 and 6.9).

We shall consider the problem of establishing the parametric series of the power for an electrical motor that drives the transmission for an aggregate of machine tools in the second case.

The power of the transmission head, which defines the nominal power on the spindle, is the basic parameter used in the selection of the transmission head for all forms of production. The initial data represent the powers of the 291 transmission head of 0.08 kW to 4 kW. They are presented in Table 9.2. Let us designate minimal power by λ_0, and maximal power by λ_N.

In this case,

$$\lambda_0 = 0.08 \text{ kW}, \qquad \lambda_N = 4 \text{ kW},$$

and $\lambda_1, \ldots, \lambda_{N-1}$ are still unknown optimal values of power. Furthermore, let us introduce the quadratic loss function

$$F_m(x, \lambda) = (x - \lambda_m)^2, \qquad m = 1, 2, \ldots, N, \tag{9.133}$$

where x represents given power values. This loss function differs from (9.100) since it has its zeros not within the intervals $(\lambda_{m-1}, \lambda_m)$ as before, but on the boundaries.

TABLE 9.2

0.080	0.110	0.120	0.120	0.180	0.180	0.185	0.190	0.200	0.220
0.245	0.245	0.245	0.250	0.250	0.250	0.257	0.270	0.270	0.270
0.270	0.270	0.270	0.270	0.270	0.270	0.270	0.270	0.280	0.300
0.300	0.300	0.320	0.330	0.350	0.350	0.350	0.350	0.350	0.360
0.367	0.367	0.367	0.367	0.368	0.368	0.368	0.370	0.370	0.370
0.370	0.400	0.400	0.400	0.400	0.400	0.400	0.400	0.400	0.400
0.400	0.400	0.400	0.400	0.400	0.400	0.400	0.400	0.400	0.400
0.400	0.440	0.450	0.500	0.500	0.500	0.500	0.500	0.500	0.500
0.500	0.500	0.500	0.500	0.500	0.550	0.550	0.550	0.550	0.550
0.552	0.600	0.600	0.600	0.600	0.600	0.600	0.600	0.600	0.600
0.600	0.600	0.600	0.600	0.620	0.700	0.700	0.700	0.735	0.735
0.735	0.735	0.735	0.736	0.736	0.736	0.750	0.750	0.750	0.750
0.800	0.800	0.800	0.800	0.800	0.800	0.800	0.800	0.800	0.800
0.800	0.800	0.800	0.800	0.800	0.800	0.800	0.800	0.810	0.810
0.850	1.000	1.000	1.000	1.000	1.000	1.000	1.000	1.000	1.000
1.000	1.000	1.000	1.000	1.000	1.000	1.000	1.000	1.100	1.100
1.100	1.100	1.100	1.100	1.100	1.100	1.100	1.100	1.100	1.100
1.100	1.100	1.100	1.100	1.100	1.100	1.300	1.400	1.400	1.400
1.470	1.470	1.470	1.470	1.470	1.470	1.470	1.472	1.472	1.472
1.500	1.500	1.500	1.500	1.500	1.500	1.500	1.500	1.500	1.500
1.500	1.500	1.500	1.500	1.500	1.500	1.600	1.600	1.700	1.700
1.700	1.700	1.700	1.700	1.700	1.700	1.700	1.700	1.700	1.750
1.850	2.000	2.000	2.200	2.200	2.200	2.200	2.200	2.200	2.200
2.200	2.200	2.200	2.200	2.200	2.200	2.200	2.200	2.200	2.200
2.200	2.200	2.200	2.200	2.200	2.200	2.200	2.200	2.200	2.200
2.200	2.200	2.200	2.202	2.500	2.570	2.800	2.800	2.800	2.800
2.800	2.800	2.800	2.800	2.800	2.800	2.800	2.800	2.800	2.800
2.800	2.800	2.800	2.800	3.000	3.000	3.000	3.000	3.000	3.000
3.000	3.000	3.000	3.000	3.670	3.670	3.680	3.700	4.000	4.000
4.000									

The expected losses are then

$$J(\lambda) = \sum_{m=1}^{N} \int_{\lambda_{m-1}}^{\lambda_m} (x - \lambda_m)^2 p(x)\, dx. \tag{9.134}$$

Here $p(x)$ is the unknown probability density function of power. The minimum of the average losses represents the goal of learning.

The average losses (9.134) are identical to (9.101) with constraints (9.132). The optimal value λ_k is simply obtained by differentiating (9.134) with respect to λ_k, and by setting the obtained result equal to zero. We then obtain the system of equations

$$-2\int_{\lambda_{k-1}}^{\lambda_k} (x-\lambda_k)p(x)\,dx - (\lambda_k-\lambda_{k+1})^2 p(\lambda_k) = 0, \qquad k = 1, 2, \ldots, N-1. \tag{9.135}$$

By introducing the characteristic function

$$\theta(\lambda_{k-1}, \lambda_k) = \begin{cases} 1 & \text{if } \lambda_{k-1} < x \leq \lambda_k \\ 0 & \text{if } x \leq \lambda_{k-1},\ x > \lambda_k, \end{cases} \tag{9.136}$$

and noticing that from (6.59) and (6.61)

$$p(\lambda_k) = \mathsf{M}\{\boldsymbol{\varphi}^{\mathrm{T}}(x)\boldsymbol{\varphi}(\lambda_k)\}, \tag{9.137}$$

we write (9.135) in a more convenient form:

$$\mathsf{M}\{(x-\lambda_k)\theta(\lambda_{k-1}, \lambda_k) + \tfrac{1}{2}(\lambda_k-\lambda_{k+1})^2 \boldsymbol{\varphi}^{\mathrm{T}}(x)\boldsymbol{\varphi}(\lambda_k)\} = 0. \tag{9.138}$$

We can now use discrete algorithms of self-learning, similar to (9.111), for obtaining the values λ_k of the parametric sequence. These algorithms have the following form:

$$\begin{aligned} \lambda_k[n] = \lambda_k[n-1] &+ \gamma[n][(x[n]-\lambda_k[n-1])\theta(\lambda_{k-1}[n-1], \lambda_k[n-1]) \\ &+ \tfrac{1}{2}(\lambda_k[n-1]-\lambda_{k+1}[n-1])^2 \boldsymbol{\varphi}^{\mathrm{T}}(x[n])\boldsymbol{\varphi}(\lambda_k[n-1])], \\ &\qquad k = 1, \ldots, N-1. \end{aligned} \tag{9.139}$$

The block diagram of a digital computer program is given in Fig. 9.34. The results obtained with the algorithms of learning (with periodic repetition of the date x) for $N = 11$ and with the normalized component functions $\boldsymbol{\varphi}(x)$,

$$\varphi_\nu(x) = \begin{cases} d^{-1/2} & \text{if } \lambda_0 + (\nu-1)d \leq x < \lambda_0 + \nu d \\ 0 & \text{if } x < \lambda_0 + (\nu-1)d, \quad x \geq \lambda_0 + \nu d, \end{cases} \quad \nu = 1, \ldots, N_1, \quad d = (\lambda_N - \lambda_0)/N, \tag{9.140}$$

are shown in Fig. 9.35. The limiting values $\lambda[n]$ with increasing n define the sought parameter values of the parametric sequence. They are given in Table 9.3 together with the values of an existing parametric sequence.

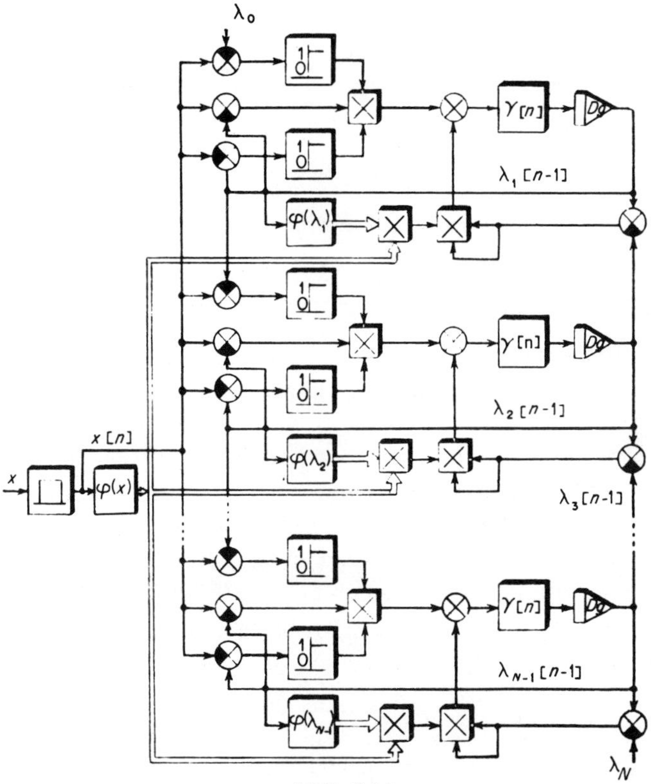

FIG. 9.34

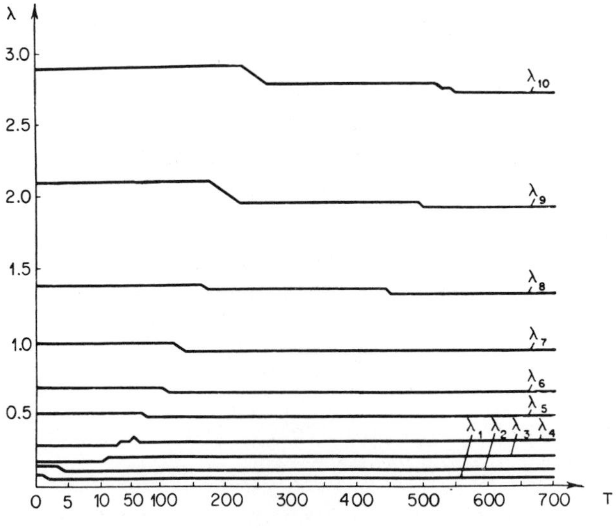

FIG. 9.35

TABLE 9.3

Parametric series according to GOSTU	0.12	0.18	0.27	0.40	0.60	0.80	1.1	1.5	2.2	3	4	Average loss 0.134
Optimal parametric series	0.14	0.22	0.28	0.41	0.57	0.75	1	1.4	2	2.8	4	Average loss 0.121

It is interesting to note that the obtained parametric sequence differs from the existing parameter sequence. The return obtained after substitution of the existing parametric sequence can be evaluated through the average losses; they are also listed in Table 9.3. By selecting different goals of learning, we can similarly obtain other parametric sequences (values of torque, dimensions, weight, displacement, and so forth). Of course, the complete solution of the problem is obtained when the goal of learning is the minimum of the total expenditures in the prediction and exploitation of the transmission heads during a certain interval with the consideration of various constraints. However, such a complete solution of similar problems deserves independent considerations.

9.15 Conclusion

This final chapter has a special importance since it represents a clear illustration of the practical possibilities of learning systems. Of course, it is difficult to describe in one chapter all possible applications of the learning systems studied by the author and his co-workers or as reported in the literature. We have attempted to present the examples that not only emphasize the variety of learning systems, but at the same time expose the general idea that lies in the foundation of the construction of learning systems.

We have also included here certain graphs and tables. This material has helped the author at one time, and it may also be helpful to the reader.

Comments

9.2 The perceptron was proposed by Rosenblatt [1]. Similar schemes of the perceptron were described by Hay *et al.* [1].

9.3 Adaline is a creation of Widrow [1]. Various applications of Adaline were described by Widrow [1] and Smith [1]. Algorithm (9.21), in which the coefficient $\gamma[n]$ is defined by (9.29), was obtained in a very ordinary way. A similar expression for $\gamma[n]$ appeared in the book by the author [1] in Chapter 1, as a result of an incorrect conclusion that follows from $K[n]$ when the observations $\mathbf{x}[n]$ are independent. But, to the surprise of the author, even this expression of $\gamma[n]$ was discussed in many papers and dissertations. This same expression of $\gamma[n]$ and Algorithm (9.21) were also presented in the book by Albert and Gardner [1] in Chapter 2 as if they were empirical results. The reader can also find there a proof of the convergence for Algorithm (9.21) and an evaluation of the properties of this "quick-and-dirty" algorithm.

9.4 The system of functions (9.23) was used by Schetzen [1] in the design of optimal nonlinear systems. A slightly different system of functions was successfully employed by Galkin and Morosanov [1] in the development of simple algorithms of identification for nonlinear elements.

9.5 Theoretical and experimental investigations of threshold receivers, presented in this section were conducted by L. E. Epstein. Similar schemes of threshold receivers were also considered by Sklansky [1], and Mond and Carayannopoulos [1].

9.6 Experimental investigations of the self-learning classifier were performed by L. E. Epstein.

9.7 Similar learning filters based on delay lines in the presence of *a priori* information about the noise or the signal were considered in the work by Chang and Teuter [1]. A learning filter of another type (Fig. 9.18) was examined by Morishita [2], where the filter was introduced on the basis of intuitive reasoning. We have borrowed from his work the experimental results obtained on a digital computer. The analysis of this filter in the book of the author [1] in Chapter 1 contained certain small errors in the derivation which since have been removed.

Similar filters, but with variations in the time delay, were considered by Powell [1] and Avedyan [1].

9.8 The learning antenna system was proposed and described by Widrow *et al.* [1]. The experimental results presented here were borrowed from this very interesting paper. The reader interested in these questions will find in the mentioned paper many important and useful details.

9.10 A learning coding system of this type was proposed by Shalkwijk and Kailath [1]. Additional descriptions of the principle of operation, numerical characteristics of the coding device both with and without the constraints on the band width were given in their papers (see Shalkwijk and Kailath [2]). These papers were given a best paper reward published in *IEEE Transaction on Information Theory* in 1965. Further studies of similar coding devices can be found in the papers by Omura [1], Wyner [1], and Kashyap [1]. Shannon's theorem discussed here was formulated in his book (see Shannon and Weaver [1]). An excellent survey of this question was composed by Shalkwijk and Kailath [2].

9.11 Learning related to optimal quantization (sampling) was considered in the book by the author [1] of Chapter 1. The literature on optimal sampling with known probability density is also given there. From the papers which became known after the publication of the author's book [1] in Chapter 1, we mention a paper by Manczak [1].

The paper by Odetti [1] was devoted to the investigation of learning in adaptive samplers.

9.12 The idea of designing a learning system that is optimal in the sense of minimum time came from Tamura and Kirokava [1]. The experimental investigations of a similar system were conducted by N. V. Loginov. The learning systems were also considered in the paper by Kotek [1] and in Fel'dbaum's book [1].

9.13 A learning diagnostic system, designed on the basis of slightly different principles, was described by Lux and Drake [1]. Our attempt to understand their algorithms was not successful.

9.14 A similar problem of constructing a parametric series for the number of revolutions in a metal-cutting lathe for a known distribution function was considered by Pasko [1, 2]. For unknown distributions, he proposed min–max solutions.

The adaptive approach to the problem of parametric series is relatively new. The application of the algorithms of self-learning for this purpose was proposed by G. B. Kats. Here, the results obtained by B. G. Kats, V. I. Rozanov, and N. V. Loginov are presented in their basic form.

We would like to turn the attention of the reader to a similar problem on optimal nominals which is posed and solved in the conditions of complete a priori information by Svecharnik [1]. Even in the case of insufficient a priori information, this problem can be solved very effectively on the basis of the adaptive approach.

REFERENCES

Avedyan, E. D.

[1] Adaptive filter based on delay lines. *Avtomat. i Telemeh.* No. 11 (1969).

Butz, A. R.

[1] Learning bang-bang regulators. *IEEE Trans. Automatic Control* **AC-13**, No. 1 (1968).

Chang, J. H., and Teuter, F. B.

[1] Adaptive tapped lag line filters. *Proc. Annu. Conf. Information Sci. System, 2nd, Princeton, 1968.*

Fel'dbaum, A. A.

[1] "Computers in Automatic Systems." Fizmatgiz, Moscow, 1959 (in Russian).

Galkin, L. M., and Morosanov, I. S.

[1] On estimation of nonlinear converters with noisy measurements. *Avtomat. i Telemeh.* No. 1 (1969).

Hay, J. S., Martin, F. S., and Wightman, S. W.

[1] The MARK I perceptron—Design and performance. *IRE Internat. Conv. Rec.* **8** (2).

Kashyap, R. L.

[1] Feedback coding schemes for an additive noise channel with a noisy feedback link. *IEEE Trans. Information Theory* **IT-14**, No. 3 (1968).

Kotek, Z.

[1] Adaptivni učici se regulator. *Automatizace* **11**, No. 6 (1968).

Lux, P. A., and Drake, K. W.

[1] Fault detection with a simple adaptive mechanism. *IEEE Trans. Ind. Electron. Control Instrum.* **IECI-14**, No. 2 (1967).

Manczak, K.

[1] Optimalizaaja kwantowania sygnalow ciaglych o znanym rozkladzie prawdoropobienstwa. *Arch. Avtomat. i Telemech.* **14**, No. 3 (1969).

Mond, F. C., and Carayannopoulos, G. L.

[1] DEMO I, a supervised or unsupervised learning receiver. WESCON Tech. Papers, Pt. 3. Comput. Comm. and Display Devices, 1968.

Morishita, I.

An adaptive filter for extracting unknown signals from noise. *Trans. Soc. Instrum. Control Eng.* **1**, No. 3 (1965).

Nolte, L. W.

[1] An adaptive realization on the optimum receiver for a recurrent waveform in noise. *IEEE Trans. Information Theory* **IT-12**, No. 1 (1966).

[2] An adaptive realization on the optimum receiver for a sporadical recurrent waveform in noise. *IEEE Trans. Information Theory* **IT-13**, No. 2 (1967).

Odetti, E.

[1] Self-organizing quantizer. *Izv. Vyssh. Uch. Zaved. Elektromelh.* No. 12 (1967) (in Russian).

Omura, J. K.

[1] Optimum linear transmission of analog data for channels with feedback. *IEEE Trans. Information Theory* **IT-14**, No. 1 (1968).

Pasko, N. I.
[1] Construction of standards using mathematical apparatus. *Standartizatsiya* No. 3, 1965 (in Russian).
[2] On quantization of control. *In* "Analysis and Synthesis of Automatic Control Systems." Nauka, Moscow, 1968.

Powell, F. D.
[1] On adapting the lags of a tapped delay line Modeller. *IEEE Trans. Automatic Control* **AC-12**, No. 2 (1967).

Rosenblatt, F.
[1] "Principles of Neurodynamics; Perceptrons and the Theory of Brain Mechanisms." Spartan Books, Washington, D.C., 1961.

Schetzen, M.
[1] Determination of optimum nonlinear systems for generalized error criteria based on the use of date functions. *IEEE Information Theory* **IT-11**, No. 1 (1965).

Shalkwijk, J. P. M.
[1] Coding for additive noise channels with feedback. Pt. 2. Band limited channels. *IEEE Trans. Information Theory* **IT-12**, No. 3 (1966).
[2]

Shalkwijk, J. P. M., and Kailath, T.
[1] A coding scheme for additive noise channels with feedback. Pt. 1. *IEEE Trans. Information Theory* **IT-12**, No. 3 (1966).
[2] Recent development in feedback communication. *Proc. IEEE* **57**, No. 7 (1969).

Shannon, C. E., and Weaver, W.
[1] "The Mathematical Theory of Communication." Univ. of Illinois Press, Urbana, Illinois, 1949.

Sklansky, J.
[1] Time varying threshold learnings. *Joint Automat. Control Conf., Seattle, Washington, 1966.*

Smith, F. W.
[1] A trainable nonlinear function generator. *IEEE Trans. Automatic Control* **AC-11**, No. 2 (1966).

Svecharnik, D. V.
[1] The problem of optimality of nominal values in the probabilistic designs. *Trudy Inst. Mashinovedenia Akad. Nauk SSSR*, No. 10 (1957).

Tamura, H., and Kirokava, T.
[1] Adaptive classifiers of patterns and their application in optimal control. Pattern recognition. Adaptive systems. *Trudy Mezhdunarodnogo Symp. po Tekhnicheskim i Biologicheskim Problemam Upravlenia, Erevan, 1968.* Nauka, Moscow, 1970.

Widrow, B.
[1] Generalization and information storage in network of adaptive neyrons. "Self-Organizing Systems." Spartan Books, Washington, D.C., 1962.

Widrow, B., and Smith, F. W.
[1] Pattern-recognition control systems. "Computer and Information Sciences." Spartan Books, Washington, D.C., 1964.

Widrow, B., Mantey, P. P. E., Griffiths, L. J., and Goode, B. B.
[1] Adaptive antenna systems. *Proc. IEEE* **55**, No. 12 (1967).

Wyner, A. D.
[1] On Schalkwijk—Kailath coding scheme with a peak energy constraint. *IEEE Trans. Information Theory* **IT-14**, No. 1 (1968).

Zaichenko, Yu. P., and Crimov, Yu. G.
[1] An improvement in the accuracy of parameter estimation using stochastic approximation. *Avtomatika* No. 2 (1968) (in Russian).

Epilogue

Noncontroversial is only that which is not of interest to us.

H. LAUBE

Learning systems, regardless of their relative youth, are leading an independent and active life. They have their areas of application, especially when it is necessary to guarantee optimal operation of systems in the conditions of initial uncertainty. Learning systems may be useful in cases when we cannot gather the information first and then process it in order to remove initial uncertainty.

On the one hand, they can be used to gather and process the information, and on the other they permit us to obtain the same results by avoiding an advanced gathering and processing of information. In a number of cases this reduces the volume of computation considerably. However, learning is not free of cost. Any learning takes time, and learning is only effective if the learning system has the potential of reaching the goal of learning. Of course, learning systems are more complicated than ordinary systems. Learning time is minimal in the case of optimal learning, but optimality requires further complication of the system. Although we already know the general principles of design and the capabilities of learning systems, much remains to be done on the realization of such capabilities. We face special difficulties in the construction of learning systems with feedback or, briefly, of the closed-loop learning systems. At one time, the problems of learning in pattern recognition and classification also appeared difficult to us. Many now speak about "triviality" of these problems. Such is the logic of development in science: the unknown, incomprehensible, and difficult can be transformed into the understandable and trivial.

All new problems considered in this book contained the elements of old, classical problems: the problems of convergence and stability, the problems of optimality. Thus, in this respect we have not followed the fashion—departing from the reliable classical results: "Extreme following of the fashion is always a sign of bad taste." It seems to us that even now the theory of learning systems greatly needs further development and generalization of these classical results. To present they have provided a great service to the ordinary systems, but now they also have to serve the learning systems.

It is difficult to predict now what the further road of the development of learning systems will be, but we are certain that such a road will bring many new and important results in the nearest future.

Author Index

Numbers in italics refer to the pages on which the complete references are listed.

Subject Index